LINGUISTIC EVIDENCE

Language, Power, and Strategy
in the Courtroom

STUDIES ON LAW AND SOCIAL CONTROL

DONALD BLACK *Series Editor*

Center for Criminal Justice
Harvard Law School
Cambridge, Massachusetts 02138

P. H. Gulliver. Disputes and Negotiations:
A Cross-Cultural Perspective

Sandra B. Burman and Barbara E. Harrell-Bond
(Editors). The Imposition of Law

Cathie J. Witty. Mediation and Society:
Conflict Management in Lebanon

Francis G. Snyder. Capitalism and Legal Change:
An African Transformation

Allan V. Horwitz. The Social Control of Mental Illness

Richard L. Abel (Editor). The Politics of Informal Justice, Vol. 1:
The American Experience; Vol. 2: Comparative Studies

William M. O'Barr, Linguistic Evidence: Language, Power, and Strategy
in the Courtroom

LINGUISTIC EVIDENCE

Language, Power, and Strategy in the Courtroom

WILLIAM M. O'BARR

Department of Anthropology
Duke University
Durham, North Carolina

ACADEMIC PRESS
A Subsidiary of Harcourt Brace Jovanovich, Publishers
New York   London
Paris   San Diego   San Francisco   São Paulo   Sydney   Tokyo   Toronto

ACADEMIC PRESS, INC.
111 Fifth Avenue, New York, New York 10003

United Kingdom Edition published by
ACADEMIC PRESS, INC. (LONDON) LTD.
24/28 Oval Road, London NW1 7DX

Library of Congress Cataloging in Publication Data

O'Barr, William M.
   Linguistic evidence.

   (Studies on law and social control)
   Bibliography: p.
   Includes index.
   1. Forensic oratory. 2. Law--Language. I. Title.
II. Series.
K2251.O22   347'.0504'014   82-6794
ISBN 0-12-523520-8   342.7504014   AACR2

PRINTED IN THE UNITED STATES OF AMERICA

82 83 84 85   9 8 7 6 5 4 3 2 1

FOR JEAN

CONTENTS

PREFACE   xi
ACKNOWLEDGMENTS   xiii

____1____
INTRODUCTION   1

The Importance of Form in Language   1
Language Strategy   5
Language and Justice   10
The Study of Courtroom Language   11

____2____
THE NATURE OF LEGAL LANGUAGE   15

Written Legal Language   16
Spoken Legal Language   23

____3____
LEGAL ASSUMPTIONS ABOUT LANGUAGE
AND COMMUNICATION   31

Legal Tacticians   31
The Courts   38
The Law, by John M. Conley   41

4
ETHNOGRAPHY AND EXPERIMENTATION   51

Deriving the Research Questions   53
Specific Procedures   56

5
SPEECH STYLES IN THE COURTROOM   61

Powerful versus Powerless Speech   61
Narrative versus Fragmented Testimony Styles   76
Hypercorrect Testimony Style   83
Interruptions and Simultaneous Speech   87

6
CONTROLLING THE EFFECTS OF
PRESENTATIONAL STYLE   93

Attempts to Control Style Effects   93
Interpretation and the Management of Style   97

7
CONCLUSIONS   113

Implications for the Law   113
Implications for Social Science   118
Further Questions   123

Appendix
1
TRANSCRIPTS OF "POWERFUL"
AND "POWERLESS" STYLES   127

Powerless Style (Female Witness)   128
Powerful Style (Female Witness)   132

Appendix
2
TRANSCRIPTS OF NARRATIVE
AND FRAGMENTED STYLES   137

Fragmented Style   138
Narrative Style   144

Appendix

3

TRANSCRIPTS OF HYPERCORRECT
AND FORMAL STYLES 149

Hypercorrect Style 149
Formal Style 153

Appendix

4

TRANSCRIPTS OF OVERLAPPING
AND NONOVERLAPPING SPEECH 157

Nonoverlapping Style 158
Overlapping Style—Lawyer Dominates 164
Overlapping Style—Witness Dominates 172

REFERENCES 181

Cases 181
Books and Articles 182

INDEX 189

PREFACE

This book reports the work of the Law and Language Project at Duke University. The project began formally in 1974 with support from a National Science Foundation Law and Social Science Program Grant (GS-42742). Although the officially designated period for the research program has ended, research and teaching about law and language continue at Duke and at several other universities where those associated with the project are now located.

When this work began less than a decade ago, the field of law and language simply did not exist. Although we are still far from understanding the full range of issues involved, concern has grown and research has developed to the point where the term *law and language* suggests several types of relations, various theoretical and practical questions, and some competing approaches.

The Law and Language Project at Duke developed out of an effort to examine the following propositions: (1) Linguistic variation in any setting is not random, but socially patterned; and (2) sets of rules of successful strategies and tactics exist for competetive arenas of all sorts, including trial courtrooms. The first of these propositions is basic in sociolinguistics; the second is widely accepted within political anthropology. The Law and Language Project was conceived as an opportunity to relate these propositions, which have seldom been considered simultaneously. Taken together and used to design a study of language in the courtroom, they have led to the study of the patterns of language used in trial courts and the strategic use of language by courtroom participants.

With the permission of a North Carolina court, more than 150 hours of courtroom speech were recorded for this study. These tapes provided a rich archive for a variety of different types of inquiry, including the ethnography of courtroom speech and social psychological experiments focused on effects of different modes of presenting information in courts of law. Four sets of linguistic variables and related experimental studies have constituted a major portion of the research: (1) "powerful" versus "powerless" speech (based on Robin Lakoff's notions of "women's language," which we found to be generally present in courtroom speech but more closely associated with social class, educational background, and previous courtroom experience than gender); (2) hypercorrect versus formal speech (inspired by the work of William Labov and other linguists on hypercorrection); (3) narrative versus fragmented testimony (based on our observations in court and opinions expressed by lawyers about the significance of long versus short answers); and (4) simultaneous speech by witnesses and lawyers (inspired by work done in the conversational analysis tradition). All four sets of studies focus on the central question of the importance of form over content of testimony.

Although specific findings vary by experiment, the general conclusion reached in all is that presentational style is highly significant in affecting the reception of courtroom testimony, possibly more important than has been generally assumed. The experiments readily confirm that seemingly minor variations in manner of testifying produce major differences in the evaluation of testimony on such key factors as credibility, competence to testify, intelligence of speaker, and the like. In a court of law, factors affecting such evaluations of speakers may in turn affect the entire decision-making process. Thus, this book demonstrates the link between language and its strategic uses in an arena of signal importance for this and most other societies. The principles it demonstrates and the questions it raises extend far beyond the particular aspects of language selected for study, the courtroom, and even the society in which the study was conducted. Yet, at a more practical level, the findings of the Law and Language Project raise fundamental questions about the degree to which certain aspects of the American legal system as presently structured serve the cause of justice.

ACKNOWLEDGMENTS

Many colleagues have been closely associated with the research reported in this book. Several have contributed so much that they are in truth coauthors. I have been greatly assisted by and have learned much from them. E. Allan Lind and Bonnie Erickson provided needed assistance in the design, execution, and interpretation of social psychology experiments. John M. Conley worked closely with the project both as a graduate student in anthropology and as a law student and provided many kinds of help over several years. He has kindly allowed me to include a portion of his Ph.D. dissertation as part of Chapter 3 of this book. Laurens Walker offered useful suggestions based on his own studies of legal behavior and served as legal consel to the project. Lawrence Rosen gave critical advice and encouragement during the years he was a colleague on the faculty at Duke. Bruce Johnson assisted in the analysis and interpretation of linguistic data. Bowman K. Atkins shared my interest in the social organization of the courtroom and its effects on speech behavior during a year-long tutorial while he was an undergraduate at Duke. Many of the insights concerning silence in Chapter 6 are results of those discussions.

In addition to members of the Law and Language research team, several other persons provided assistance to the Project. Marilyn Endriss, Debbie Mercer, Michael Porter, and William Schmidheiser assisted in the preparation of the experiments during the summer of 1975. The

Durham County (North Carolina) Courts generously cooperated with this research program. Without the help of Judges Anthony Brannon and Maurice Braswell and of Mary Tilley, the courtroom observations on which all later work depended would not have been accomplished so easily. Whereas our presence and efforts necessarily complicated their daily routines, their assistance and toleration made our work possible and much easier. Those persons whose speech we studied in court and those who served as experimental subjects must necessarily remain anonymous. For their assistance, however, we are indeed appreciative.

I acknowledge with thanks those many colleagues in the social sciences who encouraged me to undertake and to pursue the study of courtroom language. I count among those who provided this encouragement some who were my own teachers as well as others whose research has given direction to my work. In lieu of a lengthy list of names, I mention instead some ideas and principles that they contributed: a dedication to the craft of ethnography; an interest in the general relations between language and society; a specific interest in the language used in particular contexts like religion and politics; the challenge to seek out connections between law and other aspects of culture, like language; and the encouragement to consider anthropological and linguistic issues not only in exotic settings but also in my own culture.

Donald Black's conviction that the study of law and language has an important place both in the field of law and society and in his series Studies on Law and Social Control is much appreciated. The staff of Academic Press has been supportive and encouraging. In preparing the typescript, Sylvia Terrell, Anna Stinson, and Dina Grinstead have typed and retyped various drafts through what must have seemed at times to be an unending stream of revisions.

Special thanks are due to Curt Richardson and Dave Koppenhaver for helping me keep up the pace during the summer of 1981, when most of this book was written.

Several members of my family helped by providing both motives and means for completing this book. My parents, Mary and Jack, first brought questions about language and society into my awareness. My wife Jean unselfishly gave support through both the joyous and the difficult moments of research and writing. My children, Claire and Emily, tolerated my many moods and periods of seclusion and even learned to put aside their own interests to inquire politely about my progress while writing.

Permission of coauthors and publishers to adapt from the following list of earlier reports of the Duke Law and Language Project is gratefully acknowledged.

Ethnography and experimentation—Partners in legal research. W. M. O'Barr and E. A. Lind. In *The Trial Process*, B. D. Sales, ed. (New York: Plenum), 1981, pp. 181–207.

The language of the law. W. M. O'Barr. In *Language in the U.S.A.*, C. F. Ferguson and S. B. Heath, eds. (New York: Cambridge University Press), 1981, pp. 386–406.

Political aspects of speech styles in American trial courtrooms. W. M. O'Barr, L. Walker, J. M. Conley, B. Erickson, and B. R. Johnson. In *Working Papers in Culture and Communication* (Philadelphia: Temple University Department of Anthropology), Vol. 1, No. 1, 1976, pp. 27–40.

The power of language: Presentational style in the courtroom. J. M. Conley, W. M. O'Barr, and E. A. Lind. *Duke Law Journal*, Vol. 1978, No. 6, 1979, pp. 1375–1399. Copyright © 1979, Duke University School of Law.

Social attributions and conversational style in trial testimony. E. A. Lind, B. Erickson, J. M. Conley, and W. M. O'Barr. *Journal of Personality and Social Psychology*, Vol. 36, 1978, pp. 1558–1567. Copyright © 1978 by the American Psychological Association. Adapted by permission of the publisher and authors.

The social significance of speech in the courtroom. E. A. Lind and W. M. O'Barr. In *Language and Social Psychology*, H. Giles and R. St. Clair, eds. (Oxford: Basil Blackwell, and University Park, Md.: University Press), 1979, pp. 66–87.

When a juror watches a lawyer. W. M. O'Barr and J. M. Conley. *Barrister*, Vol. 3, No. 2, 1976, pp. 8–11, 33. Copyright © 1976, Young Lawyers' Division of the American Bar Association.

"Women's Language" or "Powerless Language"? W. M. O'Barr and B. K. Atkins. In *Women and Language in Literature and Society*, S. McConnell-Ginet, R. Borker, and N. Furman, eds. (New York: Praeger), 1980, pp. 93–110.

Speech style and impression formation in a court setting. Bonnie Erickson, E. Allan Lind, Bruce C. Johnson, and William M. O'Barr. *Journal of Experimental Social Psychology*, Vol. 14, 1978, pp. 266–279.

1

INTRODUCTION

The Importance of Form in Language

It is common knowledge that how something is said may be more important than what is actually said. For example, when a parent scolds a child, *Don't talk to me that way,* the emphasis is on the manner in which the message is being presented. When lovers whisper "sweet nothings" to one another, the important point is not what they are saying but that they are in intimate communication. Similarly, the accusation, *It wasn't what you said, but how you said it,* or the assessment, *His manner betrayed him,* underscore the widely held belief in this culture, and probably in most others, that FORM COMMUNICATES. This assertion does not deny or minimize in any way the importance of what is usually referred to as content. Rather, it points out that unless form—including paralinguistic features (intonation, pitch, etc.) as well as nonverbal clues (gestures)—supports and buttresses content, people question the validity and sincerity of the message. As a consequence, mannerisms can betray what a person might wish to keep secret; how one talks can communicate as much or more than what is actually said; and form may become so important on some occasions that its message overrides other content.

What is not commonly known is much about how important form really is. That form communicates is taken for granted; and that it is important, in fact very important, is generally acknowledged. For example, a popular song of a few decades ago whose words included *Please refrain from flushing toilet while train is in the station, I love you* shows the importance of form. A suitor lacking words of his own borrows from a sign in the train's lavatory. The "filler" is not heard. What matters is the expression of feelings—in this case through action and form. Most communication does not dismiss content so flamboyantly. Yet it takes only a few words like *whosoever goeth* to connote Biblical solemnity, or a phrase like *know all men by these presents* to suggest the authority of the law. To decipher such information, to hear the message communicated by form, a listener must rely on vast knowledge acquired through membership in a particular culture. Information of this sort is among the hardest to explain to foreigners and among the most difficult to acquire in another culture. But receiving such messages is not dependent on one's conscious acknowledgement or evaluation. Indeed, it is uncommon to discuss form directly. It is usually relegated to the level of feelings, intuitions, and perceptions.

This book is dedicated to the study of the importance of form. The initial working proposition is that form is, at the very least, one important component of the total message and its reception. I intend to demonstrate that form may at times be highly significant, even to the point where a change in form can alter or reverse the impact of a message. The arena chosen for investigating this proposition is the trial courtroom. Other situations might also have been chosen since this is a general proposition about the nature of communication. What makes the court especially interesting is that language strategy is generally recognized by participants, although poorly understood by them. Investigating communication in the courtroom is simultaneously an opportunity to investigate the importance of form and to seek insight into the role of language in the legal process.

Many linguists argue that form and content are inseparable, that form is a part of content.[1] I do not take exception to this position. Indeed, I intend to support it by demonstrating the inseparability of form and content in a setting where it is customary for many or most of those who normally operate in it to think of "facts" and "demeanor" as separable and different. A court may take a witness's assertion that he

---

[1] Grice (1975), for example, argues that the meaning of an utterance is more than its literal meaning; it includes as well the contextual meaning of the utterance. The difference, for example, between *I think the car hit him* and *The car hit him* might be argued to be merely a matter of style or form, or alternatively, to reflect differences in the implied meaning of the two utterances.

lacked a job as "fact" and deal with it accordingly. But human beings, who are after all the decision makers whether they be judge or jurors, also hear the manner in which a witness presents this information. Clues about trustworthiness, confidence, faithfulness of recall, and so on are to be found in paralinguistic and nonverbal mannerisms. Further information about the speaker is yielded by such seemingly minor variations as these:

(a) *I don't got no job.*
(b) *Job, I don't have one.*
(c) *I ain't got no job.*
(d) *I don't have a job.*

Unlike the others, sentence (a) suggests a speaker who comes from a background where the native language, like Spanish, requires the use of double negatives. In (b) the syntax is more likely to come from a speaker whose German or Yiddish background demands a word order quite different from ordinary English. In (c) the double negative with *ain't* might be uttered by some black Americans. Finally, (d) is what is expected from speakers of Standard American English. Thus, so-called noncontent features of language in fact carry much information—information about characteristics of the speaker, the situation, and the like which cannot be separated from other parts of the message.

There are both expected and customary forms for messages, and there are often forms that are unexpected and uncustomary. Sometimes there are even ritualized formulas for messages, as in greetings. In American English, people asking, *How are you?* expect responses like *Good* or *Fine,* not elaborate statements about health. Such packaged responses are expected, customary, and fit the required formula. How then are speakers to know that others may actually be unwell or have some sort of difficulties? Most often, this information is communicated by the manner of responding. Receivers may then draw their own conclusions and proceed to inquire further IF THEY WISH. It is important to recognize the nonobligatory and somewhat ambiguous information communicated by form. Such information is open to discussion and interpretation in a way that mere "overt content" is not. One may ignore it (not meaning, of course, that such messages of form are not heard), or one may attempt to decipher their meanings by depending on intuitions, asking for further information, checking perceptions against those of others, or using some other means. Customary and expected forms are monitored and heard as such. When expectations are not met, then participants must determine what breaks in form indicate.

The information communicated through form is primarily social.[2] Pronunciation, vocabulary, and grammar all give clues about the speaker's
education and social class. Accents, unusual words or phrases, and the
rate of speaking may reveal information about regional origin. Age and
sex are registered in myraid ways beyond pitch—older persons continue
using speech patterns common in childhood (Labov 1966) and males and
females adopt different patterns of enunciation, grammar, and vocabulary
in early years and continue these patterns in adulthood (Fischer 1958,
Thorne and Henley 1975). In addition, form conveys information about
the context or situation in which speech occurs. Although *father, dad,*
and *old man* may refer to the same parent, the situations in which the
different forms are likely to be used vary in formality, whether the parent
is present, and so on. In some situations a particular STYLE or REGISTER[3]
of language is customary, as this critic of legal language shows:

> When a man gives you an orange, he simply says: "Have an orange." But
> when the transaction is entrusted to a lawyer, he adopts this form: "I hereby
> give and convey to you, all and singular, my estate and interest, right, title,
> claim and advantages of and in said orange, together with its rind, skin, juice,
> pulp, and pips and all rights and advantages therein and full power to bite,
> suck, or otherwise eat the same or give the same away with or without the
> rind, skin, juice, pulp and pips, anything hereinbefore or hereinafter or in
> any other means of whatever nature or kind whatsoever to the contrary in
> anywise nothwithstanding" [Hager 1959:74–75, quoting from *The Tulsa Trib-
> une,* October 6, 1959].

In addition to a transmittal or rights in the orange, this phrasing gives
"legality" to the transaction.

Beyond communication of information about speaker and situation,
form can and often does communicate information about the relationship
between the speaker and the intended audience. Brown and Ford (1961)
give a convincing demonstration of how this process works in American
English. They note three basic forms of address common among pairs
of adults: (1) both persons use a title and last name in addressing the
other (*Mr. Smith, Mr. Jones*), (2) both use the other's first name (*John,
Frank*), or (3) one uses a title and last name while the other reciprocates
with the first name (*Mr. Smith, Frank*). The three situations are likely
to be observed in different contexts: Mutual use of titles with last names
indicates formality and tends to occur among recently introduced per-

---

[2] An extensive discussion of social information communicated by stylistic variations in
speech is found in Giles and Powesland (1975).
[3] American linguists tend to use the concept of STYLE to refer to co-variation on many
levels of language (Ervin-Tripp 1964) while British linguists tend more often to use the
concept of REGISTER (Ellis and Ure 1969) for much the same purpose.

sons; one-sided use of title and last name coupled with use of first name by the other party typifies relationships between persons of unequal status; and reciprocal first names—most common of all—is usual between adults of roughly equal status. In addition to these basic possibilities, Brown and Ford report other variants: last names only, suggestive of a "military" type of relationship; special terms for spouses, relatives, and lovers (the saccharine terms: *honey, sweetie, sugar*; and the animal ones: *kitten, tiger*); and terms for those whose first names would be used if known: *Mac, Buddy*. Coded within forms of address, they argue, is information about the formality and equality of the relationship.

Form may thus reflect and reinforce social relationships. But it may also create or transform them (Varenne 1978). Externally defined aspects of a relationship, like that between an employer and employee, are validated and confirmed through the use of nonreciprocal address terms, whereas a shift to mutual use of first names is likely to be a reflection of a changing relationship as well as a catalyst for further change. In choosing among the alternative forms of address, parties define a relationship as close or distant, as formal or informal, and as equal or unequal. Form is ubiquitous in language as are the messages coded within it. Even the attempt to minimize information conveyed by form is in itself a statement about the relationship between the speaker and the person spoken to.

Language Strategy

In his book on political competition, the anthropologist F. G. Bailey (1969) distinguishes two kinds of rules. NORMATIVE rules are statements expressing publicly acceptable values. They reflect the public face of politics and carry strong moral valuations. PRAGMATIC rules, by contrast, are statements not about whether a particular line of conduct is just or unjust, but about whether or not it will be effective. These rules are the private wisdom of political success and are morally neutral. Bailey suggests that both types of rules coexist in competitive situations. There are the agreed upon, public rules about how to win, and there are—as everyone knows—other rules of effective strategy.

Although Bailey does not deal in *Stratagems and Spoils* with either the courtroom as a competitive arena or with strategies involving language, it requires only a short step to do so. Rules of procedure are in effect normative rules. They outline the agreed upon, approved means for introducing evidence, ruling on admissibility, examining witnesses, and so on. They outline the sorts of issues that are objectionable: Hearsay, for example, is normally excluded; expresssions of opinions and conclusions by witnesses are normally disallowed; and leading questions are usually limited to cross-examination or dealing with children, persons with impaired abilities, and certain other types of witnesses. All such rules of procedure are, in Bailey's sense, normative rules. They are the accepted, publicly acknowledged rules for conducting a trial.

But there are also rules about successful courtroom tactics and what works. Although they are not found in any treatises on procedure, successful lawyers know many such rules. For example, it may be worthwhile to introduce evidence while knowing that it will be objected to and ruled inadmissible. Doing so may be strategically useful IN ORDER TO BRING SUCH INFORMATION TO THE ATTENTION OF THE JURY. Even though instructed to forget inadmissible evidence, lawyers know that jurors cannot and do not in fact do so. Moreover, objections of the opposition counsel may only serve to call more attention to the material. Such are pragmatic rules of courtroom procedure.

Although not codified in any strict sense, these rules of successful strategy are sometimes described in trial practice manuals, the books on courtroom tactics written by successful lawyers. In their book, *Successful Techniques for Criminal Trials* (1971), F. Lee Bailey and Henry B. Rothblatt discuss several such rules. For example, they have this to say about using the special vulnerabilities of children to advantage:

> Young children are prone to suggestion. The child is likely to answer "yes" to a question that suggests a yes answer. For example, where you want to establish that his story was carefully rehearsed, phrase your examination as follows: "Of course, you talked to your mommy and daddy about what you would say in court today . . . . Now, how many times did you speak to your mommy and daddy? . . ." Once you have received a series of affirmative answers, shift your line of questioning to the central issues in the case. Continue to phrase your questions so that affirmative answers will follow, containing favorable answers for the defendant [Bailey and Rothblatt 1971:188].[4]

Nothing of this sort is contained in the rules of evidence. This is not a public rule, but a private one about how to win.[5]

Even though they might not be able to articulate principles as consciously or specifically as Bailey and Rothblatt, most people know intuitively that skillful use of form can help achieve their goals. Two examples show the generality of language strategies.

[4] This and subsequent quotes cited to Bailey and Rothblatt 1971 are reprinted from *Successful Techniques for Criminal Trials* by F. Lee Bailey and Henry B. Rothblatt by special permission. Copyrighted © 1971, by The Lawyers Co-operative Publishing Company.

[5] Trial practice manuals, especially the advice offered in them about language strategies, are discussed at length in Chapter 3, pages 31–38.

A minister is disturbed by the fact that the public continues to use the church parking lot while shopping in nearby stores. As a consequence there are usually not enough spaces available for church meetings on weekdays. His efforts, although diligent, continue to fail until he comes up with a sign that reads: *Thou Shalt Not Park.*

At an informal meeting in his office, a departmental chairman says to another member of the university faculty: "John, I've got a problem—or, I should say, we've got a problem and I think you can help solve it."

The minister's phrasing, following the format of religious commandments, seems to carry some of their authority. His is a simple, but effective language strategy. And the chairman's shift from *I* to *we* is an effort to increase solidarity. It is a small change, but one that communicates quite a different message about power structure in the organization.

The point of these examples is straightforward: Whether consciously planned or merely the result of native intuition, form communicates. As form varies, the messages communicated vary as well. Some forms are strategically more useful because of the connotations they carry. In themselves, these are not new insights. Classical rhetoric and oratory are based on this knowledge as are rules of journalistic style, advertising practice, media presentation, and such everyday rules as the etiquette of social interaction. Yet, such a perspective on the legal process is neither widely recognized nor understood by the public, by social scientists who study it, nor even by lawyers and their witnesses who regularly employ such strategies. Accordingly, this book seeks to bring about a wider recognition of the existence of language strategies and an understanding of how they work in trial courtrooms.

Neither language nor strategy are new concerns for anthropology. Both American and European anthopologists have put considerable energy into efforts to understand the relation of language to culture and society.[6]

---

[6] In American anthropology, it is customary to date significant interest in language and culture as beginning with the work of Whorf in the 1920s. Several of his essays are collected and published in Whorf (1956). Linguistic anthropology is generally recognized as one of four major subfields American anthropology. In France, the work of Claude Levi-Strauss relies heavily on analogies of culture to language (see, for example, Levi-Strauss 1968). In Britain, Malinowski (1935) focused on the instrumental role of language in achieving magical results as does Tambiah (1968) more recently. Several major collections, among them Ardener (1971) and Bloch (1975), attest to the growing interest of British anthropologists in language and society. In addition, many anthropologists rely heavily on the idea of linguists and philosophers of language such as de Saussure (1916), Austin (1962), and Searle (1969).

And within the subfield of political anthropology, significant attention has focused on understanding strategy.[7] However, researchers have rarely considered language and strategy simultaneously, and consequently not much is known about language strategies per se.

During the 1960s, sociolinguistics developed and flourished, at least in part, as a reaction to and criticism of Chomskian linguistics. A few years earlier, Chomsky (1957) had proposed a basic unity of the underlying structures of all human languages. He made particularly strong argument for the basic similarity of grammar across languages. "Deep" structure was universal; much of what varied was "surface" structures. His theories and the research efforts they inspired have greatly advanced the understanding of the nature of language itself and of many specific aspects of it such as language acquisition, disorders, and so on. In his arguments for the universality of language structures, Chomsky (1965) dismissed most variation in language as superficial and therefore not worthy of much attention by linguists in their quest for language universals. Such matters as the differences between English and German verb phrases or internal variation in style or form tended to be seen as rather uninteresting matters that could in any case be explained by transformations of the underlying structures. Differences among the four sentences on page 3 would be explained similarly. Part of the impetus for the development of sociolinguistics was a conviction on the part of many linguists that such differences are consequential in social life. Speakers of different languages, despite any basic similarities in all human languages, do not as a matter of course understand one another; and speakers of varieties within a language gain essential information from differences in form. Sociolinguistics thus emerged in the 1960s as the study of variation, not of universals, in language. In its short history, many elegant and impressive descriptions of patterns of variation in language have been produced. For example, it has been possible to show the systematic nature of variation between old and young speakers of a language, between men and women, between native and nonnative speakers, and so on. Yet, in all this, the common procedure has been the discovery of regularities within language variation and the relation of these to social factors which explain how the patterns of variation work— hence, the term sociolinguistics.

Most sociolinguistic researchers show a clear preference for the use of social factors in explaining language variation. It is uncommon to find researchers using language to understand social phenomena. In working

---

[7] Bailey (1969) contains one of the most extensive treatment of strategy to date. See also Barth (1966) and the papers in Kapferer (1976) for other studies of strategy.

toward an understanding of the relation between two such matters as language and society, it is difficult to attempt to explain both. Rather, in relating phenomena not usually considered together, explanation of one must be the goal while the other is the means. For most sociolinguists, then, explaining language is the goal whereas social factors are the means used. It is in linking language and society in this manner that the field of sociolinguistics has been so successful.

The other way the relationship might be conceived—using language to explain society—has received a great deal less attention. Many linguists who identify themselves as sociolinguists claim that the goal of linguistics is the understanding of language, and that questions about society are properly left to social scientists. Although this view has been rather widely accepted in practice by the linguists, social scientists have not assumed much responsibility in studying the relationship of language to society.

Why and how then has political anthropology largely ignored language strategy? First, there is little agreement among political anthropologists about the most important issues deserving attention. Cultural anthropologists interested in politics have primarily been interested in the nature of political systems and especially in questions of the evolution of different types of systems. Social anthropologists have largely ignored or dismissed these concerns and focused instead on the internal operation of political systems and on efforts to understand general properties of leadership, coercion, sanctions, factionalism, and the like. These matters in turn have been given only limited attention by cultural anthropologists whose interests in the political systems and evolution per se did not allow detailed attention on the operation of political processes within systems. For this reason, most cultural anthropologists would simply not focus on strategy in the first place. The matter of language strategy would consequently get no attention at all.

A second, and actually more important reason, has to do with the tradition among social anthropologists of studying language and politics. In the introduction to *Political Language and Oratory in Traditional Society,* Maurice Bloch (1975) considers why political anthropologists have paid so little attention to language and politics. His incisive answer is a sharp commentary on the reality of anthropological fieldwork. Most of what is known about political life in traditional society, Bloch notes, has been learned not through direct observation of politics but through listening to people talk about it; and yet, as listeners, anthropologists have been generally so concerned with attempts to cull the essence of politics in action via the indirect route of asking questions of informants that they have failed to listen to how people talk about politics, and hence they have missed one of the richest and most revealing sources of data of all: the language of politics. David Turton, a contributor to Bloch's book, suggests that one reason anthropologists studying politics have tended to underplay the role to oratory is that

> [t]he anthropologists concerned simply did not, and indeed could not, understand well enough what was going on in public discussion until it was too late. For the detailed and systematic study of public meetings clearly presupposes that the investigator is already fluent in the language and has a good understanding of the issues being discussed at such meetings [1975:164–165].

Thus, despite claims of holism, neither cultural nor social anthropologists actually turned sufficient interest to language and politics for there to be any real understanding of the instrumental role of language in society.

Language and Justice

Not all legal systems are interwoven with language in the same fashion. Among the systems most different from our own is that of the Eskimo, whose dispute settlement procedures are remarkably simple institutionally: They lack courts, police, prisons, and have no formal statement of laws. Yet, disputes manage to get resolved to the satisfaction of most members of the community, and social life proceeds after resolution in an orderly manner. The traditional headbutting contest used in some Eskimo communities to settle disputes strikes most Westerners as especially barbaric and foreign to our cultural notions of justice. In the contest, the dispute is transformed into a contest in which opposing parties butt heads until one is victorious and thereby wins in the original conflict.

> [T]he opponents face each other, alternately delivering straight-armed blows on the side of the head, until one is felled and thereby vanquished. . . . The opponent moves his head forward to meet the blow. He who is upset is derided by the onlookers and comes out badly in the singing. Stealth, cunning, and ambush are not part of such contests; the strongest wins by pitted strength. The object of the boxing and butting contests is not annihilation, but subjection. Nor is there any more or less concern with basic justice than there was in the medieval wager of battle. Whatever the facts underlying the dispute, they are irrelevant to the outcome. The man who wins, wins social esteem. He who loses, suffers loss of social rank [Hoebel 1964:92].

What seems especially unjust to Americans reacting to this ancient Eskimo custom is that it favors the physically strong while putting the smaller or weaker person to disadvantage. Our sense of justice, and the cultural values on which it is based, demand that all persons be treated equally by the law, that it be blind to race, class, age, and sex. Yet, as we say all this, we know it is not in fact true. Any number of sociological studies show nonwhites do not have equal access to the legal system. Nor is social class irrelevant to access, type of punishment, and even justice in our legal system. The same is true for age and sex. Even those of us who willingly recognize such flaws in the American justice system find it difficult to accept the head-butting contest as even approaching the justice meted out by our imperfect system whose high ideals seldom find realization in practice.

I shall not attempt to evaluate the American justice system by comparing it to others like the traditional Eskimo legal system—for neither of these systems could possibly work in the other environment. Rather, I bring up the head-butting contest for consideration precisely because it seems so far from justice IN OUR CULTURE'S TERMS. Yet, when we look closely for similarities, they may not be difficult to find. In this book, I present evidence to show that, as settlements depending on physical means favor the physically strong and powerful, settlements depending on verbal means similarly favor people who are either on their own or through their advocates most able to manipulate words. A decision as to whether the two types of systems differ with respect to fairness and justice will be left to the reader.

The Study of Courtroom Language

A trial might be thought of as a situation in which many people, often as many as 10 or more, present various versions of what happened. Their versions overlap to some degree and together tell a story. As the trial unfolds and opposing sides present evidence, it becomes clear that all versions cannot be equally correct. It is the role of the jury (or judge in a bench trial) to decide which witnesses to believe and whose testimony to hold above others in reconciling differences. Underlying the trial process and ultimately the decisions made in it are the principles of communication stated in preceding pages: Form is communication; variations in form communicate different messages; and speakers manipulate form, but not always consciously, to achieve beneficial results. Practicing attorneys as well as researchers who study courtroom behavior know this. But beyond general acknowledgment that it is true, nobody has managed to be very precise. There are several reasons for this.

First, legal practitioners are, properly, concerned with planning and executing courtroom strategies and thus are unable to devote much attention to observing their own behavior or that of other participants. Even those who win most of their cases have difficulty articulating precise reasons for their success.

A second reason for why understanding the role of language in courtroom processes is limited is that social scientists have not paid much attention to language in the courtroom. Thus far, sociolinguistic studies have focused on the rich variety of socially patterned language variation but have done little with courtroom language per se. Those social scientists who have studied courtroom processes have not for the most part devoted much attention to language as a factor to be explained or as a factor that can help explain the legal process itself.

Third, and perhaps most important of all, courtroom analysts, whether legal professionals or social scientists, face considerable difficulty in breaking down and understanding the complicated processes that occur in court. Lawyers find it difficult to determine the relative importance of various causal factors in a court of law. For social scientists, the methods of conventional analysis require so much time and effort that even a great deal of effort yields understanding of only a small number of factors. Thus, despite the importance of language in the law and of language as a strategic resource to lawyers, the role of language in courtroom chemistry has been and remains poorly comprehended.

The specific objective of this book is to advance interest in the role of language in legal processes through a specific foray into courtroom language. Other aspects of language and law such as legislation about language or the specific type of language used in legal contexts are touched on only briefly. The approach to the study of courtroom language is empirical. The methods are eclectic: The participant–observational techniques of social anthropology are coupled with the analytic techniques of sociolinguistics to gather data about language use in court and to discover the patterns in it; then the experimental techniques of social psychology are used to test hypotheses about the effects of different forms of language used in court. The central part of the book reports several studies of courtroom language. A common format for discussing these studies includes an explanation of why each variable was selected, how it is patterned in the courtroom, what has been learned through experiments about it, and a discussion of related studies that have dealt with similar phenomena in other contexts.

The final chapter discusses the implications of the empirical findings about courtroom language for social science disciplines interested in language and/or legal processes and for the law where these matters raise both practical and jurisprudential concerns. Before beginning the specific study of courtroom language, however, I approach language and law at a more general level. In Chapter 2, I examine the nature of legal language, in both its written and spoken forms. And in Chapter 3, I consider some assumptions about language and communication built into the law. Both chapters provide background for the empirical investigation of language strategy in court in the chapters that follow.

2

THE NATURE OF
LEGAL LANGUAGE

An anthropologist, Charles Frake, writing about a Philippine people he studied, notes:

> The Yakan legal system is manifest almost exclusively by one kind of be-
> havior: talk. Consequently, the ethnographer's record of observations of lit-
> igation is largely a linguistic record, and the legal system is a code for talking,
> a linguistic code [Frake 1969:109].

A lawyer, David Mellinkoff, assessing the language used by legal professionals in contemporary America, describes law as a "profession of
words" (Mellinkoff 1963:vi). Similarly, a philologist, Frederick Philbrick,
analyzing forensic style among English-speaking lawyers, observes:

> Lawyers are students of language by profession. . . . They exercise their
> power in court by manipulating the thoughts and opinions of others, whether
> by making speeches or questioning witnesses. In these arts the most successful
> lawyers reveal (to those who can appreciate their performance) a highly
> developed skill [Philbrick 1949:vi].

All three observers are pointing out the preeminence of language in legal
processes, both in this culture and in others. Yet, despite the close
connection and importance of language to law, neither social scientists,
linguists, nor lawyers have paid much attention to it. This chapter focuses

primarily on American legal language. It examines legal language as it differs from ordinary English and considers how its written and spoken varieties differ from one another. A number of important studies of language and law are reviewed to facilitate an understanding of the basic issues that have attracted practical and scholarly attention, the conclusions that have been reached, and the questions that remain.

Written Legal Language

The most systematic and extensive treatment of the nature and origins of American legal language is David Mellinkoff's *The Language of the Law* (1963). Mellinkoff, a professor of law, carefully traces modern legal usages from their roots in Anglo–Saxon, Latin, French, and premodern English. In introducing his study, he observes:

> [I]n a vast literature the portion devoted to the language of the law is a single grain of sand at the bottom of a great sea. The profession is properly more concerned with rights, obligations, and wrongs, and the incidental procedures. . . . [A]t this writing, the subject of "language" is absent from most law indexes and only in capsule form in the rest. It is certainly not too early, nor is it too late, to commence a systematic examination of the language lawyers use [Mellinkoff 1963:vi].

Since most of Mellinkoff's materials are drawn from the legal literature, and only incidentally from his own observations in courtrooms, distinctions between the spoken language of the courtroom and the written language of legal documents, motions, opinions, and the like receive little attention. Nonetheless, his observations of the nature of the language of the law are astute. The following list of nine characteristics of the language of the law is abstracted from his work (1963:11–29). According to Mellinkoff, these attributes of legal language occur to some degree in everyday English, but it is their greater frequencies and co-occurrences that characterize legal language. It should also be noted that many of these attributes overlap and a given expression may illustrate several of these characteristics.

1. COMMON WORDS WITH SPECIALIZED LEGAL MEANINGS
   action for 'law suit', *instrument* for 'legal document', *of course* for 'as a matter of right', *serve* for 'deliver legal papers', etc.
2. RARE WORDS FROM OLD AND MIDDLE ENGLISH
   aforesaid, forthwith, witnesseth, and various words built on the

roots of *here, there,* and *where* (such as *hereafter, herein, thereon, therewith, whereas, whereby*), etc.

3. LATIN WORDS AND PHRASES
   corpus delicti, mens rea, nolo contendere, nulla bona, res judicata, venire, etc.

4. FRENCH WORDS NOT IN THE GENERAL VOCABULARY
   chose in action, demurrer, fee simple, esquire, voir dire, etc., plus others that are more common, but are used in legal contexts: *assault, battery, counsel, felony, heir, plaintiff, tort, suit, reprieve,* etc.

5. TERMS OF ART[1]
   contributory negligence, eminent domain, garnishment, judicial notice, injunction, negotiable instrument, prayer, stare decisis, etc.

6. PROFESSIONAL ARGOT[2]
   inferior court, issue of fact, issue of law, order to show cause, pursuant to stipulation, reversed and remanded, without prejudice, etc.

7. FORMAL EXPRESSIONS
   approach the bench, the deceased, arrested in flagrante delicto, comes now the plaintiff, Your Honor, may it please the court, know all men by these presents, etc.

8. WORDS WITH FLEXIBLE MEANINGS
   adequate, approximately, clean and neat condition, extreme cruelty, obscene, promptly, satisfy, undue interference, worthless, etc.

9. ATTEMPTS AT EXTREME PRECISION
   absolutes such as *all, none, irrevocable, never;* restrictions such as *and no more, and no other purpose, shall not constitute a waiver;* unlimiting phrases such as *including but not limited to, shall not be deemed to limit, nothing contained herein shall;* etc.

In addition to these attributes of legal language, Mellinkoff mentions four mannerisms that further characterize legal language. First, legal language is extraordinarily wordy. *Annul and set aside* is used instead of the simpler 'annul'. 'Remove' would appear to be sufficient, but the language of the law is likely to contain instead *entirely and completely remove.* And needless redundancies abound, such as *totally null and void* for 'void' and *written document* for 'document'.

Second, legal language lacks clarity. This pattern jury instruction is a good example:

---

[1] Technical words and phrases whose meanings are seldom disputed in the law.
[2] Words and phrases used for communications among lawyers.

You are instructed that contributory negligence in its legal significance is such an act or omission on the part of the plaintiff amounting to a want of ordinary care and prudence as occurring or co-operating with some negligent act of the defendant, was the proximate cause of the collision which resulted in the injuries or damages complained of. It may be described as such negligence on the part of the plaintiff, if found to exist, as helped to produce injury or the damages complained of, and if you find from a preponderance of all the evidence in either of these cases that plaintiff in such case was guilty of any negligence that helped proximately to bring about or produce the injuries of which plaintiff complains, then and in such place the plaintiff cannot recover [Mellinkoff 1963:26].

Paraphrased, Mellinkoff suggests it might read this way: "If Mrs. Smith's injury was caused partly by Mr. Jones's negligence and partly by her own negligence, she cannot recover [1963:26]."

Third, legal language is pompous. Words like *solemn, supreme,* and the like are used to evoke respect. Contrary opinions and evidence tend to be characterized as *absurd, mere,* and *unconscionable.* And legal language is filled with self-righteous expressions: *clearly pointed out, excluded in unmistakable language, dispose of the argument.*

Finally, legal language is above all simply dull. Mellinkoff puts it this way: "It is sometimes assumed that an important subject deserves ponderous treatment, and this dread of inappropriate levity has saddled the law with a weight of equally inappropriate dullness [1963:29]".

Nearly 20 years after it was first published, Mellinkoff's study of legal language remains the most extensive analysis to be published. A few efforts by linguists have complemented his work by pointing out some additional characteristics of written legal language that he either does not consider or treats only briefly. The British linguists Crystal and Davy devote an entire chapter of *Investigating English Style* (1969) to the language of legal documents. They share Mellinkoff's interest in the special vocabulary of legal language and its history. In addition, they focus on certain features of the structure and organization of legal texts. Among their observations are the following:

1. Legal language is INSTRUMENTAL language. It is used to make and to record contracts, to impose conditions, to confer rights and privileges, to register information for future scrutiny, etc. Legal language therefore intends to be unambiguous. Since it is frequently possible to interpret ordinary language in multiple ways, lawyers must make an effort to at least reduce this ambiguity, to communicate just one set of meanings while excluding many others. Whether they manage to do so is, of course, open to question. Crystal and Davy point out the conscious effort and

intention on the part of lawyers to do so. In addition, legal language is intended to be read. Rarely is a legal document composed spontaneously; rather, established formulas are drawn from standardized form books. Further, legal language is intended to be read (or deciphered!) by other persons with legal training. Almost no concern is given to whether it is comprehensible to lay people since it is not really intended that they should read legal documents.

2. Legal documents have some peculiar qualities not common in most other styles of English. For example, sentences tend to be long, self-contained units with minimal linkage to other sentences (either preceding or following them) in order to convey essential information. Documents contain only complete sentences that, despite their wordiness, can be reduced to an essential structure like *If X, then Y shall do Z* or other variations on this basic theme.

3. Legal English has many distinctive characteristics. There is extremely limited use of anaphora (pronouns, truncated verb phrases, demonstratives, etc.) in favor of repetition of full phrases and references as necessary to minimize confusion and ambiguity. Adverbial qualifiers that state conditions, qualifications, and so on (e.g., *on expiration, subject to any authorized endorsement*) are frequent as are nominalizations (e.g., *declaration, termination*) which often have postmodification (as in *any part then remaining unpaid*). Adjectives are infrequent, and intensifying adverbs (*very, rather*) are absent. In addition, Crystal and Davy discuss the distinctive vocabulary of legal language in terms similar to Mellinkoff's analysis.

4. The language of legal documents employs some semantic principles not used in ordinary English. These include:

(a) *Ejusdem generis:* General words following specific words apply only to things of the same class already mentioned (e.g., in *house, office, room, or other place,* the final item may not refer to an uncovered enclosure although it would be a "place" in ordinary English).

(b) *Expressio unius est exclusio alterius:* If a list of specific words is not followed by a general term, then all other things not mentioned are specifically excluded (e.g., *house, office, or room* allows no other places that do not fit one of these terms to be included).

(c) *Noscitur sociis:* The context in which any word appears may enter into the definition of its meaning.

(d) *The Golden Rule of interpretation:* The ordinary sense of words is to be used unless it would lead to some absurdity or inconsistency with the rest of the document.

Mellinkoff stresses the origins of contemporary American legal language that help explain many of its more peculiar characteristics. *The truth, the whole truth, and nothing but the truth*—poetic and rhythmic to be sure—is related to the ancient oaths of Old English. The influence of Anglo–Saxon, Latin, French, and older forms of English are reflected throughout contemporary usage in legal language. The use of many words when fewer would suffice is related to the multilingual origins of English law. *Acknowledge* (Old English) is often coupled with *confess* (Old French), *act* (French or Latin) with *deed* (Old English), *breaking* (Old English) with *entering* (French), and so on. The habit of using synonyms also includes terms originating from the same language, as in *by and with, each and every, have and hold* (all from Old English) and in *aid and abet, cease and desist, null and void* (from French or French–Latin).[3] Lengthy sentences and sparse punctuation—hallmarks of legal writing— owe their origins, at least in part, to the lack of faithfulness in copy- making prior to the advent of printing, in part to the influence of printers who, because of the nature of their craft, could not slough over squiggles and dots but had to make decisions about what, if any, forms of punc- tuation to use, and in part to the weight of tradition, once the precedent of lengthy, sparsely punctuated sentences had been established.

Studying the etymology of the language of the law gives one some sense of justification for its peculiar forms and usages. But the fact is that neither lawyers nor lay people, for the most part, are either schooled in philology or interested enough in it to develop much appreciation for the origins of twentieth-century American legal language. Lawyers are engaged in practicing the law, not studying it; and lay people—be they litigants, witnesses, or jurors—tend to be interested in the instrumental aspects of language, not in its history.

From time to time, the suggestion is made that simplification of legal language would improve its utility for both legal professionals and the public. Such suggestions are usually countered quickly by those who defend legal language as being more precise, actually shorter, and more

---

[3] In a study of language in religious contexts, Ferguson (1976:105) notes the high fre- quency of word pairing in the English of the *Book of Common Prayer* used in the Anglican Church. He finds the same two types of pairing as described for written legal language, namely, the combination of Romance loanwords with Anglo–Saxon glosses as well as the use of two synonymous words or phrases originating from the same language. In addition to occurring in at least two registers of English (religious as well as legal language), the practice of pairing is quite common in many languages. See, for example, the study of pairing in Rotinese by Fox (1974) and in Zinacantan by Bricker (1974). Their evidence suggests that pairing in other languages may also be due to borrowing, specific stylistic traditions of particular languages, or, as with English, both reasons.

durable and intelligible than ordinary English (Mellinkoff 1963). The call for change and popularization of legal language, however, is not merely a twentieth-century phenomenon. Mellinkoff reports a variety of such efforts since French was first introduced into England following the Norman Conquest. Over the centuries the populist versus elitist arguments have been remarkably similar. A pair of articles published in 1959 and 1960 serve to illustrate the nature of such arguments.

The anticonventional position is argued by John W. Hager (1959) in his article "Let's Simplify Legal Language." Admittedly overstating his case at times to point out the seriousness of the problem as he sees it,[4] Hager notes that complicated legal language (or LEGALESE[5]) is found in legislative enactments, jury instructions, documents prepared for clients' use, pleadings, and in materials used in law schools. Lawyers, judges, and law professors are the ones responsible for perpetuating use of these forms. Arguing that most complicated legal pronouncements have far simpler and more easily understood equivalents in everyday English, Hager believes that changes in such a direction would serve both lawyers and law students as well as the public. The place to introduce such changes is, in his opinion, the law school.

Hager argues that four main problem areas are in need of change: (1) using archaic, obsolete forms that have passed out of ordinary usage; (2) using Latin and French words and phrases when English terms could be used instead; (3) assigning unusual legal meanings to ordinary English terms; and (4) writing unusually long sentences which often have little or no punctuation and contain many exceptions and qualifications. Learning to use this kind of language is an arduous task for law students. It results in obscuring simple, everyday ideas and puts understanding them beyond the reach of "most people."

Hager's essay contains some specific suggestions for transforming legal language into a form more like that of everyday English.

> Most language used in law can be simplified so that it needs no official interpreters. Its meaning could be made clear to almost everyone. There is nothing heretical or anti-literary in this idea. . . . Law is one device for social control. It should be written in plain, ordinary English so that the average layman understands it. Nor is this argument that legal language should be simplified a new one. As early as 1776, Jeremy Bentham demanded that laws be codified in such clear language that the ordinary man could understand his legal rights [1959:85].

[4] The example cited on page 4 appeared in Hager's article.
[5] This popularly used term for legal language seems most often to refer to written rather than spoken legal language. For greater precision, the terms WRITTEN LEGAL LANGUAGE and SPOKEN LEGAL LANGUAGE are used in this book instead of LEGALESE.

Hager's objectives amount to making legal usage more intelligible to lay people, who are, after all, the consumers of the work of lawyers. He contends that the suggested reforms would also benefit lawyers, who are unnecessarily burdened by the complexity of the language they use. Why then, if there is any validity to these claims, has legalese persisted? What purposes does it serve?

Hager suggests at least one reason for the persistence of legalese. In discussing jury instructions, he notes that most of them "would seem to be prepared with an eye toward an eventual appeal. Instructions would seem to be phrased to gain approval by an appellate court and not written to be understood by the jurors for whose guidance they, theoretically, at least, are given [1959:80]." This orientation of linguistic usage within the law toward legal institutions rather than toward the public at large is one of the most basic reasons why its special form appears to have been preserved. The goal is legal accuracy and consistency, not popular understanding and ease of comprehension.

Hager's article was followed in the same journal a few months later by an article entitled, "Let's Not Oversimplify Legal Language" (Aiken 1960). In his defense of legal usages, Aiken argues that "it will not do to re-tailor the legal lexicon to fit the transient tempos of each succeeding popular age [p. 363]." Aiken finds "such terms as *res, ipsa loquitur, caveat emptor,* proximate cause, indenture, bequeath, devise, and hereof, whereof, whence, hence, foregoing, said, etc., as entirely appropriate and acceptable modes of expression, properly used. Properly used, they are often the decided superior of ordinary words which have no associated specialization of meaning [p. 362]." He, like Hager, finds "a rampant and progressing decline of legal literacy, characterized by redundancy, obscurity of meaning, poor grammar, and practical abandonment of every classical virtue of the compositional art [p. 363]." His recommendations and solutions carry none of Hager's populist tones. Instead, he suggests: (*a*) elevating the standard of ordinary English by improving the primary and secondary educational processes to the point where the average number of words in a person's vocabulary has at least quadrupled; (*b*) placing a heavy emphasis on multilingual proficiency to permit frequent usage of more precise and meaningful foreign words and phrases than are contained in English; (*c*) requiring both legal and unabridged English dictionaries as texts in law schools; (*d*) requiring a demonstration of superior competence in English composition skills as a prerequisite for taking bar examinations; and other similar measures.

This exchange between Hager and Aiken is typical of the positions taken by lawyers in assessing the state of legal language. Similar exchanges have occurred at other times in the legal literature (cf. Beardsley

1941, Morton 1941, Gerhart 1954, Bowman 1970, Younger 1976). Often witty and amusing, the two sides tend repeatedly to make the same basic arguments. The reformers suggest that legal language is unnecessarily complex and should be simplified to make it more intelligible to the public at large and of less burden to legal professionals. They argue that the same ideas, for all intents, can be uttered in everyday English with greater clarity and no loss of meaning. The traditionalists argue that the importance of consistency in interpretation by the courts of particular words, terms, and even entire legal forms outweighs the advantages of popularizing and simplifying legal usage. Those who wish to preserve the form of legal language point out that departing from conventions could cause serious legal difficulties as a result of courts giving unpredicted or unexpected interpretations to any new usage.

Those who argue for the preservation of the nonordinary form of legal language are more concerned with how other legal professionals will interpret the language of the law than they are with whether the public will comprehend it. Much of courtroom dialogue is addressed "to the record" (i.e., couched with the potential of an appeals court in mind). Legal documents are prepared according to standard form books—not because these are tried and tested for lay comprehension—but because they ensure a greater ability to predict how the courts will interpret such documents.

Finally, the self-serving interests of lawyers are involved to some degree. On the reluctance of thirteenth-century lawyers in the British Isles to purge the English courts of French, Mellinkoff observes: "What better way of preserving a professional monopoly than by locking up your trade secrets in the safe of an unknown tongue? [1963:101]." The political scientist Murray Edelman, commenting on twentieth-century American legal language, has made essentially the same observation: "It is precisely its ambiguity that gives lawyers, judges, and administrators a political and social function, for unambiguous rules would, by definition, call neither for interpretation nor for argument as to their meaning [1964:139]." The language of the law is viewed as protecting both the law and the lawyer.

Spoken Legal Language

In contrast to the attention devoted to written legal language, little systematic effort by social scientists, linguists, or legal scholars has focused on spoken language. As a consequence, relatively little is known about the nature of spoken legal language, especially about ways in which it differs from written legal language.

Most treatises on legal language by lawyers either ignore spoken language or make the tacit assumption that spoken language in legal contexts is merely the actualization of the written variety.[6] How little concern lawyers tend to place on spoken language is amply demonstrated by a quick perusal of a major textbook dealing with language and its relation to the law, Bishin and Stone's *Law, Language, and Ethics* (1972). The authors make considerable effort to understand such topics as reasoning processes, the structure of language, the meaning of words, and the nature of ambiguity in language. Almost nothing is said in several hundred pages about spoken language, and hence the language of the courtroom and the law office. Attention is directed here, as elsewhere within the law, to opinions, documents, and treatises—not to the courtroom nor to the lawyer–client interaction as domains where the role and influence of language need consideration.

Social scientists and linguists have not done much better. Passing attention is paid here and there to spoken legal language, but there are virtually no attempts to deal directly and extensively with it.[7] Crystal and Davy's (1969) treatment is typical. They note, for example, the inappropriateness of considering spoken and written legal language as being closely related. The language of legal documents is, they point out,

> essentially a visual language, meant to be scrutinised in silence: it is, in fact, largely unspeakable at first sight, and anyone who tries to produce a spoken version is likely to have to go through a process of repeated and careful scanning in order to sort out the grammatical relationships which give the necessary clues to adequate phrasing [1969:194].

Crystal and Davy hint in a brief section of their book containing SUGGESTIONS FOR FURTHER ANALYSIS that spoken language might be regarded as essentially a fairly normal variety of conversational English that contains some fixed and familiar legal formulas (p. 244). Beyond this, however, they have nothing of substance to say about its characteristics nor how it differs from the language of written legal documents.

---

[6] The problem of relating written and spoken varieties of legal language is similar to that of dealing with the language–speech dichotomy. For a general discussion of language and speech, see de Saussure (1916) where a distinction is clearly drawn between SPEECH (or *parole*) as the actual utterances produced by speakers and LANGUAGE (or *langue*) as the shared pattern of regularities used by individuals in producing speech. Most contemporary linguists follow de Saussure's original distinctions between language and speech.

[7] Danet (1980b) contains an extensive bibliography and review of social scientific studies of language in legal processes.

My colleagues and I studied language varieties used in an American courtroom that we studied (O'Barr *et al.* 1976). Our description, although brief, suggests the range of language varieties likely to be found in other courtrooms (and by implication other legal contexts). We found four varieties of legal language:

FORMAL LEGAL LANGUAGE: The variety of spoken language used in the courtroom that most closely parallels written legal language;[8] used by the judge in instructing the jury, passing judgment, and "speaking to the record"; used by lawyers when addressing the court, making motions and requests, etc.; linguistically characterized by lengthy sentences containing much professional jargon and employing a complex syntax.

STANDARD ENGLISH: The variety of spoken language typically used in the courtroom by lawyers and most witnesses; generally labeled COR-RECT English and closely paralleling that taught as the standard in American classrooms; characterized by a somewhat more formal lexicon than that used in everyday speech.

COLLOQUIAL ENGLISH: A variety of language spoken by some wit-nesses and a few lawyers in lieu of standard English; closer to everyday, ordinary English in lexicon and syntax; tends to lack many attributes of formality that characterize standard English; used by a few lawyers as their particular style or brand of courtroom demeanor.

SUBCULTURAL VARIETIES: Varieties of language spoken by segments of the society who differ in speech style and mannerisms from the larger community; in the case of the particular courts studied in North Carolina, these varieties include Black English and the dialect of English spoken by poorly educated whites.

These varieties of spoken language in the courtroom constitute all REGISTERS of court-talk actually observed. No speaker was ever found who used all four registers, but most speakers were noted to shift among possibilities within their own repertoire in response to situational changes. Divisions among the varieties are not clear-cut, and the varieties for any individual may form a continuum or may be mixed in actual usage. For example, lawyers are likely to address prospective jurors during *voir dire* colloquially, as though seeking solidarity with them. They may joke frequently during this aspect of a trial and emulate the speech styles of

[8] This variety is the closest spoken actualization of written legal language. Sometimes, written legal language is actually read aloud in court. Other times, it is emulated and mimicked in speech, This mimicking of style is similar to that which may be observed in some religious contexts where biblical language is copied in speech.

"ordinary folks." When questioning witnesses, they are likely to remove themselves from hostile witnesses either by attempting to make the colloquial or subcultural varieties of language appear "stupid" and unlike their own speech, or by attempting to suggest that expert witnesses for the opposition are using "big words to obscure relatively simple matters."

Even a brief look at the language of the courtroom is sufficient to reveal the richness of variety found there and to suggest that the language spoken in court and other legal contexts deserves its own treatment similar to that made for written legal language. Although an effort on a scale paralleling Mellinkoff's treatment of written legal language has yet to be undertaken, since the early 1970s a variety of attempts have been made by social scientists and linguists to study how spoken language is related to various aspects of the legal process. The remainder of this section will review some of these studies.

It is perhaps reasonable that anthropologists should have devoted more attention to spoken than written language. This interest is due in large part to the types of societies and legal systems they have traditionally studied. Where law is unwritten, the only language of the law is necessarily spoken. In fact, it is important to keep in mind that all legal systems rely on spoken language whereas only some use written language as well. In 1965, Laura Nader cautioned anthropologists against too narrow a focus when attempting to study a legal system. Arguing for a holistic perspective, she pointed out that although law and politics are often considered together, it has been rare for much attention to be given to the relations between law and other aspects of social life such as economics, language, ecology, and stratification, and rank systems (1965:17). Over a decade and a half later, the situation is scarcely different. Although studies of anthropology (and sociology) of law have increased considerably, only a small number have examined language and law directly.

The exceptions fall into three major groups: LANGUAGE AND COMPREHENSION, LANGUAGE AND CONCEPTUALIZATION, and LANGUAGE AND BEHAVIOR.

LANGUAGE AND COMPREHENSION

Similar to the difficulty faced by the public in dealing with written legal language is the issue of the assumptions made within the legal system concerning comprehensibility of spoken language in the courtroom. Although it has been argued both by the legal profession and by members of the public that jury instructions are "mumbo jumbo" to even well-educated Americans, the court operates as though there is full comprehension of the instructions issued to the jury by the judge. To say that jurors do not, or even more critically that they cannot, understand the language of jury instructions is to admit that one of the legal system's fundamental premises is false. At least two studies by teams of linguists and psychologists have, however, provided empirical information sufficient to warrant serious examination of the validity and appropriateness of the assumption that jurors comprehend instructions.

This research has attempted to investigate the degree to which instructions are understood, and, in instances where there is less than full understanding, to isolate the particular aspects of legal language most significantly related to difficulties in comprehending formal legal language. Both teams concentrated on pattern or standardized jury instructions, and both hypothesized that the form of language used in the instructions, particularly its syntax, is the basis of the incomprehensibility of typical jury instructions.

The difficulties lie, they conclude, in certain neurological aspects of language processing and in the particular way in which jury instructions are formulated. Most English sentences, for example, tend to be right-branching (i.e., the verb comes early in the sentence and complex constructions follow it). An examination of uniform jury instructions as used in many jurisdictions reveals a high frequency of left-branching sentences (i.e., ones in which complex constructions precede the verb). Such sentences are more difficult for English speakers to process. The combination of abstruse vocabulary and complex syntactic forms makes the language of jury instructions especially difficult to understand.[9] Both research teams have demonstrated that standard jury instructions are poorly understood by most jurors and that alterations of some of the more troublesome linguistic features significantly increase comprehension (Sales *et al.* 1977; Elwork *et al.* 1977; Charrow and Charrow 1979a, 1979b).

LANGUAGE AND CONCEPTUALIZATION

Where law is not written, how people talk about the law is the primary means for getting at how people conceive of it. Working within the framework of cognitive anthropology, Frake (1969) studied Yakan con-

---

[9] Among the specific characteristics found by the Charrows as causing comprehension difficulties are these: several types of passives, unusually placed phrases, phrases beginning with *as to*, nominalizations, certain types of embeddings, and other discourse features found in many pattern jury instructions (Charrow and Charrow 1979a).

cepts of litigation and showed how this Philippine people distinguish between talk that characterizes legal discourse and talk that characterizes other behavior. He is thus able to show what constitutes legal procedure in this particular society.

Since this problem of understanding law in societies that lack writing is long standing within anthropology, a few other studies have used similar approaches, although their attention on language per se is not as well developed. Black and Metzger (1965), for example, offer a method for eliciting native categories for use in studying the law ethnographically. From the perspective of social anthropology, Fallers (1969) explores how the Soga of East Africa conceptualize actual events in terms of rule infractions that the court will consider. Although Bohannan (1969) and Gluckman (1969) disagree on the proper approach to the problem of understanding and interpreting native categories, their debate reflects the great concern social anthropologists have devoted to systems of categorization in the cross-cultural study of law.

Although work on legal categories in Western legal systems has not been empirically oriented for the most part, at least one study points in a direction in which others are likely to follow as interest in language and law increases. Danet conceives of the legal process as involving the "fitting of words to deeds" as the various stages of the legal process unfold from first contact between lawyer and prospective client through public trial. Danet reports, for instance, a case in which an aborted fetus is referred to variously as *the fetus, the baby,* and other terms (Danet 1980a). She argues that these differences in terms of reference reflect successive transformations of "reality" in the evolution of court cases. This perspective is illustrated as well by Danet's earlier work (1976) with some of the language used in the Watergate hearings.

All these studies, despite some differences in approach, analyze systems of categorization or conceptualization of law in particular societies. Their emphasis on concepts is of course closely related to language and thought, and they attempt to show how the organization of the law and legal processes is reflected in the structure of the language used in legal contexts.

LANGUAGE AND BEHAVIOR

Since the law is a profession of words and since much of what legal processes involve is speaking (in this culture as elsewhere), understanding how language operates is critical for understanding the legal process. Perhaps it is even the most important component of a genuine understanding of the way conflicts, disputes, and problems are brought to resolution through the courts or other legal institutions. This belief in the importance of understanding language behavior in legal settings links a series of otherwise varied studies conducted during the 1970s.

Atkinson and Drew (1979) employ an ethnomethodological approach, specifically using the techniques of conversational analysis to study the structure and organization of behavior in court. They contend that to understand SPEECH INTERACTION (which is after all the essence of court-room action) is to understand how the court itself works. In justifying their concern with language as a means for a fundamental (and different) understanding of the legal process, they say:

> [T]he main emphasis of court-room studies has tended to be on what courts are claimed to do to defendants (e.g., intimidate, bewilder, oppress, alienate, label, stagmatise, etc.) rather than on the details of how they work. Indeed, the fact that courts work at all, and apparently do so rather smoothly, appears to have been regarded as a passing and essentially uninteresting matter of fact [Atkinson and Drew 1979:4].

By dealing with the way order is achieved in court hearings and the ways accusations, excuses, and justifications are produced in the course of a trial, Atkinson and Drew are using language to reveal the structure and workings of the legal process and in doing so have embarked on a radically different and promising approach to the study of the behavior of the law.

Loftus makes one of the most convincing demonstrations of the consequences and power of words in her work on eyewitness testimony. In a series of ingenious experiments, she reveals a great deal about the relation of language and legal processes. From the very moment people begin to talk about an event, she argues, their words capture, encode, and shape memory of the event. Through an experiment in which subjects viewed films of automobile accidents and later answered questions about events occurring in the films, Loftus and Palmer (1974) were able to show that questions using different verbs to describe the action elicited different answers. The question, "About how fast were the cars going when they *smashed* into each other?" elicited higher estimates of speed than questions using the verbs *collided, bumped, contacted,* or *hit* in place of *smashed.* Questions of the form "Did you see *the* broken head-light?" as opposed to "Did you see *a* broken headlight?" encouraged experimental subjects to say "yes" more frequently (Loftus 1974:118). Thus, these studies and others reported in Loftus (1979) provide important evidence about the significance of language and behavior in legal processes.

3

LEGAL ASSUMPTIONS
ABOUT LANGUAGE
AND COMMUNICATION

In this chapter, we turn to an examination of assumptions made within the legal system about language and communication. In order to have as complete a view as possible, we shall examine the claims of legal tacticians about techniques that enhance or diminish one's chances of winning in court, certain implicit assumptions made by courts about the nature of courtroom communication, and the attitude of the law about the significance of language style and verbal demeanor in the process of legal decision making. As we shall discover, each component in the legal system makes a great many assumptions about the nature of language and communication—assumptions which by the standards of social science are frequently unfounded or unwarranted. Yet, lawyers, courts, and the law itself proceed as though these assumptions are valid.

Legal Tacticians

In this section, we review some advice about effective courtroom tactics contained in TRIAL PRACTICE MANUALS ("how-to" books by successful members of the legal profession). Careful study of five widely used manuals (Bailey and Rothblatt 1971; Jeans 1975; Keeton 1973; McElhaney 1974; and Morrill 1971) reveals much about how lawyers think about language, communication, and courtroom processes. Of particular interest are discussions of language factors in trials and the epistemological basis for these conclusions. A brief examination of some of this advice illustrates typical assumptions made by legal tacticians about language and communication.

Some speech characteristics said to be associated with witness impact include the following (Morrill 1971:34–39):[1]

1. Overly talkative witnesses are not persuasive.[2]
2. Narrative answers are more persuasive than fragmented ones.
3. Exaggeration weakens a witness's testimony.[3]
4. Angry, antagonistic witnesses are less convincing.[4]
5. Overly dramatic witnesses may come across as phonies.
6. Extreme slowness in responses is not convincing.[5]
7. Too many qualifications of an answer are not good.
8. Using unfamiliar words to make an impression may be seen instead as insincerity.[6]
9. New, original, or personal descriptions and analogies are more convincing than conventional, hackneyed ones.[7]

[1] References to trial practice manuals are intended as illustrative rather than exhaustive. Since the masculine, third-person pronoun is used generically in all these books, that usage is often followed in the text of this chapter. In the few places where female witnesses are singled out for special consideration, feminine pronouns are used. The nine speech characteristics which follow are discussed in Morrill (1971:34–39) and in additional manuals as noted.

[2] See also Keeton (1973:36, 38).

[3] It is also said to be bad for a lawyer to exaggerate (see Bailey and Rothblatt 1971:126).

[4] It is also said to be detrimental for lawyers to become angry (McElhaney 1974:25) but said to be useful when a hostile witness gives some favorable testimony by making it more acceptable to the jury. However, a lawyer who is hostile evokes less sympathy from the jury, so it is dangerous unless the lawyer's hostility can be used to make a witness more hostile (see Keeton 1973:75). The lawyer is advised to have hostility expressed toward the client rather than toward the examiner. Bailey and Rothblatt (1971:202) suggest that the hostility of a witness toward one's client can be turned to advantage by having the witness express the hostility toward the lawyer. This is said to have the effect of diminishing the credibility of a hostile witness.

[5] Morrill (1971:36) suggests slowness in answering is often interpreted by the jury as indicating that a witness is unsure or is thinking up a lie. Jeans (1975:70) advises witnesses to think before answering. Keeton (1973:29) states that a jury is impressed by spontaneity of a witness in answering questions.

[6] Keeton (1973:41) notes the necessity of having expert witnesses explain themselves "in juror's language" but without appearing to condescend to a manner of speaking to which they are unaccustomed.

[7] McElhaney (1974:123) suggests that "graphic word pictures" can be a good technique for the lawyer, too, as do Bailey and Rothblatt (1971:245), who advise judicious use of illustrative examples and recommend that "simple, homey ones" be used.

The list could go on, for there is more advice offered about what characteristics are associated with convincing, persuasive, effective witnesses. Careful examination of this advice, however, shows that the authors frequently qualify the kinds of effects each technique is supposed to have with words like *generally* or *often*. They also suggest discretion in the use of these techniques and strategies, and the evolution from the state of an inexperienced trial lawyer to an experienced trial lawyer with a "feel for what to do" is suggested as a natural process.

In qualifying their statements about effectiveness of particular styles and techniques, it is interesting to note that in many cases the same technique is said to have a positive and beneficial effect on some occasions and a negative and harmful one on others. For example, the hesitant witness may be viewed in at least two ways: The witness may be proceeding cautiously to recall the facts correctly and to give precise answers in this important forum; or the witness may be pausing to fabricate and keep the story straight. What interpretation is to be placed on such techniques is largely the responsibility of the trial lawyer. It is the lawyer's job to propose, in summation if not before, what particular meanings should be associated with these forms by suggesting why a witness behaved in a particular fashion and what it means.[8] If it is the lawyer's own witness who hesitated, then it was in order to formulate precise answers. If it was the opposition witness who faltered, then it was due, perhaps, to the fact that the exact truth was not being told!

The flavor of the style in which this advice is often presented can be seen in the following passage, which advises lawyers to use finesse and postpone at least some interpretation until closing argument.

> You have become righteously angered by the inconsistencies of his testimony. . . .[Y]ou have elicited some damning concessions and now you are ready for the kill or to mix the metaphor (and run the risk of a damning Freudian analysis) you are ready for the climax. And so it is that the neophyte rushes into the trap and hoping to emulate Perry Mason by reducing the witness to a blubbery shambles and consummate the case, the one last question is asked that undoes all previous efforts. . . . Remember, the consummation comes at closing argument. . . . When the urge arises to go all the way, remember, "coitus interruptus isn't half bad" [Jeans 1975:325].

To be effective, lawyers are also offered a great deal of advice about their own verbal behavior. The following is a highly selective list of some of this advice contained in the trial practice manuals.

1. PERSONALIZE YOUR OWN WITNESS; DISTANCE YOURSELF FROM AN OPPOSITION WITNESS. For example, Bailey and Rothblatt (1971:126) suggest

---

[8] Linton (1965) contains an interesting discussion of this topic.

that a defendant should be personalized by referring to him the first time as *the accused Joe Smith* and thereafter as *Joe Smith* or just *Joe*. Prosecution witnesses should be made to appear mechanical by referring to them in such terms as *prosecution witness Jones* and the like. Morrill (1971:3–4) suggests calling nearly every client by his first name. McElhaney (1974), however, suggests many exceptions to this practice. It may not be good when the witness is older than the lawyer or is a member of an ethnic or racial minority where use of the first name may be construed by some members of the jury as disrespectful and demeaning. In addition, there is some difference of opinion as to how soon the personalization of a witness should take place. McElhaney suggests that a slow progression to the use of a witness's first name "helps the jury feel they are becoming acquainted with someone they did not know before, rather than having familiarity thrust upon them [p. 124]."

2. MAKE EFFECTIVE USE OF VARIATIONS IN QUESTION FORMAT TO GET THE MOST FAVORABLE RESPONSES FOR YOUR CLIENT. Trial practice manuals have much to say about the proper and appropriate use of leading questions and about the kinds of questions that should not be asked at all (e.g., see Bailey and Rothblatt 1971:172–173; Jeans 1975:315–316; Keeton 1973:50; and Morrill 1971:56). For example, lawyers are often cautioned against asking questions to which they do not already know the answers. In fact, enough is written about how to phrase questions and when particular kinds of questions should and should not be asked that this topic alone would make an interesting study.[9]

Suggestions about the uses of questions phrased either in the affirmative or in the negative serve to illustrate the point. Bailey and Rothblatt (1971) are direct in giving unabashed advice on this topic including:[10]

a. The biased witness is vindictive. . . . He can be relied upon to give an answer contrary to the one you want. . . . You can take advantage of his desire to hurt the defendant. He can often be led into giving a favorable answer for the accused. For example, if you want him to say it was light when the incident took place, ask him if it was not a fact that it was dark when the incident took place. He is apt to say, "No, it was light." Such tactics are justified by the nature of the witness [p. 197].

b. Women are contrary witnesses. They hate to say yes. . . . A woman's desire to avoid the obvious answer will head her right into your real objective—contradicting the testimony of previous prosecution witnesses. Women, like children, are prone to exaggeration; they generally have poor memories as to previous fabrications and exaggerations. They are also

[9] All the manuals treat this in great detail for both direct and cross-examinations.
[10] See also the advice on dealing with young children from Bailey and Rothblatt's book, as reported earlier on page 6 of Chapter 1.

stubborn. You will have difficulty trying to induce them to qualify their testimony. Rather, it might be easier to induce them to exaggerate and cause their testimony to appear incredible. An intelligent woman will very often be evasive. She will avoid making a direct answer to a damaging question. Keep after her until you get a direct answer—but always be the gentleman [pp. 190–191].

3. MAINTAIN TIGHT CONTROL OVER WITNESSES DURING CROSS-EXAMINA-TION; ALLOW MORE OPPORTUNITY TO YOUR WITNESSES TO GIVE LONGER NAR-RATIVE VERSIONS OF THEIR TESTIMONY. The importance of the lawyer's retaining tight control is expressed in a number of ways: admonitions against asking questions for which answers are not already known (Morrill 1971:3–4), advising one's own witnesses to stop talking immediately if interrupted (Jeans 1975:70), asking the trial judge to instruct a witness to restrict the answer to the specific question asked (Bailey and Rothblatt 1971:193), and so on.

4. CONVEY A SENSE OF ORGANIZATION IN YOUR PRESENTATION TO THE JURY. Bailey and Rothblatt suggest that although jurors tend to be impressed with spontaneity in witnesses, they are not impressed with spontaneity in lawyers (see also Keeton 1973:23). Instead, they respond best to tightly organized presentations, both in the organization of questions and in summation. The "hop–skip–jump" method of asking questions, however, is sometimes suggested as a means to confuse witnesses on cross-examination, and therefore to get at the truth more easily through confusing their rehearsed answers (Bailey and Rothblatt 1971:192, 200–201). McElhaney (1974:27) suggests that those who advocate the "hop–skip–jump" technique may more often be rationalizing their lack of preparation; but there is disagreement about who is most confused by this technique—the witness or the jury itself.

5. ADOPT DIFFERENT STYLES OF QUESTIONING AND INTERACTION WITH DIF-FERENT KINDS OF WITNESSES. Different techniques are suggested for women and men, the elderly, children (Bailey and Rothblatt 1971:188–191; Keeton 1973:148–150), expert witnesses,[11] and others.

6. REMAIN POKER-FACED THROUGHOUT; DO NOT REVEAL SURPRISE EVEN WHEN AN ANSWER IS TOTALLY UNEXPECTED, AND SAVE DRAMATIC REACTIONS FOR SPECIAL OCCASIONS (Bailey and Rothblatt 1971:169–170; Keeton 1973:74).

---

[11] In addition to a lengthy discussion in Bailey and Rothblatt (1971:192–196) on expert witnesses, the four other manuals have extensive remarks about techniques for dealing with expert witnesses during both direct and cross-examinations.

7. RHYTHM AND PACE ARE IMPORTANT. Trial lawyers are warned by Bailey and Rothblatt (1971:126, 178–179, 188–190, 247–248) not to bore the jury with extreme slowness, not to break the pace of the examination, especially when surprised, to use silence strategically, and to speak more slowly when complicated facts are being presented. The importance of pace and rhythm is indicated in their advice about using silence:

> Some witnesses are vulnerable to a "silent treatment." The one who has been lying or telling half-truths will be nervous and uneasy on the stand. As you begin, look at him sternly, in silence for a few moments until the courtroom becomes tense. Then shoot a question at him that will throw him off balance [p. 178].

8. REPETITION IS USEFUL FOR EMPHASIS, BUT IT SHOULD BE USED WITH CARE. Bailey and Rothblatt (1971:126, 223) warn against a lawyer's repeating the answers a witness gives, since its effect will be to bore the jury and make the trial excessively long. Jeans (1975:224), however, notes that repetition is a convenient form of educating jurors.

9. AVOID INTERRUPTING A WITNESS WHENEVER POSSIBLE. One way to do this is to phrase questions in such a way as to limit the answers to what is desired. Use of *why* questions may be a bad idea because they open the door to full explanations (Keeton 1973:140). Although most trial judges would permit a lawyer to interrupt an answer to restrict a witness to answering what has been specifically asked about, the interruption of a lengthy response may be as damaging as the answer itself. Jeans (1975:79–80) notes some of the circumstances under which interruption may be appropriate.

10. USE OBJECTIONS SPARINGLY. They have the effect of calling attention to what is objected to and may suggest to jurors that a lawyer wishes to hide some of the facts (Bailey and Rothblatt 1971:205).

In addition to all of this advice—and much more—which is offered openly, unabashedly, and without much documentation, these authors also unknowingly offer other pieces of advice about effective verbal techniques through the models and patterned remarks they provide. Especially impressive is Bailey and Rothblatt's skillful use of pronouns in the models of summation arguments they present in their book. Solidarity and distance are effected subtly through inclusive and exclusive pronouns and ambiguous antecedents are used to great advantage. Here are some examples from Bailey and Rothblatt:

> We are in an American court of law and justice. We try our cases in a democratic manner. We do not try our cases by lynch mobs [p. 271].

Ladies and gentlemen, in your examination before you were selected as jurors, I asked whether you could put aside feelings of prejudice, passion, revulsion and pity, and decide this case on the evidence. Each of you swore you would do just that. . . . You made that pledge [p. 272].

If someone were to accuse you falsely of a crime and were to produce no credible evidence to support this accusation, you would proudly face your community and this jury and say: "They have made out no case against me to answer. I do not have to testify." So this accused man stands before you and, as his spokesman, I say to you no case has been made out for him to answer or explain [p. 298].

Brown and Gilman (1960) long ago pointed out the effective use of pronouns to bring about solidarity and inclusiveness or to effect distance and exclusiveness. Bailey and Rothblatt are, in effect, through their many models of summation remarks, suggesting that successful lawyers do use pronouns for these purposes. *We* is often used in the context of appealing to common values; the mobile *you* shifts between the jury as a collective body and each juror as an individual; *I* refers to both the advocate who speaks for his or her client and, through direct quotation, to others; *they* is the unknown, undescribed accusor in juxtaposition to the personalized, hypothetical *I* with whom jurors are asked to identify as they envision themselves falsely accused of a crime and on trial for their own lives or liberty.

This advice, although provided through models rather than dicta, is nonetheless important, and those of us interested in how language is used in legal contexts would do well to pay attention to these models and paradigms of language use as well as to the more overt suggestions contained in trial practice manuals.

Now that we have reviewed some of the advice offered in trial practice manuals, we turn to the bases for these claims about what works, how, and why. In every case, the answer is the same—experience. But this is not to be minimized, for the authors of these manuals are among the most successful trial lawyers in America. They win many, or most, of their cases, and their opinions are worthy of attention. In their foreword, Bailey and Rothblatt offer this justification for their assertions and claims: "Most of the techniques have been tried and tested by our own court experience time and again. This book is a distillation of those bits of knowledge and advice that years of law practice have shown us are crucial to a good defense [p. iii]."

Experience is the primary credential offered by most of the others as well. However, Jeans's analogy of the trial to sexual intercourse points out one of the difficulties in wholesale acceptance of the advice he and the others offer. They speak about a relationship between lawyer and legal decision maker (usually the jury). They describe their technique, at least those aspects they consider impressive and successful, in somewhat intimate detail. They also make claims about what pleases their partner, the jury. What they do not say is whether or not they asked the partner how—to follow the analogy—she reacts. What do juries think about Jeans's technique? Is he as great an authority on jury reaction as he claims to be? Or are he and perhaps the others making unwarranted assumptions about jury reaction?

The tendency in all these manuals to focus on trial outcome, on winning or losing, may obscure for the casual reader the lack of evidence on which assertions about what is and is not effective are in fact based. Although the overall success of these authors is to be respected, it does not qualify them to make specific assertions about the effects of particular variations in language, demeanor, and courtroom presentation. Although these authors must be right at least some of the time, are they right all of the time? The overall chemistry of the courtroom is so complex that assertions about effects of particular techniques or variations in form or style should not stand without challenge. The lack of certainty about the precise effects of the language variables lies behind the many qualifications and cautions these authors make. What they are proferring are really hypotheses about what works; they are not conclusions based on evidence social scientists are willing to accept without more detailed examination and more careful and controlled studies.

Thus, this brief review of some advice about courtroom strategy points out the large number of specific assumptions about human nature, language, and communication that at least some lawyers make. In addition, it shows the more general assumption upon which this advice is based: Overall success is sufficient to permit conclusions about the effectiveness of quite specific techniques and strategies. Scientific inquiry demands that conclusions such as these be drawn only after efforts have been made to rule out all other possible explanations. It is therefore not possible to accept as scientific the basis upon which these conclusions are drawn. All specific conclusions are questionable.

The Courts

In addition to the views of the tacticians, the legal system contains another set of assumptions about language and communication. These are the assumptions that underlie and guide the court as it goes about its daily processes of fact finding and decision making. Few, if any, of them tend to be articulated. Rather, they are implicit in the regularities of courtroom procedures and may be discovered through detailed observation of courts in action. Like the claims of legal tacticians, these assumptions are also numerous and specific.

In attempting to understand courtroom communication, it is important to keep in mind that nearly everyone has at least some difficulties with the language of the courtroom. Perhaps most obvious are the problems of those who, in a society like the United States which uses only a single official language for most public purposes, do not speak that language or at least do not speak it well enough to use it in legal contexts. But in addition, there are those who speak the official language—or rather some varieties of it—but who do not sufficiently command the language variety used in the courtroom. Although a relatively small percentage of the American population falls into the first category, most of us belong, to some degree, to the second.

During the 1970s, there was an increased concern with communication difficulties faced by non-English speakers in the courts. In 1978, after 4 years of hearings on the problem, the U.S. Congress passed a law designed to ameliorate some of the difficulties faced by non-English speakers in dealing with the courts and the law.[12] And at least one state, California, commissioned its own study of the language needs of non-English speakers in the state's justice system.[13] Prior to the enactment of the federal law, the treatment of non-English speakers in various federal, state, and local jurisdictions had been highly variable. In some situations, well-qualified interpreters were available, whereas in others the interpretation role had been limited to only some aspects of the legal process (e.g., in court, but interpreters are not systematically provided in lawyer–client conferences). Who pays, adequacy, checks on the quality, form of interpretation, and who interprets are still subject to much variation within the American legal system since the 1978 legislation applies to federal courts only. However, the problem is being recognized, and those who worked in support of the federal law hope that many

---

[12] Legislation dealing with court interpretation for both bilingual proceedings and persons with hearing impairments was first introduced in the 93rd Congress (1974). Neither the original bill (Senate Bill 1724 in the 93rd Congress) nor a slightly revised version (Senate Bill 565 in the 94th Congress) was approved by the full Congress prior to adjournment. In 1978, a further revised bill entitled "Court Interpreters Act," was approved by the full Congress and signed into law. See U.S. House of Representatives Report 95-1687; U.S. Senate Report 95-569; and Public Law 95-539 (approved October 28, 1978). The law provides the consecutive interpretation of bilingual proceedings and of proceedings involving hearing impaired persons in federal courts. Pousada (1979) contains a useful discussion of the history of court interpretation in the United States.

[13] The State of California commissioned a study of the needs of non-English-speaking persons in the State's justice system. See *Judicial Council of California* (1976).

states will enact similar legislation to deal with these issues in state courts.

In contrast, the problems faced by speakers of English who do not fully understand the language variety spoken in courts have unfortunately received little attention and are not generally considered to constitute a serious problem. Yet, as noted in Chapter 2, especially in the recent studies of the comprehension of the language of jury instructions, the problem may indeed be of equally serious proportions. In the congressional hearings preceding the enactment of the Court Interpreters Act, the plight of the nonnative speaker in court was likened to that of a person enclosed in a glass booth, seeing but not hearing the court proceedings. Some of the impetus for the legislation had come from an appeals court ruling that a defendant not able to understand the language of the court had been denied a fundamental American right—the right to confront one's accuser(s) face to face in a court of law as guaranteed under the sixth ammendment. Not speaking the language of the court, it was reasoned, erects a barrier between the defendant and the courts, one that effectively denies the defendant this right. Although the judicial opinion in the case did not consider the problems of nonfluent speakers of "courtroom language," it requires only a short leap to see that often when fluent speakers of ordinary English find themselves in a court they may face an essentially similar problem. In fact, close examination shows that the courts tend to make a number of assumptions about language abilities of English speakers that are clearly untested and in at least some instances probably unfounded. These assumptions include such notions as

(a) Anyone who speaks English does not require interpretation of COURT-TALK.[14]

(b) In any instance where English court-talk requires interpretation, such interpretation is the responsibility of legal counsel, not of the court.

(c) Unless jurors call problems of hearing due to noise, volume, etc. to the court's attention, they may be assumed to have heard all the evidence.[15]

(d) Jurors are not usually allowed to ask any questions of witnesses, especially to clarify something a witness or lawyer says which may not be entirely clear.

---

[14] COURT-TALK is used here to refer to language varieties spoken in trial courtrooms.

[15] Although it is customary for judges to instruct jurors to call such problems to the attention of the court, few jurors actually do so.

(e) "English-speaking" jurors understand "English-speaking" witnesses, regardless of cultural background and differences in dialect.
(f) "English-speaking" witnesses understand "English-speaking" lawyers, regardless of cultural background or differences in dialect.
(g) Pattern jury instructions—which have been carefully scrutinized
for their legal accuracy—are understandable to jurors.
(h) Variations in presentational style on the parts of witnesses and
lawyers, although possibly important, are not matters with which
the law should concern itself since these are not questions of fact,
but of idiosyncratic, stylistic variation.

This list is by no means exhaustive in considering either the communication difficulties faced by English speakers in courts or the underlying assumptions made about the nature of language and communication (such as the instruction to "forget" information when the judge
orders it stricken from the record). Rather, this list serves to point out
the great discrepancy that may exist between the operating assumptions
and the reality of how communication processes actually work. Many
legal professionals, of course, know that these assumptions are unwarranted and frequently produce great difficulties. Yet, the courts continue
to operate as though these assumptions are valid.

The Law
JOHN M. CONLEY

*You are the sole judges of the credibility of each witness. You must
decide for yourselves whether to believe the testimony of any
witness. You may believe all or any part or nothing of what a
witness said while on the stand. In determining whether to believe
any witness, you should apply the same tests of truthfulness which
you apply in your own everyday affairs.*

The above excerpt is from a jury instruction given by a judge in a
North Carolina criminal court. In most jurisdictions, jurors receive a
similar instruction—namely, that they should use their own judgment in
deciding who to believe, how much weight to give to any particular piece
of testimony, and which evidence to place above other. Decisions of this
sort cannot always, or even most of the time, be based merely on the
content of testimony. They are also based upon the demeanor of the

witnesses. One needs no training in the law to determine whether a witness is relaxed or nervous, seems sure of the facts being reported or has difficulty answering the questions, or even, most important of all, whether the witness seems to be telling the truth or lying. Since all versions of the facts presented in a trial cannot be reconciled by giving equal credence to the testimony of all witnesses, each juror must decide who is to be believed and who is not.

Although trial juries evolved from the autonomous local fact-finding bodies in medieval England, the modern jury bears only limited resemblance to them. Medieval juries had the authority to engage in independent investigation of facts. Today in especially notorious cases juries are sequestered to prevent members from acquiring additional information through personal contacts or from the mass media. Even in relatively simple cases like traffic violations, the members of a jury are specifically forbidden to make independent visits to the scene of the incident. The selection of the facts to be presented in a case is left entirely to the parties through their lawyers and their witnesses. The jury is thus expected to go into the trial with a clean slate.

The only vestige of the investigative function of the ancient jury is the present jury's authority to consider the demeanor of witnesses. That is, although the jury may consider only the facts presented to it and may not go into the community itself to seek the truth, it need not accept those facts without any reference to the context in which they are presented. Rather, the jury is to take those facts as presented by real human beings, and its members may rely on their own human experience in assessing those making the presentation. In this way, the application of an often inflexible law depends in the last analysis on intuitive human value judgment.

The rules of civil and criminal procedure allow legal decision makers to rely on "demeanor evidence," that is, to use style, paralinguistic cues, and nonverbal behavior to reach a decision about a witness's credibility. An illustration of how the law deals with demeanor evidence can be found in the 1951 case *National Labor Relations Board* v. *Dinon Coal Co.*[16] The case involved a complaint brought by the National Labor Relations Board against a coal company for the discriminatory firing of union members. The Board found evidence of an unfair labor practice and entered an order for the members to be rehired, which the company appealed to the Second Circuit of the United States Court of Appeals.

In an administrative proceeding, the agency—the NLRB in this case—

---

[16] Complete citations to legal cases are contained in a special section of the References beginning on page 181.

initially holds a hearing which is much like a trial before a judge sitting without a jury. The hearing officer who presides makes a recommendation which forms the basis of the agency's final order. The key issue in the case was the hearing officer's recommendations, which went against the weight of the evidence taken at face value. The officer justified his findings on the basis of his assessment of the witnesses' credibility. He explained:

> On the entire record, INCLUDING HIS OBSERVATIONS OF THE WITNESSES, the undersigned [hearing officer] is not persuaded that [the employee] was discharged by the [employer] for the reasons advanced. . . . THE UNDERSIGNED DOES NOT CREDIT HOLLAND'S TESTIMONY, to the effect that he ordered [the employee's] discharge because defective material had been made in and shipped from [the employer's] plant [*National Labor Relations Board* v. *Dinon Coal Co.* 1951:487].

The Second Circuit sustained the Board's order, relying on the general rule applied to trial courts.

> Repeatedly, the courts have said that, since observation of such "demeanor evidence" is open to a trier of the facts when witnesses testify orally in his presence, and since such observation is not open to a reviewing tribunal, the fact-trier's findings, to the extent that they comprise direct or "testimonial" inferences, are ordinarily unreviewable [p. 487].

Thus, the hearing officer, as the trier of fact (the jury analog), had a right to consider demeanor evidence. Since the reviewing court had no opportunity to view the demeanor in question, findings based on it would not be altered.

The Court of Appeals' opinion was supported with a reference to the long history of the demeanor evidence rule. As far back as Roman law, the court noted, great stress had been placed on the judge's ability to form an opinion about the trustworthiness of witnesses. Demeanor evidence continues to be recognized by the law as valid evidence. But because of the very nature of such evidence, it is all but impossible for an appellate court to review the weight given to demeanor evidence by the trier of fact. The only applicable rule is that the trier of fact may use demeanor evidence; there are no rules limiting the way in which it may be used. Judge Jerome Frank, who wrote the opinion, commented: "This lack of rules ('un-ruliness'), with its concomitant wide discretion in the fact-trier, yields inherent difficulties not surmountable by a reviewing court, regardless of whether the fact-trier be a judge, a jury, or a trial examiner [p. 490]." The court concluded, in essence, that demeanor of witnesses is so significant that it cannot be disregarded, but the nature of this significance is so obscure that no rules can be established for assessing such evidence. Thus, an element at the very center of the functioning of the legal system is outside the law's control.

An earlier, although still valid statement, of the extent to which demeanor evidence may be used was made in the frequently cited 1908 Missouri case of *Creamer* v. *Bivert*. The case involved an unsuccessful business deal between an estranged brother and sister. Creamer, the brother, had apparently been threatened with a suit for breach of promise to marry by an exfiancée. To hide his assets, he conveyed his land to his sister, gratuitously, upon her promise to give it back to him when the threat had passed. When the time had come, the sister insisted that she had bought the land and refused to return it.

Creamer sued to recover the land, and was successful on the trial level. The suit, since it sought the recovery of land, was brought in what was then characterized as an equity court—that is, the judge sat as trier of fact without jury. The judge heard oral testimony and reached a verdict just as a jury would. On appeal to the Missouri Supreme Court, the sister succeeded in having the trial verdict overturned, for reasons having to do with property law technicalities. Of special interest here are the appellate court's comments about its ability to criticize the trial judge's factual conclusions.

A critical factual issue was whether the sister had actually paid for the property. The appellate court sustained the lower court's finding that she had not, emphasizing the latter's opportunity to assess not only the substance of the evidence but also the manner of its presentation.

> Here there was a maze of testimony affecting the credibility of some of the witnesses on both sides; there were currents and cross-currents in it sharply affecting the probability and the improbability of the stories told on the stand. . . . [D]eference should be given to the trial chancellor [judge]. He SEES AND HEARS MUCH THAT WE CANNOT SEE AND HEAR. We well know that there are things of pith that cannot be preserved in or shown by the written page of a bill of exceptions. Truth does not always stalk boldly forth naked, but modest withal, in a printed abstract in a court of last resort. She oft hides in nooks and crannies visible only to the mind's eye of the judge who tries the case. To him appears the furtive glance, the blush of conscious shame, the hesitation, the sincere or flippant or sneering tone, the heat, the calmness, the yawn, the sigh, the candor or lack of it, the scant or full realization of the solemnity of an oath, the carriage and mien, the brazen face of the liar, the glibness of the schooled witness in reciting a lesson, or the itching overeagerness of the swift witness, as well as the honest fact of the truthful one, are alone seen by him. In short, one witness may give testimony that reads in print, here, as if falling from the lips of an angel of light, and yet not a soul who heard it, nisi [at trial] believes it [*Creamer* v. *Bivert* 1908: 1120–1121; emphasis added].

The court thus provides an extensive catalog of expressive human be-
haviors, an awareness of the critical importance of what can be loosely
categorized as demeanor—but no hint of guidelines for assessing it.
Another application of the same general approach is seen in the 1953
case, *Bartholomew* v. *Universe Tankships, Inc.*, which came to the
federal district court on a motion to set aside the jury's verdict as contrary
to the weight of the evidence and motivated by passion and prejudice.
Specifically, the defendant claimed that the plaintiff's behavior on the
witness stand had been so bizarre as to preclude a rational decision by
the jury.

> Defendant bases his contention upon the demeanor of the plaintiff upon the
> witness stand. It is true that he appeared nervous. He was a difficult witness
> to examine; he hesitated for some period of time on some questions; closed
> his eyes, and incessantly tapped with his foot while seated in the witness
> chair. . . .At one time when he was telling of the assault upon him, he became
> hysterical, rose in his chair, shouted and cried. Hysterical is the word. It
> was near the end of the day and I adjourned the court. In the absence of the
> jury I admonished him on his conduct and also admonished his attorneys.
> The next day and for the rest of the trial he was calmer but a rather nervous
> witness. At another point, I adjourned court when it appeared to me that he
> was about to lose control of himself while seated in the courtroom, although
> I am not sure that anyone else noticed it [*Bartholomew* v. *Universe Tankships,
> Inc.* 1953:159].

Notwithstanding this extraordinary display, the judge found no grounds
for limiting in any way the jury's fact-finding prerogative. The jury was
allowed to evaluate the demeanor of this witness, according to whatever
rules its members saw fit to recognize, and according to whatever views
on human behavior its members subscribed to: "On the whole, after
serious consideration, I do not feel that passion and prejudice dictated
the verdict of the jury. They might have been justified in taking a cant
the other way. I don't know [p. 159]." This statement epitomizes the
American judicial attitude toward the effects of courtroom demeanor:
It is important, although not explainable.

Despite the prevailing rule that there are no rules, a few highly specific
restrictions on the use of demeanor evidence have developed. *Kovacs*
v. *Szentes* presented the unusual situation of a husband suing his mother-
in-law for alienating the affection of his wife by threatening to disown
her if her daughter remained with her husband. Remarkably, the husband
won a verdict for money damages at trial.

The mother-in-law appealed to the Connecticut Supreme Court and
won the right to a new trial, largely on the basis of several errors in
admitting evidence made by the trial judge. One such error is of interest

here. The trial judge, who sat as the trier of fact without a jury, as is normal in domestic cases, was apparently overcome by the strange drama facing him, and stepped outside the usual rules of judicial restraint.

In his findings of fact, the trial judge noted that he attached significance to behavior exhibited by the wife and the mother-in-law when NOT on the witness stand. Specifically, he observed that "the wife continually sat beside the defendant, and it was very evident that she was under the domination of the defendant; and that it was fairly apparent that if left to themselves the plaintiff and his wife would get along together [*Kovacs v. Szentes* 1943:126].''

On the basis of this abuse of demeanor evidence, the Connecticut Supreme Court called for a new trial. Specifically, it objected that:

> In effect the trial court, as a basis for these findings, made of himself a witness, and in making them availed himself of his personal knowledge; he became an unsworn witness to material facts without the defendant having any opportunity to cross-examine, to offer countervailing evidence or to know upon what evidence the decision would be made [p. 126].

Thus, although the trier of fact may do whatever it chooses in assessing demeanor evidence, it must close its eyes to any human behavior occurring beyond the physical confines of the witness stand, that is, to behavior that is not technically evidence.

These cases show the prevailing attitude of the courts toward demeanor evidence. The courts repeatedly recognize and respect its importance, yet they are unable to impose any restrictions on its use. A judge or jury member may use the demeanor of a witness as the basis for believing or disbelieving any or all of the testimony, or even for reaching a conclusion that is contrary to the weight of the evidence. And in doing so, the trier of fact is given no established guidelines to follow.

Limits on the expansiveness of the demeanor evidence rule have been imposed in only limited instances, as for example in the *Kovacs* case where it was held that the legal decision maker may rely only on demeanor which occurs on the witness stand. In refusing to limit or guide the assessment of demeanor evidence, the law thus preserves a vestige of the jury's origin as a local fact-finding body.

The modern jury, as representative of the community from which it is drawn, is permitted, indeed encouraged, to bring the full measure of its humanizing influence to bear on the judicial fact-finding process. Unimpeded, the jury must be allowed constantly to assess style, paralinguistic cues, and nonverbal behavior to determine trustworthiness, credibility, and so on, using the same evaluative criteria used in daily life.

Having dealt with the general issue of demeanor, we turn briefly to a consideration of a specific type of speech demeanor to illustrate how the American courts have dealt with more specific matters. We consider now the issue of HEDGES or QUALIFIERS, a topic that will be considered from a behavioral perspective in some detail in Chapter 4. What we consider here is not the consequence hedges or qualifiers may have when used in a courtroom, but the courts' prevailing view of them. The pattern noted here is similar to that exhibited by the courts in considerations of other paralinguistic and nonverbal demeanor characteristics.

The prevailing judicial attitude toward qualifications is illustrated by the case of *Abbott* v. *Church*. The case involved a challenge to the validity of a will on the ground that the deceased man's lawyers had exercised undue influence over him at a time when he was weakened by illness and domestic stress. The suspicion arose because one of the lawyers was a beneficiary of the will and the other was named executor.

One of the challengers' key witnesses was Lewis, a young lawyer employed in the office of the lawyers who drew the will, who was a witness to the signing of the will. His testimony was necessary to establish that the beneficiary–lawyer was in fact the one who had drawn the will. The pertinent part of his testimony follows.

> Q. Where was this will executed?
> A. In our office. . . .
> Q. Who drew the will; do you remember?
> A. Well, I don't remember positively, but, judging from the form of the certificate, I THINK Frank Shepard.
> Q. You did not draw it?
> A. No, I don't THINK I did. I may have but I THINK not.
> Q. How long had you known [the deceased] before this time?
> A. Oh, I had known him about 15 years.
> Q. Do you know who drew this will?
> A. Why, I THINK Mr. Shepard—Frank L. Shepard [*Abbott* v. *Church* 1919:307; emphasis added].

At trial, all of the foregoing was objected to as being an incompetent opinion. The trial court sustained the objection and ordered all of Lewis's testimony stricken from the record. It relied on the rule of evidence that nonexpert witnesses may testify only as to what they have actually observed, and are not permitted to state what they THINK about a particular issue. The court focused on Lewis's use of the word *think,* inferring from his uncertain language that he was merely rendering opinions on matters about which he had no personal knowledge.

On appeal, the Illinois Supreme Court rejected this interpretation of Lewis' qualifying language:

"Think" means "believe," and when a witness prefaces his testimony with "I think" he is to be taken as testifying to what he remembers. . . . The witness Lewis might have been able to have given a number of good reasons for thinking Shepard . . . drew the will if he had been further questioned [p. 308].

To summarize, the trial court treated the qualifying language as evidence of a lack of knowledge—a sign that the witness was rendering an opinion on what had happened, not relating a personal observation of the event, as the law of evidence requires. This holding was reversed on appeal, because the Illinois Supreme Court took what has become the more widely accepted view. According to this view, the presence of words of qualification is not cause for disallowing testimony. Rather, such words are to be taken into account by the jury in deciding what weight to give to the testimony. Neither *Abbott* v. *Church* nor the subsequent case law, however, has established guidelines for determining how such weight is to be apportioned.

As early as 1920, the *American Law Reports* (*A.L.R.*) series, in an annotation on the *Abbott* v. *Church* case, was able to cite over 50 cases that reached the same result in similar circumstances.[17] Reviewing cases from every state and federal jurisdiction, the *A.L.R.* stated this general rule:

Though a witness is uncertain as to either the observation or the recollection of a fact concerning which he is asked to testify, and gives his testimony qualified by a phrase or phrases expressive of something less than a positive degree of assurance, the admissibility of his evidence is not affected thereby [*A.L.R.* 1920:979].

More recent cases illustrate the persistence and varied applicability of this general rule. In *Murphy* v. *Roux* (1958), Murphy brought suit as a result of an automobile accident in which her car was struck by Roux's. At the trial, Murphy presented evidence in an effort to show that Roux had run a stop sign on an intersecting street, forcing her off the road. At the close of her evidence, the court granted defendant Roux's motion for a directed verdict. This means that the court held that Murphy had presented no evidence that could conceivably have supported a finding of negligence on Roux's part. The case was therefore dismissed.

On appeal, the Michigan Supreme Court expressed shock at this result: "Upon these facts why is there any doubt about a *prima facie* case?"[18]

---

[17] See *American Law Reports* (1920:979 note). The *A.L.R.* service provides commentary on significant cases and references to related cases each year.

[18] In any lawsuit, the party bearing the burden of proof (the plaintiff in a civil case) must present a prima facie case, meaning that the party must present legally admissible evidence that, if believed, would prove the claim being asserted.

It went on to answer its own question: "It was because Mrs. Murphy was a very poor witness [*Murphy* v. *Roux* 1958:533]." As the court's elaboration of this conclusion makes clear, she was a poor witness because of the manner in which she spoke. The Supreme Court characterized Murphy's testimony as follows:

> How wide was the traveled portion of South Merrill Road? She didn't know. How wide was Calvin Road? She didn't know. How fast was she going? That she didn't know. She had glanced off and on at her speedometer. It was between 50 and 55 miles per hour. What speed was defendant going on Calvin Road? She didn't know. She did know that he slowed up. Slowed to what speed? "I don't know," she replied. How far north of the intersection was she when she saw him slow down? Again, no idea. "I'm very poor with feet" was the way she put her inability to gauge the distance [1958:533–534].

Notwithstanding Murphy's lack of certainty, the court held that her testimony should be treated as competent, admissible evidence.

> Yet even litigants who, as Mrs. Murphy, are "very poor with feet" may have a cause of action. How far may we retreat from the precision of the well-drilled witness with his mental stop watch and yardstick before we must hold that the case has dissolved into such vagueness and uncertainty as not to merit submission to the jury? We probably answer very little when we say that it depends upon the nature of the case, and showings made, and the reasonable inferences to be drawn therefrom [1958:534].

Similar statements have been made by courts all over the country, for example:

> Witnesses are not required to speak with absolute positiveness, but may testify as to their thought or belief . . . some uncertainty of memory goes rather to the credibility of the witness than to the admissibility of the testimony [*First Federal Savings & Loan Ass'n.* v. *Commercial Union Ins. Co.* 1967:103].

As in the demeanor evidence cases, in *Murphy* v. *Roux, First Federal Savings & Loan Ass'n.* v. *Commercial Union Ins. Co.,* and many similar cases the courts have endorsed the rule that legal decision makers may and in fact should make common sense behavioral judgments in evaluating the credibility of witnesses.

4

ETHNOGRAPHY AND
EXPERIMENTATION

Anthropology and social psychology are uncommon partners in research. Social scientists trained in one of these approaches seldom have significant facility with or appreciation for the other. Yet, ETHNOGRAPHY and EXPERIMENTATION can combine to enhance the ability of both disciplines to study certain questions of common interest.

The term ETHNOGRAPHY came into wide usage when anthropologists began conducting extensive field studies of non-Western peoples and their cultures scarcely more than 50 years ago. Documentation of the cultures is termed ETHNOGRAPHY (from the roots *ethno-*, meaning people or cultural group, and *-graphy*, meaning writing on a particular subject). Today, when anthropologists work in Western as well as non-Western cultures, the techniques of participant-observation, coupled with a predisposition for inductive generalization, are also referred to as ethnography.[1] An ethnographic approach to the study of trial courtrooms thus means long-term, careful observation coupled with detailed recording through note taking and mechanical devices, toward the goal of making as accurate a description as possible. Many anthropologists who study

[1] Extensive discussions of anthropological research methods can be found in Naroll and Cohen (1973) and Pelto and Pelto (1978). In addition, most basic cultural anthropology textbooks contain discussion of the ethnographic approach. See, for example, Keesing 1981:5–7.

language behavior consider themselves to be ethnographers of language.[2] Their methods are similar to those of a more general ethnographer, but in this case attention is focused on the observation and description of speech behavior.

EXPERIMENTATION is widely used by social psychologists to test hypotheses about human behavior. First, a causal relationship between two variables, or factors, is hypothesized. The experimenter manipulates the independent variable (suspected to be the causal one) by creating, controlling, or changing it. Then, he or she systematically measures the effects of the manipulation on some other behavior or condition—the dependent variable. For example, to test the hypothesis "speech style affects listener response," the experimenter manipulates speech style (the independent variable) to determine whether listeners respond differently (the dependent variable). If responses are more positive or negative as style varies, then the researcher may conclude that variation in speech style CAUSES differences in listener response. Since differences can occur as a result of chance—as, for example, a tossed coin may not land an exactly equal number of times on both sides, differences observed in the experiment must be large enough to rule out the likelihood that chance variation is responsible. When the differences are sufficiently large to rule out chance, they are said to be statistically significant.[3]

The specific research problem on which we focus is the influence of language factors on legal decision making. Understanding this relationship involves answering the following questions:

1. What variations in language forms occur in legal contexts?
2. What are the effects of these variations in form on trial processes?

The ethnographic method is especially well suited to deal with the first of these questions whereas the second is best answered through experimentation. Although similar questions could be said to underlie many problems of interest to social scientists (e.g., first, how is variation in behavior patterned?; second, what are the effects of such variation on

---

[2] A good introduction to recent work in this tradition is Bauman and Sherzer (1974). *Ethnography of Speaking* owes a great debt to the influence of Dell Hymes at whose urging many anthropologists began to turn their attention to such matters. His early programmatic essay (Hymes 1962) is still useful 20 years after it was first published.

[3] A difference between two experimental conditions is tested for statistical significance by comparing the magnitude of the difference to the variation within each condition. The difference is said to be "significant" if it would occur less than five times out of a hundred by chance alone (written as $p < .05$). Smaller values of p provide greater assurance that the difference was not the result of chance. Only differences that are reported to be significant should be regarded as "true" or real differences.

social processes?), these complementary methods are too seldom used together in research. The consequence is that anthropologists, frequently masterful in describing patterns of variation, are unable to answer convincingly the question, *So what?* Similarly, social psychologists skilled in refined techniques of controlled social experimentation often appear to have contrived the questions they research to such a degree that the empirical validity of their findings seems to be mundane to outsiders. When the approaches of ethnography and experimentation are joined they reinforce and strengthen one another.

Deriving the Research Questions

In recent years there has been an increasing interest among social scientists in studying the American legal system as well as an increasing willingness in the legal community to make use of the results of social science studies. For the most part, these studies have investigated issues relevant to judicial procedure and substantive issues of trial law.[4] It is in the area of procedural law that social science research appears to have had its greatest impact upon legal developments.[5] Although social science techniques, especially those of anthropology, have been applied to the study of speech styles in legal systems other than our own,[6] the study of language used in American courtrooms is only beginning.

The specific research questions through which we seek to understand the more general problem of the relation between language and legal processes have been derived from several sources. Sociolinguistics, anthropology, and social psychology have provided important theoretical directions. For each of them, the study of language in the courtroom provides a means for inquiring about more general processes. Lawyers and judges, both in interviews and in their writings, have suggested issues for study. And ethnographic observation of courtroom interaction suggested additional ideas for study.

[4] See Kalven and Zeisel (1966), Thibault and Walker (1975), Lind *et al.* (1976). For studies by anthropologists involving topics concerning the American legal system, see Rosen (1977) and Nader (1980).

[5] The issues of jury size and unanimity of verdicts have been the subjects of many legal cases (e.g., *Ballew* v. *Georgia, Apodaca* v. *Oregon, Johnson* v. *Louisiana,* and *Williams* v. *Florida*) and of social scientific studies (see Padawer–Singer *et al.* 1977).

[6] The best known of these is Frake (1969). Two collections of articles also contain many examples of speech styles appropriate to legal contexts in non-Western societies (see Bloch 1975 and O'Barr and O'Barr 1976).

SOCIOLINGUISTICS. Sociolinguistics is founded on the premise that much variation in language is socially patterned and reflects both personal and contextual factors.[7] Personal variables include age, sex, social class, and ethnic or regional background. Contextual variables include differences in formality, situational appropriateness, and the like. The study of speech styles in court is a natural extension of research on styles of speaking in nonlegal contexts. This research has revealed that across a wide variety of situations it is possible to distinguish definite styles of speaking and to trace these styles to the social background and the immediate surroundings of the speaker.[8]

ANTHROPOLOGY. Anthropology contributes at least two important questions to this study of courtroom language. First, the long-standing interest in the empirical study of dispute settlement procedures across many cultures provides an important precedent for questions about how courts actually work. Second, the concern with such matters as strategy leads rather directly to an interest in how courtroom participants attempt to win and avoid loss. The distinction noted in Chapter 1 between normative and pragmatic rules is especially useful in the study of courtroom behavior. Although the law places considerable emphasis on normative rules (in this case, the rules of procedure), the existence of pragmatic rules of successful courtroom strategy which may even vary from accepted procedural rules is only covertly acknowledged.

SOCIAL PSYCHOLOGY. Social psychological theories of attribution, influence, and justice suggest hypotheses about the probable impact of speech style on decision makers.[9] Studies have shown that responses to influence attempts are affected by beliefs about motivations and the situation in which the attempt occurs.[10] Specific studies of speech style in nonlegal contexts repeatedly show listeners forming strong impressions of speakers based on the manner of speaking.[11] In some studies, the

---

[7] For a general introduction to the field of sociolinguistics, see Trugill (1974). For a comprehensive review of social psychological studies employing sociolinguistic variables, see Giles and Powesland (1974).

[8] Labov's (1972b) work on English in New York City provides many examples of sociolinguistic patterns.

[9] A useful introduction to these studies can be found in Kelley (1967), Jones and Davis (1976), and Thibaut and Walker (1975).

[10] See, for example, the especially illustrative studies by Mills (1966) and Mills and Jellison (1967).

[11] Social scientists have shown that the same information presented in different speech styles may be perceived and evaluated differently. In a classic experiment, W. Lambert et al. (1960) asked bilingual Montrealers to speak once in English and once in French in a conversation recorded for experimental study. The experimental subjects judged the

degree to which others accept a person's arguments depends on his or her style of speaking.[12] Based on such findings in nonlegal contexts, it was expected that presentational style in court would affect the jury's impressions of witnesses and lawyers.[13]

INTERVIEWS WITH LEGAL PROFESSIONALS. Many lawyers and judges gave generous amounts of time to discuss our research. Interviews of one to two hours in length were insufficient to gain much specific information of relevance. Most of those interviewed were quick to understand the general problems of interest, but few proved helpful in providing much understanding of these issues. Although lawyers and judges expressed the opinion that language strategies are important in the courtroom, they

---

French speaker significantly more negatively on most dimensions than they did THE SAME speaker when repeating the same information in English. This "matched guise" technique has become a useful means for controlled studies of the effects of language varieties. Many studies using Lambert's model, pioneered by Lambert and his associates, are reported in Giles and Powesland (1975).

[12] Giles and Powesland (1975) is a comprehensive review of social scientific studies on the influence on social evaluation of speakers of different styles of language such as accents, use of one or another language in bilingual societies, and educated or uneducated varities of language. Despite the large number of studies conducted by psychologists in this general area, Giles and Powesland concede that almost nothing is known about the effects of different language varieties in legal contexts: "Almost certainly, nonstandard usage can also affect forensic situations such as police and courtroom decision-making. . . . For example when members of the public are stopped in the street or on the highway by the police for inquiries, do standard speakers undergo a less severe interrogation than non-standard users of the language? Is evidence by standard speakers generally regarded by courts as more reliable and substantial than evidence given by nonstandard speaking witnesses? Are juries prejudiced by the speech style of accused persons? How does the speech style of a lawyer affect his advocacy? AT PRESENT THERE ARE NO ANSWERS TO THESE QUESTIONS [1975:111; emphasis added]."

[13] Although we focus in this book more on the speech styles of witnesses than lawyers, an equally important problem is that of the presentational style of counsel. By virtue of their obvious position as intermediaries between the legal authority of the state and the lay public, and their presumed command of legal language, lawyers may assume an aura of quasijudicial authority in the eyes of the jury. The jury often hears that lawyers are "officers of the court," suggesting their intermediate position between the court and the lay public. This role is confirmed in a variety of other obvious ways: Lawyers enjoy a unique freedom of movement in the courtroom; they control the flow of information; they are able simultaneously to converse with judges in the obscure language of the law and with jurors in everyday English. Even in dress, lawyers are likely to occupy an intermediate position between the archaic formality of the judge and other court officers and the casual appearance typical of jurors. Accordingly, opinions and conclusions expressed by lawyers may often be perceived as having some official standing. Resort by counsel to stylistic extremes thus creates a particularly serious danger that the jury will be diverted from its theoretical role of evaluation of the facts and induced to engage in speculation and emotional reaction.

could seldom identify with any precision what styles they thought were significant. This is hardly surprising, since the styles studied ethnographically typically involved quite subtle variations in particular features of speech. The difficulties experienced by the legal professionals in articulating strategies involving language use in court were further justification for using ethnographic and experimental techniques. Our conclusion after many interviews was that speech style factors operate beneath the level of consciousness of most legal professionals. Most seem generally unaware of the specific strategies they employ in courtroom practice since their usual efforts are devoted more toward the design of arguments, the content of evidence, and other substantive matters.

TRIAL PRACTICE MANUALS. In addition to interviews, the writings of members of the legal professionals who have focused on courtroom practice proved helpful in understanding the role of language and communication factors. A study of trial practice manuals provided many specific statements about language strategy.[14]

OBSERVATIONS IN COURT. Observations of 10 weeks of trials provided an additional source of information about how people speak and behave in court. As noted on page 58, these observations were the basis of additional hypotheses about effective courtroom strategies.

Specific Procedures

A program of research combining ethnography and experimentation entails a series of steps that must follow one another in a particular order. Ethnographic observation and analysis necessarily precede experimentation. In this way, ethnography can provide the raw materials for the formulation of specific hypotheses taking into account actual patterns of language use in the court. Then the experimental studies that follow are based on real not contrived situations and thus provide a means to test hypotheses about what has been observed.

The first step in our study of courtroom language was to select the particular courts to study. Preliminary observation of courts in Durham County, North Carolina had provided sufficient basis for designing the research program. After the project was funded, additional observation in several other North American cities and towns was conducted before

---

[14] An extensive discussion of the views contained in trial practice manuals can be found on pages 31–38 of this book.

it was finally decided to continue working in the North Carolina courts. In addition to their typicality, these courts had the advantage of being close to both Duke University and the University of North Carolina at Chapel Hill where the anthropologists, linguist, lawyers, and psychologists associated with the project were located.

The presiding judges of the Durham County courts during Summer 1974 gave their permission to make audio tape recordings of the proceedings with the specific proviso that the tapes would be used only for research and not made available to the parties in the cases, and would not be played in any public forum nor made available to members of the press or broadcasting services. In addition, it was asked that anonymity of persons and their cases be preserved through appropriate changes in any published references. After trying several types of tape recorders, we determined that a reel-to-reel machine with the capacity to record stereophonically at a slower-than-usual speed was best. A slow speed maximized time between changing tapes, and stereophonic recordings, when played back through two speakers, helped separate speech and noise that were otherwise mixed in the single channel. Similar to that normally used by court reporters, this recorder was less intrusive than other types. At the court's suggestion, the court reporter operated it so as to minimize disruption of proceedings. This left members of the research team free to observe and take notes on courtroom interaction. This means of recording presented few problems.

Ten weeks during the summer of 1974 were devoted to recording and observing trials. During this time, at least one member of the research team was always in the courtroom making notes for use with the recordings. More than 150 hours of trials were recorded. Because language proved to be more varied in criminal court, more time was spent in the Superior Criminal Court. Trials that were taped included a variety of misdemeanor, felony, and capital charges. The parties came from different social, economic, ethnic, and linguistic backgrounds. Notes made by observers proved invaluable in identifying speakers and in explaining some of the gestures, demeanor, and courtroom events that were impossible to capture in the audio tape recordings. They also helped keep track of time of day, bench conferences, recesses, and so on. When cross-referenced with the tapes, they became an important source of information as well as an index to the trials.

In addition to the tape recordings and the observations made in the courtroom, another important means for gaining useful insights into courtroom processes emerged fortuitously. During the summer, I received a summons to appear to jury duty in the very court being studied. The matter was discussed with the presiding judge who pointed out that he was unable to excuse anyone from jury duty for occupational reasons—although he did admit that "anthropologist studying the court" was one of the more unusual occupations he had ever encountered. Thus, for 1 of the 10 weeks I spent many long hours waiting in the jury pool room until I was finally called and eventually seated on two cases, both involving appeals of traffic violations. This opportunity, highly desirable for any serious participant–observer of the court and strictly the result of chance, generated many beneficial ideas and insights for the project.

The ethnography of courtroom language also involved the analysis of the recordings. Each night members of the team went over the events of the day. We indexed the tape against the notes and took special notice of both unusual patterns of speech and those that began to emerge as ordinary and expected for the court. These discussions helped us identify and select issues for more detailed analysis. There was not much time for analysis during the collection phase. However, these preliminary observations later proved to be valuable since it takes far more time to analyze tapes than to record them.

By the end of the collection phase, the multidisciplinary team was fully assembled. Several courtroom speech patterns were identified and selected for intensive study. Specific portions of the recordings were subjected to detailed linguistic analysis to discover the characteristics of observed patterns. Discussions among team members who were drawn from several disciplines—anthropology, linguistics, social psychology, and law—led to the selection of four patterns of speech variation for intensive investigation: "powerful" versus "powerless" speech style, narrative versus fragmented testimony, hypercorrection, and simultaneous speech.[15]

By this point, the team was ready to begin the experimental phase and planned a series of experiments using a common design. In each instance, an excerpt of testimony of 10 to 15 minutes in duration was selected. These segments on which experiments would be based were selected after careful consideration of many possibilities. Working jointly, the team produced "doctored" versions of the original testimony segments as required. These altered versions represented other ways in which the witnesses might have testified or the interactions might have occurred. For example, the segment of testimony delivered in the hypercorrect style was rewritten so as to remove all hypercorrect features; the originally fragmented testimony style of the witness selected was revised to be more narrative; and so on.

[15] Many other patterns beyond these were noted and studied in some detail. However, for reasons to be explained in Chapter 5, these were deemed among the most interesting for purposes of the research.

After deciding what to include in the experimental tapes, the team set about the process of producing them. We originally thought that actors would be able to listen to the original tapes, follow directions for modifying them, and produce the needed versions. It was a disappointment to find that almost no amount of effort on the parts of the actors resulted in tapes that sounded much like the original ones. The actors had, alas, been trained to project voices, to wait until other speakers finished talking, and generally to "play act." Although these techniques might be good for the stage, they produced experimental tapes that were too artificial and dramatic to replicate the court. After several actors showed similar difficulties, we turned to lay people who had not been trained in drama. This was clearly what was needed, for they were able to reproduce rather faithfully and without so much effort what they heard on the original tapes as well as the required variants. The lawyer was played by an able, advanced law student who also lacked dramatic training.

It often took as much as 2 weeks to produce satisfactory experimental tapes. Pronounciation and timing were carefully monitored; mistakes of any sort could not be allowed. Once the tapes were made, the linguist analyzed them to describe the experimental conditions.

At this point, we began the experiments. Test subjects were university students, as is customary and conventional for much social psychological research.[16] In each experiment, students reported in small groups and were given general instructions and specific background for the particular experiment. They were told that they would hear a segment from an actual trial and would be asked questions about it afterward. Each subject heard only one tape in a single experiment. Responses were aggregated for those hearing each version. The different treatment groups were compared with one another to determine whether the differences in impressions about and evaluations of speakers are statistically significant.[17]

In the chapter that follows, we report the four specific studies of speech style in the courtroom. Unless otherwise noted, the general approach outlined above was used in each study.

---

[16] Although it might be objected to that students are quite different from actual jurors, it should be noted that other programs of sociolegal research have shown similar effects occurring in both student and nonstudent populations (for example, see Thibaut and Walker 1975).

[17] See footnote 3 in this chapter.

5

SPEECH STYLES
IN THE COURTROOM

In this chapter, ethnographic and experimental studies of four specific styles of courtroom speech are reported. Each of the four (powerful versus powerless speech, narrative versus fragmented testimony, hypercorrection, and simultaneous speech) occurs frequently in court and represents one or more salient issues in the study of courtroom interactions. The tape recordings of the 10 weeks of observed trials provide a means for discovering and analyzing the patterning of each style as it actually occurs in the courtroom. This in turn facilitates the design of realistic experiments to test for possible effects of the speech styles. For each of the four, a specific experiment was designed to test the general hypothesis that variation in testimony style evokes significant responses in legal decision makers.

Powerful versus Powerless Speech

The phenomenon termed here POWERLESS SPEECH was derived from an initial investigation of differences between male and female witnesses. The term POWERLESS SPEECH is gaining currency among other researchers, suggesting both the appropriateness of this concept for discussions of courtroom speech styles and the saliency of the style across a wide variety of contexts.[1]

BACKGROUND

Differences in the speech characteristics of men and women have been reported by anthropologists and linguists in the United States (Fischer 1958) and in other cultures (Haas 1944). The proliferation of studies of language and gender during the 1970s was due both to the general development of sociolinguistic interest in patterns of language variation and to the women's movement (Philips 1980). Robin Lakoff's book, *Language and Woman's Place* (1975), provided a catalyst and encouragement for many other researchers with rudimentary interests in the way women and men speak differently. By the mid 1970s, the fact that there are gender-based differences in speech was beginning to be recognized by people who had previously given little or no thought to it.[2]

For the study of language in the courtroom, Lakoff's work heightened awareness of possible differences in the speech of men and women and provided a beginning point for investigation of empirical differences in court. Unlike many other studies, this effort was not primarily an attempt to understand language and gender differences. Rather, gender-related differences were one of the kinds of variation that current sociolinguistic issues led us to focus on and to consider. In addition, interest in the way women in particular speak in court was further kindled by the discovery that many trial practice manuals often contained special sections on how female witnesses behave differently from males and what special kinds of treatment they require as a consequence. This advice includes the following:

1. BE ESPECIALLY COURTEOUS TO WOMEN. "Even when jurors share the cross-examiner's reaction that the female witness on the stand is dishonest or otherwise undeserving individually, at least some of the jurors are likely to think it improper for the attorney to decline to extend the courtesies customarily extended to women [Keeton 1973:149]."

---

[1] For example, see Philips (1980:535) and McConnell-Ginet (1980:18;25, footnote 35) for more general discussions of the power associated with speech styles and Newcombe and Arnkoff (1979) and Poythress (1979) for more specific applications of the concept of POWERLESS speech styles in social psychological and legal contexts.

[2] Philips (1980) and McConnell–Ginet *et al.* (1980) contain useful reviews of the development of these interests. A bibliography of major writings on gender-based differences in language can be found in McConnell–Ginet (1980:20–21, footnote 2).

2. Avoid making women cry. "Jurors, along with others, may be inclined to forgive and forget transgressions under the influence of sympathy provoked by the genuine tears of a female witness [Keeton 1973:149]." "A crying woman does your case no good [Bailey and Rothblatt 1971:190]."

3. Women behave differently from men and this can sometimes be used to advantage. "Women are contrary witnesses. They hate to say yes. . . . A woman's desire to avoid the obvious answer will lead her right into your real objective—contradicting the testimony of previous prosecution witnesses. Women, like children, are prone to exaggeration; they generally have poor memories as to previous fabrications and exaggerations. They are also stubborn. You will have difficulty trying to induce them to qualify their testimony. Rather, it might be easier to induce them to exaggerate and cause their testimony to appear incredible. An intelligent woman will very often be evasive. She will avoid making a direct answer to a damaging question. Keep after her until you get a direct answer—but always be the gentleman [Bailey and Rothblatt 1973:190–191]."

These comments about women's behavior in court and their likely consequences in the trial process further raised our interest in studying the speech behavior of women in court. Having been told by Lakoff that women do speak differently from men, we interpreted these trial practice authors as saying that at least some of these differences can be consequential in the trial process. Thus, one of the kinds of variation we sought to examine when we began to observe and tape record courtroom speech was patterns unique to either women or men. We did not know what we would find, so we started out by using Lakoff's discussion of women's language as a guide. First, it would be necessary to determine ethnographically how women's speech in court is different from men's— if indeed it is. Second, one or more experiments would need to be designed and conducted to determine what, if any, consequences women's language has on the reception of testimony. The stage was thus set for the examination of the first pattern of language use and its role in the legal process.

LAKOFF'S MODEL OF WOMEN'S LANGUAGE

What Lakoff proposed was that women's speech varies from men's in several significant ways. Although she provided no firm listing of the major features of what she terms women's language (hereafter referred to as WL), the following features were said to occur in high frequency among women. This set of characteristics provided a baseline for investigating gender-related speech patterns in court.

1. HEDGES: *It's sort of hot in here; I'd kind of like to go.; I guess . . . .; It seems like . . . .;* and so on.
2. (SUPER)POLITE FORMS: *I'd really appreciate it if . . . .; Would you please open the door, if you don't mind?;* and so on.
3. TAG QUESTIONS: *John is here, isn't he?* instead of *Is John here?;* and so on.
4. SPEAKING IN ITALICS: Intonational emphasis equivalent to underlining words in written language; emphatic *so* or *very*; and the like.
5. EMPTY ADJECTIVES: *Divine, charming, cute, sweet, adorable, lovely,* and others like them.
6. HYPERCORRECT GRAMMAR AND PRONUNCIATION: Bookish grammar and more formal enunciation.
7. LACK OF A SENSE OF HUMOR: Women said to be poor joke tellers and frequently to "miss the point" in jokes told by men.
8. DIRECT QUOTATIONS: Use of direct quotations rather than paraphrases.
9. SPECIAL LEXICON: In domains like colors where words like *magenta, chartreuse,* and so on are typically used only by women.
10. QUESTION INTONATION IN DECLARATIVE CONTEXTS: For example, in response to the question, *When will dinner be ready?,* an answer like *Around 6 o'clock?,* as though seeking approval and asking whether that time will be okay.

"WOMEN'S LANGUAGE" OR "POWERLESS LANGUAGE"?

Although most lawyers observed in the North Carolina courts were men, the sex distribution of witnesses was more nearly equal. On looking for the speech patterns described by Lakoff, it was readily apparent that some women spoke in court in the manner described, but it was also apparent that the degree to which women actually exhibited these characteristics varied considerably. Cases observed during the 10 weeks included a variety of misdemeanors and felonies—traffic ordinance violations, drug possession, robbery, manslaughter, and rape—and varied in length from a few hours to a week or more. The cases covered a good cross section of the kinds of trials, and hence witnesses, who regularly appear in a superior criminal court. Despite the number of hours of testimony included, 10 weeks is not enough to produce a large number of witnesses. It is not unusual for a single witness to testify in direct and cross-examinations for several hours. Add to this the fact that the court spends much time selecting jurors, hearing summation remarks, giving jury instructions, and handling administrative matters. Thus, the 150 hours of tapes collected provide a better basis for understanding the range of speech typical in the court than a means for making a precise frequency count of persons falling into various stylistic categories. The discussion in this section thus concentrates on a description of the range of variation and complements it with some nonstatistical impressions regarding frequency.

Observation of courtroom speakers show a continuum[3] of use of the features described by Lakoff. Initially, it was not clear why some speakers should conform rather closely to Lakoff's proposed model of speech characteristic of American women while others depart in critical ways from it. Before suggesting an interpretation of this finding, let us examine some points along the continuum from high to low incidence of WOMEN'S LANGUAGE features.

A

Mrs. A,[4] a witness in a case involving the death of her neighbor in an automobile accident, is an extreme example of a person using WL in testifying. She displays nearly every feature described by Lakoff and certainly all those appropriate for the courtroom. Her speech contains a high frequency of INTENSIFIERS (*very close friends, quite ill,* etc., often with intonational emphasis); HEDGES (frequent use of *you know, sort of like, maybe just a little bit, let's see,* etc.); EMPTY ADJECTIVES (*this very kind policeman*); and other similar features. This typical example[5] of her speech shows the types of intensifiers and hedges she commonly uses:

Q. *State whether or not, Mrs. A, you were acquainted with or knew the late Mrs. X.*
A. *Quite well.*
Q. *What was the nature of your acquaintance with her?*

[3] Each feature should actually be treated as a separate continuum since there is not perfect covariation. For convenience, we discuss the variation as a single continuum of possibilities. However, it should be kept in mind that a high frequency of occurrence of one particular feature may not necessarily be associated with a high frequency of another.

[4] Names have been deleted and are indicated by a letter only in order to preserve the anonymity of witnesses. However, the forms of address used in court are retained.

[5] These examples are taken from both direct examinations and cross-examinations of the witnesses, although Table 5.1 uses data from only direct examinations. Examples are selected to point out clearly the differences in style. However, it should be remembered that the cross-examination of a witness is potentially a more powerless situation than a direct examination.

A. *Well, we were, uh, very close friends. Uh, she was even sort of like a mother to me.*

By contrast, this rewritten version of the same testimony illustrates what her speech MIGHT be like without these features.

Q. *State whether or not, Mrs. A, you were acquainted with the late Mrs. X.*
A. *Yes, I did.*
Q. *What was the nature of your acquaintance with her?*
A. *We were close friends. She was like a mother to me.*

Table 5.1 summarizes the frequency of several features attributed to WL by Lakoff. Calculated as a ratio of WL forms per answer, this witness's speech contains 1.14 — among the highest incidences we observed.

B

The speech of Mrs. B, a witness in a case involving her father's arrest, shows fewer WL features. Her ratio of features per answer drops to .84. Her testimony contains instances of both WL and a more assertive speech style. Frequently, her speech is punctuated with responses like: *He, see, he thought it was more-or-less me rather than the police officer.* Yet it also contains many more straightforward and assertive passages than are found in A's speech.

C

The speech of Dr. C, a pathologist who testifies as an expert witness, exhibits fewer features of WL than either of the other two women. Her speech contains the lowest incidence of WL features among the female witnesses whose speech was analyzed. Dr. C's ratio of WL features is .18 per answer. Her responses tend to be straightforward, with little hesitancy, few hedges, a noticeable lack of intensifiers, etc. (see Table 5.1). Typical of her speech is this response in which she explains some of her findings in a pathological examination:

Q. *And had the heart not been functioning, in other words, had the heart been stopped, there would have been no blood to have come from that region?*

A. *It may leak down, depending on the position of the body after death. But the presence of blood in the alveoli indicates that some active respiratory action had to take place.*

What all this shows is that some women speak in the way Lakoff described, employing many features of WL, whereas others are far away on a continuum of possible and appropriate styles for the courtroom. It

Table 5.1
Frequency Distribution of Women's Language Features[a] in the Speech of Six Witnesses

	Women			Men		
	A	B	C	D	E	F
Intensifiers[b]	16	0	0	21	2	1
Hedges[c]	19	2	3	2	5	0
Hesitation forms[d]	52	20	13	26	27	11
Witness asks lawyer questions[e]	2	0	0	0	0	0
Gestures[f]	2	0	0	0	0	0
Polite forms[g]	9	0	2	2	0	1
Use of *sir*[h]	2	0	6	32	13	11
Direct quotations[i]	1	5	0	0	0	0
Total (all powerless forms)	103	27	24	85	47	24
Number of answers in interview	90	32	136	61	73	52
Ratio (powerless forms per answer)	1.14	0.84	0.18	1.39	0.64	0.46

[a] The particular features chosen for inclusion in this table were selected because of their saliency and frequency of occurrence. Not included here are features of WL that either do not occur in court or that we had difficulty operationalizing and coding. These data are based on the direct examinations of the six witnesses.

[b] Forms that increase or emphasize the force of assertion, such as *very, definitely, very definitely, surely, such a.*

[c] Forms that reduce the force of assertion allowing for exceptions or avoiding rigid commitments, such as *sort of, a little, kind of.*

[d] Pause fillers such as *uh, um, ah,* and "meaningless" particles such as *oh, well, let's see, now, so, you see.*

[e] Use of question intonation in response to lawyer's questions, including rising intonation in normally declarative contexts (e.g., *thirty?, thirty-five?*) and questions asked by witness of lawyer like *Which way do you go . . . ?*

[f] Spoken indications of direction such as *over there.*

[g] Includes *please, thank you,* etc. Use of *sir* counted separately due to its high frequency.

[h] Assumed to be an indication of more polite speech.

[i] Not typically allowed in court under restrictions on hearsay which restrict the situations under which a witness may tell what someone else said.

was quickly observed that men, too, vary considerably in their courtroom speech styles and specifically in the degree to which WL features are present in their speech. Three examples follow which illustrate how the speech of male witnesses also varies along a continuum of high to low incidence of WL features.

D

Mr. D exhibits many but not all of Lakoff's WL features.[6] Those WL features he employs, like intensifiers, for example, occur in especially high frequency—among the highest observed among all speakers, whether male or female. His ratio of WL features per answer is 1.39, actually higher than Mrs. A. The following excerpt, an extreme example of Mr. D's use of WL features, illustrates the degree to which features attributed to women are in fact present in high frequency in the speech of some men.

Q. *And you saw, you observed what?*
A. *Well, after I heard—I can't really, I can't definitely state whether the brakes or the lights came first, but I rotated my head slightly to the right, and looked directly behind Mr. Y, and I saw reflections of lights, and uh, very, very, very instantaneously after that, I heard a very, very loud explosion—from my standpoint of view it would have been an implosion because everything was forced outward, like this, like a grenade thrown into a room. And, uh, it was, it was terrifically loud.*

E

Mr. E, more toward the low-frequency end of the continuum of male speakers, shows some WL features. His ratio of features per answer is .64, comparable to Mrs. B. Many passages from the testimony of this speaker show few WL features while others contain quite a large number. The following answers to separate questions show the variation in this witness's speech.

---

[6] This speaker did not use some of the intonational features that we had noted among women having high frequencies of WL features in their speech. The only major discrepancies between Lakoff's description and our findings were in features that the specific context of the courtroom rendered inappropriate, for example, TAG QUESTIONS (because witnesses typically answer rather than ask questions) and JOKING (because there is little humor in a courtroom, we did not have occasion to observe the specifically female patterns of humor to which Lakoff referred).

A_1. *After I realized that my patient and my attendant were thrown from the vehicle, uh, which I assumed, I radioed in for help to the dispatcher, tell her that we had been in an accident and, uh, my patient and attendant were thrown from the vehicle and I didn't know the extent of their injury at the time, to hurry up and send help.*

A_2. *I felt that she had, uh, might have had a sort of heart attack.*

F

Officer F, among the males lowest in WL features, virtually lacks all features tabulated in Table 5.1 except for hesitancy and use of *sir*. His ratio of WL forms per answer is .46. His no-nonsense, straightforward manner is illustrated in the following excerpt, in which a technical answer is given in a style comparable to that of Dr. C.

Q. *You say that you found blood of group O?*

A. *The blood in the vial, in the layman's term, is positive, Rh positive. Technically referred to as a capital r, sub o, little r.*

Taken together these findings suggest that the so-called women's language is neither characteristic of all women nor limited only to women. A similar continuum of WL features (high to low) is found among speakers of both sexes. These findings suggest that the sex of a speaker is insufficient to explain incidence of WL features.

Once it had been noted that WL features were distributed in such a manner for witnesses of both sexes, the data were examined for other factors that might be associated with a high or low incidence of the features in question. First, it was noted that MORE women fall toward the high end of the continuum. Next, it was discovered that all the women who were aberrant (that is, who used relatively few WL features) had something in common—an unusually high social status. Like Dr. C, they were typically well-educated, professional women of middle-class background. A corresponding pattern was noted among aberrant men (i.e., those high in WL features). Like Mr. D, they tended to be men who held either subordinate, lower status jobs or were unemployed. Housewives were high in WL features whereas middle-class males were low in these features. In addition to social status in the society at large, another factor associated with low incidence of WL is previous courtroom experience. Individuals C and F testify frequently in court as expert witnesses, that is, as witnesses who testify on the basis of their professional expertise. However, it should be noted that not all persons who speak with few WL features have had extensive courtroom experience. Thus, a powerful position may derive from either social standing in the larger society and/or status accorded by the court. Careful ethnographic observation revealed these patterns to hold generally.[7] A little more about the background of the persons described confirms the observed pattern.

A is a married woman, about 55 years old, who is a housewife.

B is married, but younger, about 35 years old. From her testimony, there is no information that she works outside her home.

C is a pathologist in a local hospital. She is 35–40 years old. There is no indication from content of her responses or from the way she was addressed (always Dr.) of her marital status. She has testified in court as a pathologist on many occasions.

D is an ambulance attendant, rather inexperienced in his job, which he has held for less than 6 months. Around 30 years old, his marital status is unknown.

E is D's supervisor. He drives the ambulance, supervises emergency treatment, and gives instructions to D. He has held his job longer than D and has had more experience. About 30–35 years old, his marital status is unknown.

F is an experienced member of the local police force. He has testified in court frequently. He is 35–40 years old and his marital status is unknown.

These data indicate that the variation in WL features may be related more to social powerlessness than to gender. Both observational data and some statistics show that this style is not simply or even primarily a gender-related pattern. Based on this evidence, it appears that the phenomenon described by Lakoff is more appropriately termed POWER-LESS LANGUAGE, a term that is more descriptive of the particular features involved and of the social status of those who speak in this manner, and one that does not link it unnecessarily to the sex of a speaker.

Further, the tendency for more women to speak "powerless" language and for men to speak it less is due, at least in part, to the greater tendency

---

[7] We do not wish to make more of this pattern than our data are able to support, but we suggest that our grounds for these claims are at least as good as Lakoff's. Lakoff's basis for her description of features constituting WL are her own speech, speech of her friends and acquaintances, and patterns used in the mass media (1975:4).

of women to occupy relatively powerless social positions.[8] Social status is reflected in speech behavior. Similarly, for men, the greater tendency to use the more powerful variant (which we will term POWERFUL LANGUAGE) is probably linked, at least in part, to the fact that men much more often tend to occupy more powerful positions in society than women.

SOME CONSEQUENCES OF USING POWERLESS LANGUAGE

Part of our study of courtroom language entailed experimental verification of hypotheses about the significance of particular forms of language used in court.[9] We conducted this part of our research by designing social psychological experiments based on what we had actually observed in court. First, we located on the original tapes recorded in the courtroom a segment of testimony delivered by a witness in the powerless style. For this study, we chose the testimony given under direct examination by witness A described on pages 65 and 66. Her original testimony was used to generate the test materials needed for the experiment.

The original, powerless-style testimony was edited slightly to make it more suitable for use in the experiment.[10] The testimony was then recorded on audio tape with actors[11] playing the parts of the lawyer and the witness. In this recreation of the testimony the actors strove to replicate as closely as possible the speech characteristics found in the original testimony. Another recording was then made using the same actors, however, most of the features that characterize the powerless style—the hedges, hesitation forms, intensifiers, etc.—were omitted from the witness's speech, producing an example of testimony given in the

---

[8] That a complex of such features should have been called WOMEN'S LANGUAGE in the first place reflects the generally powerless position of many women in American society, a point recognized but not developed extensively by Robin Lakoff (1975:7–8).

[9] This research on powerful versus powerless speech as well as experimental studies of other speech variables reported in this chapter have been discussed in previously published journal articles (Conley *et al.* 1978; Erickson *et al.* 1978; Lind *et al.* 1978; O'Barr and Conley 1976), conference proceedings (O'Barr *et al.* 1976), and book chapters (Lind and O'Barr 1979; O'Barr and Atkins 1980; O'Barr and Lind 1981).

[10] This editing involved only minor changes in the testimony. Specifically, we changed the names, dates, and locations mentioned in the original testimony to fulfill our promise to the court that we would protect the privacy of those involved in the actual taped trials. In addition, we removed attorney objections and the testimony to which the objections were addressed. The removal of this material was prompted by our observation in an early stage of the study that objections tended to divert attention from the relatively brief segment of testimony used in the experiment. We are currently investigating the effects of objections as a style topic in its own right.

[11] See the discussion about the use of actors in Chapter 4, page 59.

Table 5.2
Comparison of Linguistic Characteristics of the Four Experimental Tapes (Powerful versus Powerless Language)

	Female witness		Male witness	
	Powerful	Powerless	Powerful	Powerless
Hedges[a]	2	22	2	21
Hesitation forms	13	73	18	51
Witness asks lawyer questions	2	5	2	6
Use of *sir* by witness	0	3	0	4
Intensifiers	0	35	0	31
Running time of tape[b]	9:12	11:45	9:35	12:10

[a]For definitions, see Table 5.1.
[b]Time given in minutes and seconds.

powerful style. It is important to note that the powerful and powerless experimental testimony differed only in characteristics related to the speech style used by the witness. In both samples of testimony exactly the same factual information was presented.

The first two columns of Table 5.2 present the results of linguistic analyses of the two experimental testimony tapes described earlier. As may be seen, they differed markedly on each of the features that distinguish the two styles. Differences between powerful and powerless modes are illustrated by the original (powerless) and the rewritten (powerful) excerpts on pages 65 and 66.[12]

The original testimony on which the experimental tapes were based was delivered by a female witness. To have conducted the experiment only with a female witness would have limited the conclusions to be drawn from the results. To determine whether any particular effects of the speech style factor were restricted to only one sex, the process described above was followed using a female and a male acting as the witness. The FOUR tapes thus produced presented the same information from the point of view of content. The differences consisted of a female and a male witness speaking in either the powerful or the powerless style.

As may be seen from Table 5.2, for both witnesses the intended differences between powerful and powerless styles are present in the tapes used in the experiments. The characteristics summarized in Table 5.2 show that powerful versions of the testimony taped by the male and

[12] Transcripts of the tapes used in this and other experimental studies are contained in Appendix 1, pages 127–135.

female actors are quite similar. The male and female versions of the powerless tapes, however, contain some important differences. The male version has relatively fewer powerless characteristics than the female. It contains, for example, fewer hesitations and intensifiers. In general, the male powerless tape contains many elements of powerless language, but it is a less extreme variant of the style than that used by the original witness and replicated in the female experimental version. These differences between male and female powerless version were built into the experimental tapes because members of the research team were in agreement that a faithful replication of the original female witness's speech style and powerless mannerisms—although suitable for a female witness—were not within the normal range of acceptable male verbal usage.

Once the four experimental tapes had been produced, it was possible to proceed with the experimental test of the results of the two styles. Ninety-six undergraduate students at the University of North Carolina at Chapel Hill served as mock jurors in the experiment.[13] The participants reported to the experimental laboratory in groups of five to seven at a time. Upon arriving, they were given written instructions describing the experiment. Read aloud by the experimenter, these instructions explained to the participants that they would hear a segment of testimony from an actual trial. The instructions then briefly outlined the details of the case and the major issues to be decided.

The case involved a collision between an automobile and an ambulance. The patient in the ambulance, already critically ill and en route to the hospital, died shortly after the collision. The experimental participants were told that the patient's family was suing the defendants (both the ambulance company and the driver of the automobile) to recover damages for the patient's death. The participants were also told that the witness they would hear was a neighbor and friend who had accompanied the now-deceased patient in the ambulance and was therefore present during the collision. The participants were informed that they would be asked questions about their reactions to the testimony after listening to the trial segment. Note taking was not allowed.

The participant–jurors then listened to only one of the four experimental tapes described above. After the participants had heard the testimony, the experimenter distributed a questionnaire asking about the participants' reactions to the case and to the individuals involved. The responses to these questions formed the basis for several conclusions concerning the effects of the style in which testimony is delivered.

---

[13] Of the 96 participants, 46 were males and 50 were females. The experiment was later repeated at the University of New Hampshire with essentially similar findings.

Table 5.3
Average Rating of Witness Using Powerful and Powerless Language

	Female witness		Male witness	
	Powerful	Powerless	Powerful	Powerless
Convincingness	3.00^a	1.65	3.52	2.09
Truthfulness	3.70	1.88	4.24	2.86
Competence	2.61	0.85	2.44	0.18
Intelligence	2.57	0.23	1.80	0.18
Trustworthiness	3.04	1.65	3.48	2.00

^{a}All differences are significant at $p \leq .05$.

The average-rating-scale responses to each of five questions about the witness are shown in Table 5.3. For each of these questions, a rating of $+5$ indicates a very strong positive response to the question, whereas a rating of -5 indicates a strong negative response. The effects of the testimony style on impressions of the female witness may be seen by contrasting the first and second columns of the table. The results for the male witness are presented in the third and fourth columns of the table.

Statistical analyses[14] confirm the patterns of testimony style influences seen in the table. These analyses permit us to state with a generally high degree of certainty that "jurors" who heard the female use the powerful style indicated that they believed the witness more ($p < .01$), found her more convincing ($p < .001$), and more trustworthy ($p < .02$) than did those who heard her give her testimony in the powerless style. Obviously, the female witness made a much better impression when she used the powerful than when she used the powerless style.

The same pattern of results was found in the comparison of the male's use of powerful versus powerless testimony styles. Again the statistical analyses indicate with high certainty that participants who heard the powerful style responded more favorably than those hearing the powerless style to questions asking how much they believed the witness ($p < .05$) and how convincing they thought the witness was ($p < .05$). As was the case with the female witness, participants thought the male

[14] The significance of the results reported in this section was assessed by the appropriate multivariate or univariate analysis of variance technique. Only differences reported to be significant should be regarded as "true" or real differences. Social scientists interested in more details of the analyses should consult the other published reports of this research; see footnote 9 to this chapter.

witness testifying in the powerful style was more competent ($p < .001$), more intelligent ($p < .005$), and more trustworthy ($p < .02$). It is therefore apparent from the results of the experiment that, for both male and female witnesses, the use of the powerless style produced consistently less favorable reactions to the witness than did the use of the powerful testimony style. Thus, this experiment demonstrates that the style in which testimony is delivered strongly affects how favorably the witness is perceived, and by implication suggests that these sorts of differences may play a consequential role in the legal process itself.

SOME RELATED STUDIES

This discussion of powerless speech concerns a stylistic complex, a set of features that tend to covary. Although it is possible that only a few of the powerless features may occur with high frequency in the speech of a particular witness while others are low in incidence or even absent, we observed ethnographically that a high frequency on one or more dimensions is usually associated with a high frequency on others. Hence, powerless language as we find it in the courtroom is an amalgam, a complex of features that together constitute a style.

The issue of powerful language need not be thought of only as a stylistic complex. Indeed, the findings of at least two other researchers who have investigated language in legal contexts have shown the power of single words. As noted in Chapter 2, Elizabeth Loftus (1979) was able to show experimentally how different verbs—*collided, bumped, contacted,* and *hit*—elicit different estimates of the speed of automobiles involved in collision accidents. Her research has also shown that questions presupposing the presence of items or events (*Did you see **the** broken glass?*) as opposed to those questions which make no such presuppositions (*Did you see **any** broken glass?*) elicit quite different responses. Another researcher, Brenda Danet (1980a), in examining the words used in a trial to refer to the "object of an abortion" found attempts by the prosecution and the defense to use terms like *fetus, person, male child,* and *baby boy* strategically to convey different impressions and connotations to the jury.

Both Loftus's and Danet's studies show the enormous power conveyed by single words. When recalling the model of a trial (proposed in Chapter 1) in which many different versions of the facts are presented—not all of which can be equally true—then we see that those STYLES that are more convincing and those WORDS that are more powerful and persuasive carry much more weight in the courtroom.

Narrative versus Fragmented Testimony Styles

The styles of speaking discussed in the previous section result from and reflect the speaker's social prestige. In the courtroom, they affect the power of a witness's testimony by decreasing or increasing its credibility and convincingness. Social power and the related issue of control are also associated with other aspects of speech. Narrative and fragmented testimony styles are another aspect of the power of speech style in the courtroom.

BACKGROUND

Ethnographic observation of courtroom interaction revealed considerable variation in the length of witnesses' responses to questions asked by lawyers. Some witnesses tended to give relatively brief answers; others were habitually more loquacious. At times, it appeared that the examining lawyer wanted the witness to speak long and fully. On other occasions, it seemed that brief, incisive, nonelaborative responses were desired. For convenience, we refer to these two styles with the terms NARRATIVE and FRAGMENTED.

The following excerpts illustrate the difference. In the first, the witness volunteers a long answer to the question. In the second, the witness is less responsive, making it necessary for the lawyer to pose additional questions to elicit the same information volunteered in the first answer.

Narrative Style

Q. *Now, calling your attention to the twenty-first day of November, a Saturday, what were your working hours that day?*

A. *Well, I was working from, uh, 7 A.M. to 3 P.M. I arrived at the store at 6:30 and opened the store at 7.*

Fragmented Style

Q. *Now, calling your attention to the twenty-first day of November, a Saturday, what were your working hours that day?*

A. *Well, I was working from 7 to 3.*

Q. *Was that 7 A.M.?*

A. *Yes.*

Q. *And what time that day did you arrive at the store?*

A. *6:30.*

Q. *6:30. And did, uh, you open the store at 7 o'clock?*
A. *Yes, it has to be opened by then.*

In actual courtroom interchanges, observation shows witnesses are rather consistent in their tendency to use one or the other of these styles. In general, there is not much variation between very long and very short answers within the testimony of a particular witness. Rather, each person tends to operate within a personal range along the continuum from a highly narrative to a highly fragmented testimony style.

Since the courtroom examination is organized so that lawyers ask the questions and witnesses answer them, ultimate control of these exchanges is vested in the lawyer. It appeared, in observations of the court, that long, narrative answers by witnesses are possible only when lawyers relinquish some control, allowing more leeway to witnesses in answering questions. When such opportunity is "offered," it is by no means always accepted. But it seems virtually impossible for it to be assumed without open conflict except when the opportunity for a narrative answer is offered. Thus, it seemed, information about both the assertiveness of the witness and the lawyer–witness relationship is encoded within the mode of lawyer–witness interaction.

Moreover, it turned out on researching the matter that writers on trial tactics have often commented on these testimony styles.[15] The general advice offered in trial practice manuals is that lawyers should allow their own witnesses some opportunity for narrative answers and should restrict opposition witnesses to brief answers as much as possible. This advice appears to be based on the implicit assumption that narrative answers are better received than fragmented ones.

HYPOTHESES FROM ATTRIBUTION THEORY[16]

In addition to what the tacticians have to say about narrative and fragmented styles and what our own ethnographic observations suggested, there are social-psychological reasons why these styles are interesting. In the Anglo–American legal system, control over the substance and form of testimony is delegated to the interrogating attorney.

[15] Morrill (1971:34) is a typical example of the tacticians who have commented on the narrative versus fragmented testimony styles.

[16] I am especially indebted to Allan Lind for bringing attribution theory to my attention and for the suggestions he has made in interpreting the results of our study of narrative versus fragmented testimony styles.

Since the delegation of control from judge to attorney to witness is a widely known and accepted principle of courtroom structure, it seems likely that narrative testimony is interpreted by jurors as reflecting voluntary, partial transfer over evidence presentation by the attorney to the witness. In permitting a witness to respond at length, we hypothesized that the attorney is perceived as surrendering some control over testimony to the witness.

Models of attribution within social psychology suggest that the style of testimony might carry, in addition to other messages through form, information about the attorney's perceptions of the witness. Attribution theory attempts to explain how individuals discover underlying motives by analyzing the behavior of others (Jones and Davis 1965; Kelley 1967). In the situation considered here, the models suggest that—if the earlier supposition about relinquished control is correct—jurors are likely to search for an explanation for the transfer of control that is reflected in narrative testimony. Such an explanation is available in the attribution that the attorney holds a generally favorable opinion of any witness allowed to testify in a narrative style. An attribution of this sort, if indeed it does occur, might influence in turn the juror's opinions about the witness. For example, a juror might accept the evaluation the lawyer seems to have of the witness. The process posited here suggests that a juror accepting the attorney's apparent evaluation would react more favorably to a witness testifying in a narrative style.

Attribution theory suggests another factor that may influence reactions to the narrative and the fragmented styles. Previous studies have shown that attributions concerning others' beliefs and evaluations are strongest when the observed behavior (used to posit causes and motives) is contrary to expectations (Jones and Davis 1965; Jones et al. 1961). It is widely recognized that men are expected to be more assertive than women in speaking (Key 1975; Lakoff 1973, 1975; Thorne and Henley 1975). Since narrative answers may be perceived as linguistic assertiveness, those hearing a female witness using a narrative style or a male witness using a fragmented one might view such behavior as a significant departure from expected norms. If so, they might interpret such behavior as revealing important information about the attorney–witness relationship.

TESTING THE EFFECTS OF NARRATIVE AND
FRAGMENTED STYLES

An experiment similar to that used to investigate the effects of powerful and powerless speech was designed to study the effects of narrative and fragmented testimony styles on social perceptions. Again, the experiment

Table 5.4
Characteristics of the Narrative and Fragmented Testimony Tapes Used in
Experiment

	Narrative style		Fragmented style	
	♂ Witness	♀ Witness	♂ Witness	♀ Witness
Question/answer pairs	30	30	131	131
Average words per question	14.1	14.1	7.9	7.9
Average words per answer	42.2	43.0	8.3	8.5

was based on a segment of actual testimony recorded in the court. As
before, actors were used to make the experimental stimuli, each of which
contained the same substantive information but varied in the style of
presentation.

Four tapes were prepared for the experiment. A female witness spoke
once in the narrative and once in the fragmented testimony style, and
a male witness replicated the experimental tapes made by the female
witness. On all four tapes, as in the preceding study, the lawyer's part
was spoken by a male. Characteristics of the four experimental tapes
are reported in Table 5.4.

In addition to narrative and fragmented styles, another element was
built into the design of the experiment. Since many cases are tried by
judges sitting without juries, we decided to attempt to discover whether
judges might respond differently to different speech styles of witnesses.
Direct study of the reactions of judges versus jurors was deemed too
difficult and costly to arrange, at least until it was known whether there
were likely to be general differences in reactions to narrative and fragmented styles. Thus, it was decided to investigate the judge–juror dimension indirectly through the use of experimental subjects with some
legal training versus those with none.

In conducting the experiment, a procedure similar to that employed
before was used. Subjects with and without legal training (law students
and psychology students, respectively)[17] listened to one of the four tapes
and then answered a questionnaire about their reactions to the testimony.
Subjects were asked to give their impressions of the witness and the
lawyer. In addition, they were asked about how they thought the lawyer
perceived the witness. This latter set of questions attempted to discover
possible attributions of the sort discussed earlier.

---

[17] Eighty-two undergraduate students (42 male and 40 female) and 43 law students (34
male and 9 female) at the University of North Carolina participated in the study.

Some major findings are summarized in Table 5.5. As may be seen from the table, for undergraduates hearing the male witness and for law students hearing the female witness, the narrative style produced higher ratings than did the fragmented one. For each rating dimension reported in Table 5.5, the differences are statistically significant. No significant differences in ratings of the narrative and fragmented styles were observed for psychology students hearing the female witness or for law students hearing the male witness.

Closer examination of the mean values in Table 5.5 reveals that the narrative–fragmented differences are due to the particularly low ratings of the ♂ fragmented tape by the psychology students and to the particularly high ratings of the ♀ narrative testimony tape by the law students. That is, for the undergraduates the ♂ fragmented testimony tape produced lower ratings on each measure than did the other three tapes, all of which received more similar ratings. For the law-trained subjects, the ♀ narrative testimony tape received ratings on each measure that were consistently higher than the ratings on all other tapes, which again did not differ significantly from one another in ratings. Measures of the witness's convincingness and of the subject's beliefs concerning the guilt

Table 5.5
Ratings of Narrative and Fragmented Testimony[a]

		Subjects' legal training			
		No legal training		Legal training	
Rating dimension	Sex of witness	Narrative testimony	Fragmented testimony	Narrative testimony	Fragmented testimony
Attribution of lawyer's	♂	1.11	−1.55	−0.55	0.23
impression of witness's	♀	0.63	0.50	2.80	−0.05
competence					
Attribution of lawyer's	♂	0.84	−1.74	−0.32	−0.41
impression of witness's	♀	0.21	−0.16	2.15	−1.23
social dynamism					
Subject's impression of	♂	0.55	−1.10	−0.73	−0.64
witness's competence	♀	0.29	0.50	2.05	−0.68
Subject's impression of	♂	−0.42	−1.52	−1.14	−0.82
witness's social	♀	0.26	−0.43	2.10	−1.82
dynamism					

[a]Higher values indicate more favorable ratings. For each rating dimension the narrative versus fragmented × legal training × sex of witness interaction is significant, $p < .01$. For an extensive discussion of these findings, see Lind *et al.* 1978.

of the defendant against whom the witness testified showed the same pattern of effects, but the statistical tests on these measures fell short of significance ($p < .12$ for the three-way interaction for both measures).

A speculative explanation of these results may be advanced using the attribution theory ideas discussed earlier. It appears that the implications of the narrative–fragmented distinction for testimony control operate as posited: The subjects hold traditional expectations concerning gender-related differences in speech assertiveness, and the subjects with legal training expect the lawyer to maintain control over the witness's verbal behavior, more so than do subjects without legal training.

We consider first the subjects trained in the law. These subjects might expect the attorney to maintain overall control of the testimony, but might not expect this control to be carried to the extreme of suppressing typical and expected assertiveness for a male witness. When such a suppression of expected assertiveness does occur, as in the ♂ fragmented tape, the subjects consider the style unusual and particularly indicative of the lawyer's negative evaluation of the witness. Stated slightly differently, the lay subjects may believe that only a lawyer who dislikes a male witness would deny him the usual opportunity to exercise male assertiveness through delivering his testimony in a narrative style. The ♂ narrative and ♀ narrative tapes, according to this line of reasoning, are not considered distinctive (and, hence, do not receive distinctive ratings) because the subjects expect only moderate lawyer control and see nothing unusual in the lawyer's permitting witnesses of either sex to speak at length. The ♀ fragmented testimony is not contrary to the subjects' gender-role stereotypes about linguistic assertiveness and, thus, does not show unexpected behavior and does not receive distinctive ratings.

In contrast, the law-trained subjects, perhaps by virtue of their schooling in the theory and practice of the adversary system, may have expected the lawyer to maintain stricter control over the witness. If so, the ♂ fragmented testimony would not be seen as exceptional by these subjects, since they would not expect norms of male assertiveness to "override" the importance of strict control by the lawyer. What may be unexpected by these subjects is a lawyer allowing narrative testimony by a type of witness usually expected to be nonassertive, the situation in the ♀ narrative testimony situation. Again following leads from social attribution theory, only this unexpected combination of stereotypes and speech behavior is viewed as particularly indicative of the lawyer's impressions of the witness, suggesting in this instance that the lawyer holds a high evaluation of the female witness AS DEMONSTRATED BY THE FACT THAT SHE IS PERMITTED TO DELIVER NARRATIVE TESTIMONY.

The effects observed on the subjects' impressions of the witness can be explained by assuming that the subjects accept the lawyer's apparent evaluation of the witness. This seems reasonable since ratings of the lawyer by subjects are generally positive, indicating that he is favorably evaluated. In addition, since the testimony used in the experiments is from a direct examination of a witness (that is, the lawyer questioned a witness whom he had called to testify), the lawyer might be thought to be reasonably well acquainted with the witness, giving further basis for the subjects to believe that the lawyer's (perceived) evaluation of the witness is accurate.

The above explanation of the results of this experiment is admittedly highly speculative, and additional research will be needed to verify the psychological processes proposed. It is clear, however, that when reactions to narrative and fragmented testimony differ they are more favorable toward witnesses giving narrative answers. Further, that the testimony type affected not only evaluations of the witness but also perceptions of the attorney–witness relationship shows that listeners use court observations to arrive at rather complex beliefs about those they hear.

RELATED STUDIES

Studies of similar phenomena show that the process reported here is a general one. Giles and Powesland (1975) report a large number of studies that show the response-matching phenomenon. For example, in a study of news conferences held by President John F. Kennedy, it was discovered that longer questions tended to get longer answers, and that shorter questions got shorter ones. Researchers have also found correlations between two speakers with regard to several speech characteristics, including rate of speech, precision of enunciation, frequency of interruptions, frequency of pauses, verbal aggressiveness, and accent. Along all these dimensions it has been found that speakers tend to match the other party in the conversation.

Although these findings are interesting in themselves, they have fairly serious implications for the legal process. Since response matching appears to be a general characteristic of verbal interactions and the style of one speaker influences that of the other, it is not only possible but even likely that lawyers quite literally put a language style into the mouths of their witnesses. For example, short questions are likely, according to the response-matching phenomenon, to elicit short answers, or the fragmented style. Similarly, longer questions might be expected to elicit more narrative responses. Since we know that the two styles are not evaluated equally, it would seem that this represents an opportunity for a LINGUISTIC LEADING OF WITNESSES, one that is consequential in the reception and evaluation of testimony.

Hypercorrect Testimony Style

A trial court is one of the most formal and intimidating situations that many people ever confront. It is no surprise therefore that many, or even most, witnesses speak considerably more formally than they do in everyday conversations. Some witnesses, however, attempt to speak in a style so much more formal than is their custom that they consequently make frequent errors in vocabulary and grammar. Witnesses who use this "hypercorrect" style do not achieve the formality intended, but speak instead in a stilted and unnatural manner. Hypercorrect testimony style was another issue chosen for intensive study.

THE HYPERCORRECT STYLE

During the ethnographic phase of the research, hypercorrection was discovered to be used rather frequently in the courtroom. A paper by the linguist William Labov (1972) provided useful guidance for the study. Labov described hypercorrection as the misapplication of imperfectly learned rules of grammar, incorrect use of vocabulary, and overly precise pronunciation. These "mistakes" can occur on one or more levels of language at once. They can be limited to sounds, words, or grammar, but frequently when hypercorrection is found in one level it is also present on other levels. Hypercorrect speech is likely to include more precise enunciation than is typical for most speakers so that it sounds overly "correct" (for example, normally silent letters are pronounced); vocabulary choices can be more formal or technical than is normally expected with some choices altogether inappropriate or "wrong"; and grammar can be "bookish" beyond the patterns used by even those who normally speak in highly formal ways. Hypercorrection is, thus, the overapplication or misapplication (usually irregularly) of the rules of formal language.

The following excerpt from one of the tape recorded trials shows a high frequency of hypercorrect vocabulary.

Q. *Immediately after the collision, what happened to you?*
A. *Well, directly after the implosion, I vaguely remember being*

hurled in some direction. I know not where, but I went, I hurdled through the air some distance. I must have been unconscious at the time. I did awake briefly, and during that interim, Mr. Norris was standing over me, uh, perhaps more than likely, getting ready to administer first aid. But, I, I relapsed into a comatose state, and, I, I can't remember anything after that for the next 72 hours or so.

For contrast, compare the following hypothetical answer to the one actually given in court.

A. *Well, directly after the collision, I vaguely remember being hurled in some direction. I don't know where, but I went, I hurled through the air some distance. I must have been unconscious at the time. I did awake briefly, and during that time, Mr. Norris was standing over me, uh, probably getting ready to administer first aid. But uh, I lost consciousness, and I can't remember anything after that for the next 3 days or so.*

Differences between the two answers point up the sorts of vocabulary differences that amount to hyperformality and "overly" correct speech. Table 5.6 suggests additional differences in the testimony between typically formal speech and the hypercorrect usages of this particular witness.

STUDYING HYPERCORRECTION EXPERIMENTALLY

In analyzing the tape recordings of trials, it was discovered that hypercorrection, although unusual, was not an infrequent style adopted by

Table 5.6
Some Lexical Differences between
Hypercorrect and Formal Speech

Hypercorrect	Formal
Seventy-two hours	Three days
Comatose	Unconscious
Not cognizant	Not aware
Opposite of	Opposite
Transport her	Move her
The patient was not ambulatory	Mrs. Davis was not able to walk
In somewhat less than a dire condition	Able to be moved

witnesses in testifying. Since it was not an idiosyncratic pattern limited to one particular witness it was selected for experimental study.

Hypercorrect speech was, in fact, the initial pattern selected for detailed ethnographic analysis and subsequent experimental study. As the team's first attempt to study the effects of speech variation on the reception and evaluation of testimony by decision makers in legal contexts, this experiment taught us a great deal about what and what not to do in successive efforts. Retrospectively, it appears that a study of hypercorrect versus formal speech (involving covariation in sounds, vocabulary, and grammar) was far too ambitious a beginning. In fact, this proved to be the most difficult of the experimental studies conducted. Nonetheless, it was possible after much effort to produce experimental tapes for the study of hypercorrect versus formal speech.[18]

The experimental tapes were based on the testimony of the ambulance attendant whose speech is excerpted above. In testifying, the witness describes his recollections of a collision involving the ambulance in which he and a patient whom he was attending were riding. His testimony was hypercorrect in that he misapplied certain rules of formal grammar and used a more formal and technical vocabulary than seemed necessary or appropriate. After transcribing the original testimony and editing it for extraneous and distracting legal technicalities, two scripts differing only in style were prepared (see Appendix 3). As in other studies, the substance of the testimony was not altered between the two versions. Then, the experiment was conducted in a manner similar to that described for the experiments previously reported. In this study, only two experimental tapes were made; both the witness and lawyer were males.

Once again, social-psychological theories suggested some hypotheses about what we might find. We expected, for example, that a witness speaking in the hypercorrect style would be evaluated less positively to the extent that listeners equate such a speech style with low social status (Hurwitz *et al.* 1953) or with the desire on the part of the speakers to ingratiate themselves to those listening to them (Jones 1964).

---

[18] Differences between the HYPERCORRECT and FORMAL experimental tapes can be summarized as follows. Vocabulary differs along the lines shown in Table 5.6. The formal condition contains more standard usages and eliminates all unnecessary technical or quasi-technical vocabulary. The formal tape is less "wordy" than the hypercorrect version of the same testimony. When fewer words could be used without altering referential meaning, this was done in preparing the formal version. Detailed phonological analysis of the two tapes revealed few differences. The hypercorrect version contains nonstandard word stress on a few words (*proficient, determined,* and *relapsed*), all of which occurred in the original courtroom testimony. Differences in the realization of phonological variables between the two tapes is minimal. For transcripts of the hypercorrect and formal style stimulus types, see Appendix 3.

Table 5.7
Rating of Witnesses Speaking in Formal and
Hypercorrect Styles

Dimension	Formal	Hyper-correct
Convincingness	3.2^a	2.1
Competence	2.2	-0.1
Qualified	-0.6	-3.2
Intelligence	0.4	-1.3

[a]All differences are significant at $p \le .05$.

RESULTS

Results of the experiment are consistent with our general predication that differences in testimony style elicit differences in responses of listeners. The subject–jurors evaluated the witness differently along several dimensions when he testified in the hypercorrect and formal styles. Specifically, students acting as mock jurors[19] in the experiment evaluated the witness as significantly more convincing ($p < .05$), more competent ($p < .01$), more qualified ($p < .01$), and more intelligent ($p < .01$) when he used the formal style than when he used the hypercorrect style (see Table 5.7). In addition, there was a tendency for higher monetary awards to be made against the defendant speaking in the hypercorrect style (see Table 5.8).

These findings further demonstrate the ability of jurors to perceive subtle stylistic factors and the particular tendency to discredit the testimony of and be punitive toward a witness who attempts to speak with an inappropriate degree of formality. These findings were an important beginning along a path that has consistently shown that patterns of variation in speech—even some that might be regarded as seemingly minor or unimportant—do indeed make a difference in how testimony is evaluated.

RELATED STUDIES

Other findings about the evaluation of speech styles have important implications for understanding fuller significance of testimony delivered in nonstandard speech styles. First, a series of studies reported by Giles

---

[19] Forty-two undergraduate psychology students at Duke University served as mock jurors in this experiment.

Table 5.8
Compensation Awarded against Defendant
Speaking in Formal and Hypercorrect Styles[a]

	Formal	Hyper-correct
No compensation	14	8
Compensation award to plaintiff	7	13

[a]Chi square = 3.46; $p < .1$.

and Powesland (1975:37–46) shows that people tend to be more punative in their evaluations of speakers attempting to disguise their usual speech style WHEN THE LISTENERS ARE MOST LIKE THE SPEAKERS. In specific studies, persons speaking with ethnic accents repeatedly are more able to scrutinize the speech of fellow ethnics and to know when they are attempting to deny or hide their background. It was also found that members of ethnic groups apply more strongly the stereotypes typically associated with the ethnic group. In related studies, Labov (1966) found working-class New Yorkers more critical in their evaluation of other working-class people. In adddition, other studies have shown that persons of all social classes tend to be more cooperative with those who speak standard, nonaccented speech. These studies thus suggest that a jury of one's peers may in fact behave differently from those who are not as similar linguistically. If persons most like a speaker are best able to detect disguise (as suggested by the studies reported by Giles and Powesland) and if those from similar social class backgrounds are more critical of their fellows (as suggested by Labov's findings), then a jury of one's peers may indeed react MORE NEGATIVELY to hypercorrection and similar phenomena than other people. Moreover, since hypercorrection is likely to occur (at least as described here) among speakers of nonstandard English, the additional fact that people of all backgrounds are less likely to cooperate with them than with speakers of Standard English adds additional difficulties for those whose backgrounds are more likely to make the court strange and intimidating in the first place.

Interruptions and Simultaneous Speech

In the process of testifying, a witness and the examining lawyer may become entangled in a verbal clash. This situation typically occurs only during a cross-examination, since lawyers usually prepare their own witnesses for direct examination prior to testifying and thus know, to some degree, what to expect with regard to both the substance and style of their testimony. When clashes do occur during cross-examinations, they are marked by overlapping speech in which lawyer and witness vie for control over the presentation of testimony. In a fourth study, the team turned its attention to the effects of these hostile exchanges.

THE STRUCTURE OF VERBAL CLASHES

Detailed analysis of the verbal clashes revealed a consistent structure. First, the conflicts are characterized by many interruptions of one party by the other and by periods when both parties talk at once. Second, either the attorney or the witness may initiate conflict by interrupting before the other finishes talking. Both parties may share responsibility for the overlaps, or one party may be primarily responsible for them. Third, when overlaps occur, one party typically stops while the other continues talking. Thus, one usually "gives up" to the other in any particular overlap.

Ethnographic study showed no instances of verbal clashes where one party always interrupted while the other always stopped. Although such situations can occur rarely, they do not, in fact, constitute conflicts. Interruptions occur both at "turn relevance places" (points in an utterance where one might assume the speaker has finished)[20] and at other points. In "very hostile" simultaneous speech episodes, interruptions were found to be initiated by both speakers. In such interactions there is, however, a difference in the degree to which one party acquiesces. In the court cases studied, the pattern of acquiescence varied from the situation in which the witness usually stops in favor of the lawyer to that in which the witness usually perseveres and the lawyer stops.

EXPERIMENTAL DESIGN

The experiment was designed to test whether situations of relative dominance and acquiescence are perceived as such by those who hear them in the court. The general technique developed in previous studies was used again: An instance of the speech style phenomenon of interest

---

[20] This investigation of overlapping speech was suggested in part by the work of Sacks *et al.* (1974) on turn-taking in conversation. Whenever possible without becoming overly technical, terminology used here is consistent with their usage. For a more recent treatment of turn-taking that deals specifically with the organization of courtroom verbal interactions, see Atkinson and Drew (1979).

was located in the taped trials and the stimulus tapes for the experiment were based on it. In this experiment, the testimony used occurred in a cross-examination in which the witness and the lawyer interrupted each other frequently, about equally often. The interruptions occurred both at turn relevance places in the initial speaker's utterance and at other points in the utterance. The case from which the testimony was drawn concerned criminal charges arising from a family conflict in which a young woman brought charges against her alcoholic father by accusing him of assaulting her mother.

The original speech was edited to create four experimental conditions. For the first of these, all instances of overlapping speech in the original testimony are eliminated. In this "control" condition, each speaker begins speaking only after the other speaker finishes. The remaining three conditions contain frequent instances of simultaneous speech,[21] but differ in who dominates. A second condition is created by altering the exchange so that neither dominates, both persevere equally often. In a third condition, the lawyer dominates by persevering in three-fourths of the instances of simultaneous speech. In the fourth condition, the situation is reversed so that the witness perseveres in three-fourths of the overlaps and thereby dominates. All other characteristics of the four tapes are held constant, including the presentation of the same substantive information, use of the same actors, and so on.[22]

RESULTS

Two important sets of findings resulted from this experiment. First, the lawyer's control over the presentation of testimony was perceived as low in ALL situations involving simultaneous speech—no matter who

[21] Since the experiment focused on perseverence during simultaneous speech rather than on the initiation of overlaps, the 24 instances of simultaneous speech in the experimental tapes were initiated an equal number of times by each party. Half of the overlaps occurred at turn relevance places and were distributed in random order in the excerpt. In the original exchange on which the experimental tapes are based, instances of simultaneous speech were initiated about equally by the two parties and about half occurred at turn relevance places.

[22] The subjects in the experiment were 86 undergraduate students at the University of New Hampshire (38 males and 48 females). They reported to the experiment four to eight at a time and were given written instructions concerning their role in the experiment. These instructions, which were read aloud by the experimenter, asked the subjects to assume the role of jurors and alleged that they would hear a tape of testimony delivered in an actual trial. The instructions further explained the legal situation and the issues addressed in the trial.

Table 5.9
Ratings Evaluating Lawyer in Simultaneous Speech Study

	Witness dominates	Lawyer dominates
Witness given opportunity to present evidence	1.5[a]	−.1
Fairness of lawyer to witness	2.0	.4
Intelligence of lawyer	2.8	1.7

[a]Higher values indicate more positive ratings. For all reported differences $p \leq .05$.

dominated and who acquiesced. Subject–jurors, asked about their perception of relative control by the lawyer and the witness, rated control near the midpoint,[23] indicating their perception of it as being about equally shared. Such a rating is a confirmation that the control situation represents shared control by the attorney and the witness. However, in all three situations involving overlaps, the witness is perceived as having greater control of the situation.[24] Thus, subjects' ratings show that no matter who dominates the exchange or whether the dominance in overlapping speech is equally shared, the lawyer is perceived as having far less control over the presentation of testimony. Similarly, the witness in all simultaneous speech situations is perceived as more powerful and more in control. Although these results do not show the finely tuned calibration in the assignment of responsibility as hoped for in designing the experimental conditions, they do show this important finding about the perception that an attorney loses control whenever simultaneous speech occurs in the courtroom.

Second, comparison of ratings of the lawyer and the witness in the "witness dominates" and the "lawyer dominates" situations show significant differences. When the witness dominates by persevering more often, subjects feel he has significantly more opportunity to testify and present his version of the facts. Similarly, in this condition as well, the lawyer is evaluated as being more intelligent and fairer to the witness

[23] A rating of 0 indicated equal control. Subjects could vary from this 5 points in the direction of either lawyer or witness to indicate greater control by one of the parties. The mean rating given by the subject–jurors for the control situation was actually 0.1 in the direction of the witness.

[24] The ratings in the experiment were −3.0 for the "lawyer dominates" situation, −1.9 in equal perseverence, and −2.6 for the "witness dominates" situation. The mean rating for all simultaneous speech situations is −2.5 (in the direction of the witness). This difference is significant ($p < .025$).

than when the lawyer dominates the exchange. These ratings are summarized in Table 5.9.

This experiment shows that patterns of perseverence in simultaneous speech affect listeners' evaluations of speakers. The overall findings suggest that subjects prefer and evaluate most positively the situation in which hostile verbal exchanges are absent. When such interactions do occur, subjects come down strongly in favor of the witness who perserveres. Even the examining lawyer is rated more positively when the witness is assertive in the conflict between them. These findings suggest, by implication, that an attorney who attempts to limit verbal conflict by overpowering a witness may very likely receive highly negative evaluations from the jury.

6
CONTROLLING
THE EFFECTS OF
PRESENTATIONAL STYLE

In the last chapter, some effects on legal decision makers of four speech style variables were reported. The consistency with which style affects reception and evaluation of testimony makes, we believe, a convincing case for its salience and importance in the legal process. What has been specifically demonstrated is that form of presenting information in court conveys messages that are interpreted by experimental subjects and, by implication, jurors and other legal decision makers. The experiments have shown the psychological effects of style on individuals. In this chapter, we consider various efforts to manage the meaning conveyed by style so that these effects can be mitigated, directed, transformed, or even extinguished. We first consider some additional experiments devised to test whether the effects observed in the experiments can be controlled or eliminated. Then, we consider how various participants in the legal process, especially lawyers and judges, attempt to interpret presentational style and thereby manage it.

Attempts to Control Style Effects

Two additional experimental studies were undertaken to determine whether the effects of speech style could be controlled or even eliminated. The first study focused on the consequence of presenting testimony through depositions rather than orally. The second study researched the question of whether judicial warnings could help control the effects of style.

For the deposition study, the powerful versus powerless language study was repeated using transcripts in place of audio tape recordings in the experiments. The transcripts used in the study (see Appendix 1) were prepared by a free-lance court reporter who was asked to transcribe the four experimental tapes just as she would testimony delivered orally in court. The transcripts thus produced were used to replicate the experiment. With the exception that the participants read, rather than heard the testimony, the method of experimentation used was the same as that used in the original study. We thus sought to discover whether transcribed testimony that contained only those powerful and powerless features captured in written language would show a decrease in or absence of the effects we had observed in the responses to spoken testimony given in the two styles. For example, vocabulary and grammar would be retained in the transcripts, but intonation would be lost.

The responses of the participants in the experiment showed the same patterns of evaluations as those found for the corresponding conditions in the experiment using tapes. Subject–jurors evaluated both male and female witnesses using the powerless mode as being less believable, less convincing, and less trustworthy than the powerful counterpart. These results provide compelling evidence for the validity of the original findings. They show specifically that the results are not an artifact of the actors' voices, accents, patterns of intonations, or the experimental tapes themselves, but are due to those powerful and powerless features contained in both written and spoken versions of the testimony. However, the findings are not encouraging with regard to the possibility of controlling the effects of speech style through using written testimony, or depositions, rather than oral delivery of testimony.

A second study of the possibility of controlling the effects of speech style dealt with the use of judicial warnings. One way the law attempts to control the use of information deemed unreliable is to instruct jurors to disregard such information.[1] The powerful–powerless experiment was again repeated, this time using the four experimental tapes and changing only the instructions given to the subject–jurors. One-third of the subjects

---

[1] As noted in Chapter 2, we have serious reservations about the lack of congruence between this procedure and how mind and memory actually work. Nevertheless, we followed precedent and used what is common procedure for dealing with such matters, namely a judicial instruction issued to jurors by the presiding judge.

were given a standard charge. A second third heard in addition a charge making specific reference to the fact that witnesses sometimes show a preference for or place greater credence in the testimony of particular witnesses based on the way they speak. A final third of the subjects received instructions that included not only the standard instruction and the general reference to speech styles, but also a specific reference to many of the features of the powerless style, cautioning that these features need not indicate uncertainty or deceit. The three instructions are contained in Table 6.1.

Table 6.1
Instructions Used in Attempt to Control Style Effects

Standard Instruction:[a]
Now, members of the jury, you are the sole judges of the credibility of the witnesses and of their worthiness of belief. You may believe all, part, or none of what each witness testifies to. The weight to be given to the testimony of each witness is for your decision. In determining the weight to be given to the testimony of each witness as to whether he or she is to be believed, you should apply the same test of truthfulness that you would in your everyday affairs. You may consider the manner and appearance of the witness on the witness stand; the opportunity of the witness for seeing, hearing, knowing, and remembering that concerning which he or she testifies; the interest or lack of interest of the witness in the outcome of this case; any bias or prejudice which may be shown; any statement shown to have been made by a witness in the past which is consistent with the witness's testimony given here in court as may tend to corroborate or support his or her testimony; and any statement shown to have been made by a witness in the past which is inconsistent or contradictory with his or her testimony given here in court as may tend to impeach or discredit the testimony of the witness.

General Instruction:[b]
In preparing you for the consideration of the evidence to be presented in this trial, I call your attention, members of the jury, to recent studies which have shown that the way in which people speak may affect their believability. As you know, members of the jury, there are many different styles of speaking. Many of these are related to a person's background and origin and some are merely personal or idiosyncratic. It is for you, members of the jury, to determine whether or not these differences are related to the believability of a witness.

Specific Instruction:[c]
For example, it has been shown that some people tend to begin their sentences by saying "It seems to me . . . ," or "I think that . . . ," or "I believe . . . ," or to end their sentences with rising intonation, or to phrase their answers in generally indefinite terms. Whether a particular witness is one of those generally cautious, non-committal individuals and is but following his or her usual way of expressing himself or herself, or whether he or she is a witness who really does not know what actually happened, or is deliberately evasive, is for you, members of the jury, to determine.

[a]Given to all subject–jurors.
[b]Given in addition to the standard instruction.
[c]Given in addition to the standard and general instructions.

Table 6.2
Average Rating of Witnesses Using Powerful versus Powerless Testimony Styles with Different Jury Instructions

	Type of instructions	Female witness		Male witness	
		Powerful	Powerless	Powerful	Powerless
Convincingness[a]	Standard	3.42	.90	3.95	1.74
	General	3.00	1.00	3.00	1.11
	Specific	3.86	.90	2.76	.19
Truthfulness	Standard	3.74	1.48	4.05	3.11
	General	3.74	2.08	3.09	2.10
	Specific	4.14	2.00	3.24	1.24
Competence	Standard	3.00	.52	2.37	.68
	General	1.83	.74	1.73	.74
	Specific	2.33	.19	1.94	−1.00
Intelligence	Standard	1.95	−.38	1.84	.63
	General	.91	−.56	.86	.47
	Specific	1.90	−.66	1.12	−1.00
Trustworthiness	Standard	3.58	1.57	3.63	2.63
	General	3.09	1.83	2.73	1.53
	Specific	2.76	1.33	2.71	.71

[a] The questions asked were identical to those described in Table 5.3.

After receiving one of these three instructions (called STANDARD, GENERAL STYLE, and SPECIFIC STYLE, respectively), the subject–jurors listened to one of the four experimental tapes and answered the same questionnaire used in the original powerful–powerless study. Table 6.2 presents results of this study. Overall results are similar to those in the initial study. Whether the witness was male or female, he or she was thought to be less convincing, less believable, less competent, less intelligent, and less trustworthy when the powerless style was used.[2]

The instructions concerning speech styles led to no diminution of the effects. As the figures in Table 6.2 show, powerless-speaking witnesses are viewed less favorably regardless of the type of instructions that the experimental subject–jurors received. The finding is not surprising since many other studies have already shown that jurors seldom obey instructions to disregard what seems to them to be useful information (Doob 1976:135). However, it is disappointing in terms of what it suggests about the possibilities for limiting and controlling the effects of speech style. It appears that neither the use of depositions nor the use of judicial instructions hold much promise.

[2] All reported differences are significant at $p < .01$.

Interpretation and the Management of Style

Interpretation is central to the business of the court. A court exists, among other purposes, to interpret the issues that bring people before it. It resolves in the verdict the multiple versions of the facts as reported by witnesses. It decides in the end who wins, overriding all individual opinions on the matter as well as the contending positions of the two sides. In doing this, the court interprets. Finally, lest anyone not wish to abide by the official interpretation, the court can command enforcement by the state of its interpretation and all decisions subsequent to it (fines, jail terms, monetary awards, and so on).

But this is not the only kind of interpretation that occurs in court. In testifying, witnesses interpret. They report recollections, and in doing so interpret the past. Lawyers interpret at critical points in the trial: Opening remarks and summations are interpretations—suggested interpretations lawyers hope will be accepted by the decision makers. The jury also interprets in rendering its verdict. It decides and announces publicly which version, or suggested interpretation, it accepts. Thus, the trial process is in effect a movement from multiple interpretations to a single, officially sanctioned one.

In a fundamental sense, what the court does at the public level parallels what individuals do privately—interpret the facts. Yet, the social organization of the court requires that individual decisions (about who is telling the truth, what really happened, who is right or wrong, and so on) be reconciled into a single shared decision by members of the jury. At least two issues are therefore critical in understanding the legal process that takes place in the courtroom—understanding the way individual decisions are made (e.g., how speech style conveys messages about truthfulness, competence, intelligence, and trustworthiness) and understanding how individual decisions are affected by the context or social structure within which they are made. For example, a problem that has interested many jury researchers in the last 20 years or so is understanding how decision making operates within small groups.[3] Similarly, speech style is not left by the court merely as a matter for individuals to interpret privately. Rather, the organization of the court provides many opportunities for attempts to influence the interpretive process. We turn now to a consideration of how this social process works.

---

[3] Levine *et al.* (1980) contains a useful discussion of this issue. In addition, see Kessler (1975) and Nemeth (1976) for other useful discussions of group versus individual decision-making models as applied to juries.

SILENCE—A CASE IN POINT

Silence is not a style in the same sense as powerless speech, fragmented testimony, or hypercorrection. Yet it is like all of them. It too means something. Why is one witness slow in responding? Why does another not respond at all? Silence occasions these kinds of questions, and they are similar ones to those raised by other testimony styles.

In the next several pages, we examine the interpretation of silence. Although it may seem at times that fascination with silence and how it works in court is the motivating force, it will become clear that the real reason we focus on it is to discover the complex ways in which the court as an institution and the individuals who make it up attempt to influence and manage the meaning of silence. In many ways, it is a more interesting case than any style of speaking per se—for in silence lies greater ambiguity and hence more opportunity to manage its meaning.

This study of silence proceeds in the following manner. First, consideration is given to certain specifically legal aspects of silence: the right to remain silent, the consequences of refusing to obey the usual rules regarding silence in courts, and the matter of "silencing" the official record. Second, focus shifts to the interactional level. Lawyer–witness interactions contain several types of silence that differ in terms of consequences. Finally, we focus attention directly on the means of resolving the ambiguities of silence and on the strategies for attempting to manage its interpretation in the courtroom contest.

THE RIGHT TO REMAIN SILENT

The right of a defendant in criminal proceedings to remain officially silent (i.e., to refuse to testify in a court of law) is guaranteed by the Bill of Rights. Whether the advantages of testifying (and hence exposing oneself to cross-examination) outweigh those of refusing to testify is a decision that every defendant, in consultation with counsel, must make. It is a further principle of American law that a defendant's decision not to testify—to remain silent—shall not create any presumption against the defendant. Note that this principle concerns how silence is to be interpreted. It cannot, for example, be argued that a defendant's refusing to testify is an admission that he or she has something to hide. Rather, the burden is on the State to prove its case without any assistance from a defendant who decides not to testify. What private meanings may be attached, for example, by jurors to the fact that a defendant does not take the witness stand remain unknown. It is probable, however, that some jurors may—despite the warning of the court—consider the fact that a defendant remains silent to be a negative factor.

Beyond the constitutional guarantee to remain silent under certain circumstances, some further aspects of a defendant's election to be silent may have legal significance and therefore require explanation by the court. Specifically, the situation may arise when an accused person is given an opportunity to deny an accusation of guilt. Failure to seize an opportunity for denying an accusation has frequently been interpreted by the court as an admission of the truth of such an accusation. Put simply, the court may sometimes interpret no answer as *yes*. Such a situation might arise if a defendant were to take the witness stand and were asked on cross-examination, *Did you kill the deceased?* Should the defendant refuse the opportunity to answer, the court would be on sound legal footing by ruling that no answer in such an instance is an admission of guilt. Here again the court is intervening to interpret. Few instances where such a matter might arise are as straightforward as this example. Let us examine an actual instance and the reasoning expressed by the court for the action it took.

An illustration of how the court interprets this type of silence is taken from the case of *The People of the State of Illinois* v. *Isabella Nitti et al.* in which Isabella Nitti and Peter Crudelle were charged with the murder of Isabella's husband, Frank. Testimony was presented in court regarding a reenactment of the supposed manner in which Frank Nitti was murdered. Both defendants were present during critical parts of the reenactment. Crudelle, who tended to remain silent through most of the reenactment, did respond with the words, *bull shit*, when another person present told the deputy sheriff how Crudelle had supposedly disposed of Frank Nitti's body. Mrs. Nitti, when asked through an Italian interpreter, *Did you kill your husband?*, replied: *Whatever Charlie said, that is true.* Charlie Nitti, her son, stated that his mother and Crudelle had killed Frank Nitti. The trial court, following precedent in handling reticence and silence on the parts of defendants in situations like this, allowed the facts that both Isabella Nitti and Peter Crudelle had not denied outright the accusations made against them to be ADMISSIONS of the truth of the accusations.

The convictions of both defendants were, however, reversed on appeal. The opinion of the higher court makes several points worth noting regarding the matter of a defendant's reticence or silence in matters like this. First, the court distinguishes an ADMISSION from a CONFESSION. (In criminal law, an admission is a statement by the accused of a pertinent fact, or facts, that in connection with other facts tends to prove guilt. A confession by contrast is a direct acknowledgment of guilt.) Citing precedent, the court reaffirmed the manner in which the law should deal with the silence of a person accused of a crime. Specifically, the court argued that when it is plainly evident that the accused has heard and understood the accusation and when opportunity has been provided to deny the accusation, then silence on the part of the accused may constitute a type of demeanor from which guilt may be inferred. It may be, in the court's terminology, an admission but not a confession of crime.

Second, the court pointed out that silence under such circumstances is not to be construed as proof of guilt but should be used TO GIVE MEANING TO the reply or lack of a reply from the accused. Citing precedent once again, the court argued that an accused person given adequate opportunity to deny the accusation would naturally be expected to do so—unless the accusation is in fact true.

Third, the opinion considers how different situations or contexts might affect the tendency of an accused person to be silent. Citing further precedent, the court made it clear that such an accusation made in a courtroom or other judicial proceeding would probably be handled differently from an accusation made in a situation where a denial was more likely to be expected. It noted that the expectations surrounding appropriate decorum for a formal legal proceeding (e.g., a courtroom) would mitigate the tendency of a person to shout out a denial unless, of course, the accused were on the witness stand. It further held that an accused person is not to be expected "to enter into a controversy with every idle straggler who may choose to accuse him to his face, nor is he bound to continue to shout his denial of every fugitive statement tending to implicate him that may reach his ears [*People* v. *Nitti* 1924:455]."

In this particular case, the court held that adequate opportunity had not, in fact, been given to the defendants to deny the accusations made against them, that Crudelle's uttering *bull shit* was a statement on his part of the absurdity of the claims against him, and that it was not clear that the defendants had fully understood the implications of the situations in which the accusations were made, and hence that their tendency to be silent had not been shown to be voluntary on their parts. These factors pertaining to reticence on the parts of accused persons were among the arguments given by the appeals court in reversing the conviction of the defendants in this case.

From the preceding discussion, it is clear that American law considers the right to be silent of fundamental importance, although the right does not extend to all possible circumstances involving a defendant. It is important to recognize that in both the situation where a defendant elects not to testify and where he or she refuses to deny an accusation when given an appropriate forum to do so the court is concerned with whether any meaning is to be attached to silence, and when it is appropriate to do so, what meaning shall be attached.

REFUSING TO BE SILENT

A counterpoint to the right to remain silent is to refuse to be silent in court. Although an accused person may elect to remain silent under certain circumstances it is not the case that a defendant may alternatively elect to speak at will. Customary court etiquette and established rules of legal procedure define the proper and acceptable situations during which any person may speak. Courts tend not to show much tolerance for violations of conversational decorum and have at their disposal powers of contempt citations to punish violators. The well-publicized case of the Chicago 7 illustrates the extremes to which a court may be pushed in preserving customary decorum. This case is particularly interesting because one of the original defendants, Bobby Seale, refused on several occasions to respect the court's request to remain silent.

Seale was one of eight defendants charged with conspiring to cross state lines with an intent to incite a riot. The charges stemmed from the disturbances associated with the 1968 meeting of the Democratic National Convention in Chicago. During the trial which began in 1969 and lasted into the next year, Bobby Seale was cited by Judge Julius Hoffman for several counts of contempt of court. For these, he was given jail sentences totaling 4 years. As Harry Kalven points out in an introduction to one of the many books written about this trial, the contempt citations result in jail sentences not for the crimes for which the defendants were originally charged but for "crimes" committed in the course of the trial itself (Kalven 1970:xiv). Some of Kalven's thoughts about the sociolegal implications of this are worth considering at length.

> At one of the unsettled moments during the trial, Judge Hoffman observes: "There comes a time when courtroom decorum must be observed." David Dellinger [another defendant] replies: "Decorum is more important than justice, I suppose." Dellinger's rhetorical question may prove in the end to be a real one, but the traditional answer has been that there is no conflict between decorum and justice, that decorum in the trial process is a rational value in the pursuit of justice. I have always thought the traditional answer was correct. And the contempt power has traditionally been viewed as an indispensable means to the preservation of order and decorum in the trial.
>
> Yet there are anomalies. Because the contempt power carries penal sanctions, it marks, pragmatically viewed, a kind of crime. But as in the instant case, it is a crime which can be committed while one is in the process of being tried for some other crime. It may carry more serious penalties than the original crime with which one is charged [Kalven 1970:xvii].

Although there are many instances where Seale's refusal to respect the silence demanded of him by the court are reflected in the transcript, the following excerpts demonstrate the sort of exchanges that took place.

MR. SEALE: I have a right to stand up and speak in my own behalf, I do.
              You know that.
THE COURT: You know you do not have a right to speak while the Judge
              is speaking [Dellinger 1970:1].

THE COURT: I direct you, sir, to remain quiet.
MR. SEALE: And just be railroaded?
THE COURT: Will you remain quiet?
MR. SEALE: I want to defend myself, do you mind, please?
THE COURT: Let the record show that the defendant Seale continued to
              speak after the court courteously requested him to remain
              quiet [Dellinger 1970:5].

Remarks like these, considered by Judge Hoffman to show disrespect for the ordinary rules of decorum in a trial courtroom, resulted in Seale's eventually being bound and gagged, taken from the courtroom itself, and ultimately cited extensively for contempt of court. While this is an extreme instance, it unmistakeably illustrates the right that the court, through the person of the judge, has to demand official and public silence and the power that it has to punish violators. Similar treatment is possible for lawyers, spectators, or anyone not following expected rules of customary behavior in a courtroom. Lawyers may be cited for contempt (as they were in the Chicago 7 case) and a courtroom may be cleared of noisy spectators if a judge deems it appropriate. Once again, the court through its actions is providing an interpretation of silence. Here it signifies respect for the court and for the legal system.

SILENCING THE RECORD

In some instances, the court (through the judge) SILENCES the official record or transcript of the proceedings. In a typical instance, a lawyer will move to strike from the record a portion of a witness' testimony. If the judge agrees to the motion, he might say something like: *The motion to strike is allowed. Disabuse your minds, members of the jury, of that last answer and the question and comment of counsel.* The public system of the court continues AS THOUGH the remark had not been made. But the official transcript will contain the remark, the objection, and the judge's ruling. The official record has been silenced with regard to the matter; whatever private opinions are held or events committed to memory—so long as they do not enter the public aspects of the court—are outside the domain of concern of the court.

It is interesting to consider the legal fiction of striking words from the record. The assumption that it is possible to cause jurors to forget by instructing them to do so bears little or no relationship to the way language actually works. Most lawyers tend not to take seriously the notion that such an instruction will actually result in juror's forgetting or erasing from memory what has been said. Trial practice manuals recognize this and caution against unnecessary objections on the grounds that they may actually call attention to what has been said.

> Often your objection will serve to call special attention of the jury as well as the court to the unfavorable evidence you seek to exclude, thus tending to emphasize its significance. Natural curiosity will cause a juror to speculate privately and perhaps also to share the speculations with other jurors regarding the excluded matter. . . . They may even surmise something worse than the excluded evidence [Keeton 1973:167].

Because the official record actually shows the entire exchange, the striking of remarks from the record is a legal fiction in terms of what is actually done as well as how it may relate to memory.

How then are we to understand this act of striking remarks from the record? What can it actually mean if we know that words once spoken cannot actually be erased from the minds of those who have heard them and if the actual record kept by the court stenographer includes what was said and all remarks pertaining to it? From a strictly legal point of view, it means that facts ordered stricken may not be used in determining the verdict. But is this what happens?

Our evidence here is limited, but suggestive. During the summer of 1974 when most of our courtroom observation and tape recording of trials took place, I had, from the point of view of participant observation, the good fortune to be selected as a member of the jury pool. This unusual opportunity proved to be an invaluable part of the overall study.

One of the things I discovered while serving twice as a juror was that both juries considered it highly inappropriate for any public discussion to take place of any evidence that we had been instructed to forget. In other words, each group attempted to accept the court's interpretation of admissibility. In a few instances, one or another juror would comment on such a piece of information. Almost immediately, the others would object to the discussion of such information. What did not occur, and is therefore interesting as well, was any mention that jurors as individuals should not THINK about such information. What the juries considered inappropriate was group or open discussion of stricken remarks. Thus, the court's rulings on motions to strike certain information from the official record did, in effect, define boundaries around what was legitimate for group discussion and what was not.

What emerges from all this is an understanding that there are, in fact, a great many rules regarding silence in court. They operate for the most part at the level of public, shared understandings. But there is another aspect of silence that deserves recognition. It is that in many of these instances variable meanings might be assigned to silences. In these situations, the court—usually in the person of the judge—usually goes to great length to attempt to INTERPRET the silences. For example, the court can demonstrate through its contempt powers how speaking out of turn or refusing to speak in turn indicates disrespect for the court and/or legal system. Or through the commentary the court provides at the beginning and end of trials, it can be seen attempting to guard the constitutionally guaranteed right to remain silent by making great efforts to point out both how such silence is to be interpreted and how it should not be interpreted.

This issue of interpreting silence becomes even more complex when focus is shifted to the interpersonal level. In the lawyer–witness exchanges that constitute a large portion of a trial, silences can cause two kinds of problems. First, they can interfere with the orderly nature of the lawyer–witness (hereafter L–W) interview. Second, silences in L–W exchanges—as in conversation more generally—may be subject to more than one interpretation. The interpretation of silence is, as we shall see when we shift from an institutional to an interpersonal level, not simply a matter for the court but a concern of all who aspire to manage meaning in the trial.

SILENCE DURING THE TRIAL PROCESS

Silence during a trial may present considerable problems for the court. By its very nature, silence is ambiguous and therefore messy. Questions about its meaning may lurk in the shadows unless the court or the attorneys assume an active role in resolving the ambiguities. For example, what does it mean when a witness is slow to answer or generally reticent? What meaning lies in the behavior of a hesitant witness—careful thinking in order to report recollections faithfully OR cautious planning to fabricate a false version?

Not all silences during the process of a trial are equivalent. Some "belong" to a person, others are properties of the communication system, and still others are difficult to assign. This variation in kinds of silence provides great opportunity for the manipulation of its meaning.

A brief review of some observations made by analysts of conversational exchange systems provides useful distinctions. Sacks et al. (1974), in particular, have noted that a major characteristic of conversational interaction is that there tends to be little gap or overlap between adjacent turns of talking. When intervals do occur, they are not always structurally equivalent. Based on how silence is assigned by participants in the exchange, three analytically distinct types of silences emerge: silence that is ambiguous because it comes between one turn at talk and the next; silence that is unambiguously assigned by all participants as belonging within a particular turn; and silence that is a property of the exchange system itself rather than of any particular turns or participants.

RESPONSE LAG is the period between a question and its answer (Q–A) or between an answer and the next question (A–Q). This period of structurally ambiguous silence is usually brought to an end in one of two ways: Another speaker begins talking, or the previous speaker continues. Our measurements of response lags in a large number of instances of courtroom speech revealed that the vast majority—both Q–A and A–Q— occur before 1.5 seconds have elapsed after the end of the previous utterance. Response lags between A–Q tended to be somewhat longer than Q–A intervals.[4] In many instances, however, it is hardly possible to perceive any interval between Q–A or A–Q. Frequently, the next speaker begins before the previous one has actually ceased.

This excerpt is typical of response lags:

> W: . . . *for snacks and little things like cigarettes, and little things like that.* (0.7)
> L: *Alright.* (1.7) *Now on, or about the fifth day of May, 1975, was your store open?* (0.5)
> W: *Yes, it was.*

Intervals of 0.7 and 0.5 seconds are common between utterances of different speakers. Although most response lags are relatively brief, there may be quite long ones. The following excerpt is an extreme example, but it does illustrate how far the system can be pushed to accommodate individual situations.

> L: *What happened while you were lying on the ground?* (16.8)
> W: *That's when we had sexual intercourse and . . . .*

W, an alleged victim of forcible rape, was slow to respond to many questions put to her. Some responses came more than 30 seconds after the question. These were the longest response lags we recorded. Usually, the court is not as tolerant of long silences before questions are answered

---

[4] An ordinary stopwatch was used to measure intervals, with each interval measured several times to assure as much consistency as possible. Since we were primarily interested in a reasonable, rather than highly precise measure of the length of intervals, we did not attempt to use more sophisticated measuring devices.

or new ones asked. The delicate nature of a rape case seems to have occasioned exceptional tolerance for long response lags on the part of the court.

The ambiguous nature of response lag stems from the potential lack of agreement over whether the silence is part of the next speaker's turn or is merely a period during which the previous speaker may elect to continue. In many instances, such a period is interpreted differently by the various parties involved. The same instance of silence can be interpreted as BOTH the time in which the previous speaker may continue and the time at which the next one may begin. This excerpt clearly illustrates the problem:

W: *... and I looked around, and they was behind me.* (0.7)
W: *Then*
L: <u>*Did you*</u>[5] *say anything to any of those fellows at that time about you taking part in robbing the Fast Food Store?* (0.5)
W: *No.*

W ceases talking for 0.7 seconds. At the end of this interval, both L and W begin talking simultaneously.[6] Since no additional question has been asked by L, the most likely explanation accounting for W's action is that he considers himself to be continuing with his own turn. Since W has stopped at a point where the previous utterance might be interpreted as syntactically complete (a TURN RELEVANCE PLACE), L's beginning to talk is indicative of a different assumption, namely, that W has completed his answer to the previous question. What makes response lag especially interesting from an interactional perspective is that different parties in the speech exchange system can place different interpretations on the same silence and behave accordingly.

PAUSE, by contrast, is an interval of assigned silence. It is not syntactically ambiguous like response lag since it is assigned by all participants in the exchange as belonging to a particular speaker and the respective turn. One excerpt on page 105 contains a pause within L's utterance. After claiming the turn for himself, that is, after resolving any possible ambiguity in the response lag of 0.7 seconds by uttering *Alright,* L has indicated to W and others that he accepts the previous turn as a complete answer to his question. Once L begins, it is no longer W's

---

[5] The words *Then* and *Did you* were spoken simultaneously.

[6] The notation system used to show overlapping speech follows the one devised for use in Appendix 4 (pages 157–180). Instances of overlapping speech are italicized, underlined, and—whenever needed for clarity—numbered.

turn. However, the interval of 1.7 seconds between the first word of L's turn and the next one is an interval of silence that BELONGS indisputably to L. In this case, he appears to use the interval for formulating his next question. But whatever anyone may think he is doing during that period of time, the interval belongs to L and L alone. Thus, it is a PAUSE—an unambiguously assigned silence.

Previously we noted that response lag can be brought to an end in one of two ways—another speaker can begin a turn, or the previous speaker can continue. When the latter happens, the ambiguity inherent in response lag is resolved by being transformed, in effect, into an interval or PAUSE within an ongoing turn.

LAPSE differs from both other forms of silence in that it is a property of the speech exchange system rather than of an individual. It is a period when speech exchanges in the courtroom come to a temporary halt. Recesses, bench conferences, interruptions during which the judge is called away from the courtroom are examples of how the public speech exchange system may cease temporarily. Such intervals are periods of public silence—but these intervals are neither ambiguously assigned to participants in the exchange (as in RESPONSE LAGS) nor clearly assigned to one participant (as are PAUSES).

THE MANIPULATION OF SILENCE

An important aspect of some silences in the court, especially response lags, is their potential for ambiguity resulting from the variable interpretations that may be placed on them by different participants. Since it is possible to understand many intervals of silence in more than one way, efforts to suggest a particular interpretation as opposed to another are common. For example, both utterances by L in the following testimony excerpt are attempts to induce W to continue his narrative account.

W: ... I said, "What do you want?" He said, "I want your money."
     So I say, "Well, there's the cash register." (2.7)
L: Then what happened? (0.9)
W: Then he caught the gun on the boy, the boy was kind of
     obstinate about trying to go in my cash register. So in a little
     bit I said, "Do what the man tell you to." He had a pistol. And
     then he, he, he still kept the gun over the boy and, uh, he ran
     over to the cash register. And he unloaded all that was in there.
     (1.4)

L: *Then what next occurred?* (0.5)
W: *Then he was still at the counter* . . . .

L's questions are, in effect, requests for W to continue. Thus, L is attempting to encourage W to interpret the 2.7 and 1.4 second intervals as W's own PAUSES. Had L asked for specific clarification of points made in previous answers or posed new questions, it would be difficult to interpret these intervals as anything other than RESPONSE LAGS on W's part. Careful examination of this excerpt reveals that the intervals are not clearly response lags. L appears to suggest that W interpret them as W's pauses. By his subsequent behavior, W appears to accept L's suggestions and continues his narrative account.

Similar attempts to encourage acceptance of particular interpretations are common parts of courtroom dialogue. Because there are only general notions of how the exchange system is to operate, the specifics of any particular dialogue are negotiated through the ongoing interaction. This flexibility in the system means that L might elect to seize every ambiguous interval to limit W's talk or alternatively might attempt to persuade W to interpret such gaps as W's own pauses and therefore continue. Possibilities for manipulating the system, for placing a desired interpretation on silences, exist for both L and W. The most severe limitations on these possibilities appear not to be properties of the system itself but rather of the skill of those who may manipulate it to advantage.

THE INTERPRETATION OF SILENCE

The speech exchange system of the courtroom is structured such that witnesses testify by answering questions posed by lawyers, opposition lawyers suggest alternative interpretations of the evidence, and jurors ultimately decide between competing views by sanctioning one interpretation as their verdict. En route to the final interpretation which the court upholds with its powers, many managers of meaning attempt to influence the process.

In addition to summation remarks, there are many opportunities on a smaller scale during the course of a trial for interpreting silence. Remarks like, *Take your time and tell us as best as you can remember,* said to a nervous witness whom a lawyer has called are short-run interpretive remarks that may soften the slowness of responses. Or, a lawyer may express disgust and contempt by tone of voice when an opposition witness refuses to answer. Skillful lawyers do not fail to seize opportunities to influence understanding. During a trial a lawyer might say:

Your honor, let the record show that on repeated occasions this witness did not answer the questions put to him when he was courteously requested to do so.[7]

And in summation, the same point may be made again:

Ladies and gentlemen of the jury, you saw before you that every opportunity was given to this witness to tell his version of the facts. He said very little. Sometimes nothing at all. I suggest to you that there is a very good reason why . . . .

Astute lawyers, recognizing the potential for variable interpretation of speech behavior as well as substantive evidence, make great efforts to lay the foundation along the way for the interpretation they intend to provide at the end.[8] The range of interpretations that may be suggested for reticence or silence are perhaps greater in most instances than the meanings that could be attached to almost anything a witness might say, but the process that occurs is essentially similar to that of interpreting and garnering meaning from speech style. Silence can be a manifestation of the witness's concern for accuracy; it can be interpreted as uncertainty; or it may reflect any number of other things. A reticent witness provides an opposition lawyer with a remarkable opportunity—for it is the lawyer who has almost free range to interpret the witness's spoken intentions. Consider the potential for variable interpretation reflected in the following remarks in a rape case.

PROSECUTION
LAWYER: *This experience of being here in court was a most difficult experience for this young woman. You saw her embarrassment as you heard her describe how she was*

---

[7] This and subsequent references to remarks by lawyers in the remaining pages of this chapter are not verbatim but rather reconstructed from notes taken by members of the research team. Because the court reporter operated the tape recording equipment as noted in Chapter 4, only those parts of the trial normally recorded by the court reporter were consistently tape recorded during the 10 weeks of observations. Summation remarks, in North Carolina courts, are not usually a part of the official transcript. Hence, we were sometimes forced to rely on notes taken during the remarks.

[8] It should also be remembered that concerned judges may offer interpretive remarks at many points during the trial. Depending on the particular jurisdiction, these may be before the actual trial begins (as in opening remarks to the jury), during the trial (in various instructions regarding how events such as stricken testimony should be treated), and at the end (e.g., in the charge where the judge reminds jurors not to hold against a defendant the fact that he or she did not testify).

raped. Think of how difficult it was to go to the police
and to tell about it in the first place. Think of what it
must have been like when . . . . How would you react
if you were in her place?

DEFENSE
LAWYER: *You saw how slow the prosecution witness was to*
testify. Was it perhaps because she didn't know the
answers to the questions she was asked? Was it be-
cause it didn't happen the way she says? Or, perhaps,
because it didn't happen at all?

Like speech, silence is communication. And like words, their absence may have many meanings. Ultimately, each individual may be in a position to place a personal interpretation on silence. But there may be many attempts along the way to influence this understanding. In a court of law, a jury may search together for a common interpretation of its meaning. Critical participants—judges and lawyers in particular—may attempt to suggest how silences should be interpreted. Seldom is the individual left to interpret the meaning of silence without many managers of meaning attempting to intervene.

In this chapter we have examined whether the effects of speech styles can be controlled. Two experimental efforts to do so, using either written as opposed to oral testimony or specific judicial warnings against overreacting to the messages communicated by form showed little promise. Then we turned attention to quite a different matter, the social context within which the effects of style operate. We noted through the examination of a specific instance of a stylistic factor some of the ways in which the law, the judge, the lawyers, and even the witnesses attempt to make sense out of style. By the very nature of silence, its meaning is neither inflexible nor insensitive to context. Silence does not have a single meaning, but there are many who attempt to suggest what meaning it should have. Similarly, a narrative answer does not, indeed cannot, mean the same on all occasions. One witness's testimony may be MORE narrative or MORE ''powerful'' than another's. As in the case of silence, the effects these factors have under controlled experimental conditions may be mitigated to some degree by the context in which they occur. At least, we cannot expect to apply the conclusions from tightly controlled experimental conditions directly to conditions in the courtroom. Rather, what we know is that these factors do matter—in fact, they matter a great deal. But we also know that they do not exist in isolation from one another nor from various attempts to control or mitigate or even magnify their significance.

What we must seek to understand is how the psychological and the social dimensions interact. We see in the concern about silence and its interpretation expressed both by the lawyers and by the law a good deal of evidence for the belief that style matters. Yet, they lack specific knowledge—as do we without experimental study of its effects—about the degree to which style actually matters. Here is a concrete instance, then, of how psychological studies can enhance understanding of the legal process. In the same way, as we have already suggested, the psychological processes that can be demonstrated through controlled experimentation must ultimately be contextualized within the limits and constraints which operate upon them in reality. A combination of the social and the psychological are as essential to a full understanding of courtroom processes as ethnography and experimentation are for the method we proposed in Chapter 4.

___7___

CONCLUSIONS

In this chapter, we consider implications of the findings of this research for the many disciplines whose theories and methods have contributed to it. First, we deal with implications for the law, including both the practical issues of concern to those lawyers whose daily professional activities center on courtroom strategies and some of the more general legal issues of concern to jurisprudence. Second, we consider the implications for the several social sciences that have in one way or another been a part of this project. They include anthropology, linguistics, social psychology, and sociology of law. Finally, we raise some further questions for future research.

Implications for the Law

These findings about the effects of speech style on legal decision making have both practical and jurisprudential implications for the law. On a practical level, the discovery of a consistent set of effects due to testimony style makes a substantial contribution to trial practice theory. As was shown by the reactions of the experimental subjects in their roles as legal decision makers, witnesses who speak in a powerful style, avoid unnaturally formal speech patterns, testify with minimal assistance from the lawyer, and resist efforts by the opposing counsel to cut short their remarks will enhance their credibility because they will make more favorable impressions on the jury. Obviously, it is good strategy for an attorney who has more than one witness able to present essentially the same testimony to rely on the one whose speech style most closely approaches the optimal profiles defined by these experiments.

The results also strongly suggest that extensive pretrial witness education or coaching with respect to testimonial style may improve a witness's credibility in the eyes of the jury. For example, many of the problems pointed out by the studies as occurring during direct examinations (that is, powerless speech, hypercorrection, and fragmented testimony) might be avoided if the lawyer takes the time to make witnesses as relaxed and confident as possible. These stylistic tendencies could receive special attention during pretrial conferences and rehearsals of the testimony.[1] Most lawyers are accustomed to paying specific attention during pretrial meetings with witnesses to the probable substance of testimony. How many pay equal attention to the probable style in which the testimony is likely to be delivered? Do they include in calculations of courtroom strategy a careful consideration of the probable effects of their witnesses' speech styles on the jury? The problems illustrated by the simultaneous speech study—a situation specific to cross-examinations and therefore difficult to plan for ahead of time—might be reduced and minimized if lawyers undertake conscious, on-going reviews of their own behavior. Finally, where witnesses prove incapable of avoiding powerless, hypercorrect, or fragmented speech, lawyers may mitigate their effects by interpreting the style for the jury in opening statements, summation remarks, as well as during the trial. It requires relatively little effort to calm a witness by suggesting that he or she take enough time to remember what happened, to tell the story in one's own words, and even to relax. Nor is it out of order to remind the jury in closing that they too might be nervous, have difficulty remembering, or be intimidated if they were called on to testify in court. The lawyer might even undertake a "translation" of testimony delivered in an unfavorable style.[2]

---

[1] A number of lawyers who are familiar with earlier published reports of the findings on speech style effects have reported success in educating witnesses about one or another of the styles known to have negative effects on testimony reception. A few have even made the claim that such efforts altered the outcome of the trial in their favor.

[2] This frequently occurred in the courts we studied in North Carolina. Lawyers often "elevated" the style of poorly educated black and white witnesses by restating their testimony in more standard and formal English. For example, a witness might say, *I ain't got no usual job.* The lawyer on hearing this might restate it as, *You don't have any regular job,* and then proceed to the next question.

To persons without legal educations, these suggestions about the practical uses to which the findings on speech style might be put may appear gratuitous. But lawyers know that principles such as these are not much taught in law schools. There are at least two major reasons for this.

First, a legal education especially for trial lawyers often seems to teach little of relevance to future professional activities. Law school curricula tend to be oriented not toward the training of trial lawyers, but toward teaching for the practice of law in other contexts. Clinical programs are typically small, at least in the more prestigious law schools, and few courses focus on trial practice. First-year law students are often told by their teachers something to the effect: *We are not here to teach you to be a courtroom lawyer, but how to think.* Although the specific language may vary, the message that comes through is the same: The law is comprised of a set of ideals; the practice of law can be acquired once legal thinking is mastered; and trial practice is low in prestige. A first step in effecting any serious change would be to add more elective courses on methods of trial practice to the typical law school curriculum. Although in the last several years there has been a substantial increase in the number and quality of trial practice courses offered within most law schools as well as a growing emphasis on continuing education for practicing legal professionals, the Chief Justice of the United States in a public speech recently questioned the professional competence of many American lawyers. Despite increased emphasis and concern, the quality of the clinical education a law student receives today does not begin to compare favorably with the clinical experience considered necessary in the professional education of a physician.

Second, the rudimentary state of social science knowledge about legal processes makes it difficult to teach law students much about such matters. The ability to do so more fully in the future depends on the degree to which social science studies produce findings that may be put to use by practicing attorneys. The successful incorporation of courses in such fields as sociolinguistics depends heavily upon the degree to which social scientists are able through current and future research programs to demonstrate the usefulness of such information for the professional activities of lawyers. If lawyers are to be expected to teach about the relations between language and law, basic and applied research efforts must better demonstrate the nature of this relationship.

However, the general implications of these studies are also important for the law. The results demonstrate how relatively subtle variations in courtroom speaking styles can influence jurors' reactions and deliberations. Although additional studies would strengthen this assertion and help delineate the precise influence of stylistic differences in various courtroom situations, it is clear from the present studies that the issues of presentational style deserve far greater attention than they have previously received from either legal scholars or social scientists.

In determining the form that future research and action should take, the critical question is whether the courts have an obligation to respond to problems of style. The propensity to use a "powerful" or "powerless" style, for example, might be considered merely another aspect of a person's mode of self-presentation, much like dress or appearance. The courts have never been responsible for compensating for interpersonal or intergroup differences with regard to such features.[3] But it is also the case, as we have attempted to demonstrate, that a witness's social status and previous courtroom experience appear to be significant determinants of this propensity. Given the fact that witnesses who speak in one or the other of these modes thereby affect their credibility and thus their chances for a fair hearing in court, the issue takes on a different light because it raises questions about equity and fundamental fairness.

The problem of dealing with non-English speakers in the courts provides a useful analog for considerations of difficulties occasioned by speech style. Until recently, the use of interpreters for both non-English speakers and deaf persons had been left to the discretion of trial judges in both federal and state jurisdictions. In 1978, Congress enacted legislation designed to regularize judicial treatment of such persons. Many states are considering similar legislation regarding the use of interpreters and the standardization of interpretive procedures.

Diversity in speech style can plausibly be viewed as a subspecies of the problem of interpretation between English and another language. Both situations involve functional differences in the language used by the court and the litigant, with the distinction being one of degree rather than kind. However, the extensive documentation of prejudicial impact that inadequate interpretation has for the non-English speaker is lacking a parallel in the case of stylistic differences. Findings such as those in the powerful–powerless, narrative–fragmented, and hypercorrect style studies reported here are first steps in such a process of documentation. With the development of more extensive research to supplement these data, it is conceivable that protective judicial responses and legislative actions might ensue.

---

[3] For example, although the courts have held that individuals may not be excluded from jury pools on the basis of race, the concept of trial by a jury of one's peers has never been extended to require that jurors be peers of the accused in terms of education, economic background, and the like. See *Swain* v. *Alabama* (jury pools must include an appropriate representation of the racial background of the community) and *Turner* v. *Fouche* (real property ownership held invalid criterion for school board membership).

A number of remedial procedures for dealing with the possible effects of speech style on the reception of testimony are available to trial courts. Judges who are sensitive to the significance of style might exercise flexibility in dealing with witnesses who speak in nonstandard styles. For example, existing law gives judges the authority to depart from the usual rules prohibiting leading questions during direct examinations to prevent unfair prejudice. There is also ample precedent to support trial judges in intervening directly to question witnesses themselves when they determine that the interests of justice require it.[4]

In addition, a court may avail itself of the opportunity to incorporate information such as that reported here into its routine management of the trial. For example, just as judges frequently give witnesses preliminary encouragement to speak loudly and slowly and to tell their stories as clearly as possible, they might also advise witnesses that it is in their best interests to speak in a natural, straightforward fashion (that is, not to use hypercorrect or "powerless" speech) and to use a narrative format whenever possible. Furthermore, knowing that the presence of interruptions may color jurors perceptions of the facts, courts may wish to assume an active role in cutting off simultaneous speech episodes early. Finally, it may be reasonable for the courts to draw somewhat more extended inferences from these findings. For example, more attention might be focused on the speech patterns of lawyers on the assumption that jurors are likely to be sensitive to the subtleties of their speech as well.

The possible remedial responses of courts discussed here are not intended to be exhaustive but rather to be indicative of the types of solutions that are well within the range of discretion of the courts operating under existing law. It must be recognized, however, that these solutions depend first on a recognition of the problem by a trial judge who has a willingness to exercise judicial discretion in attempting to remedy them. Points may arise where the effects of speech style become so extreme that communication in the courtroom is frustrated and the substantive issues are obscured. At that point, the only meaningful response might require a recognition of the essential similarity between the situation of

---

[4] For cases bearing on a judge's authority to permit leading questions on direct examination, see *United States* v. *Littlewind* (leading of young rape victims who "responded hesitantly" and were "reticent"); *Rotolo* v. *United States* (leading of teenage girl who was "nervous" and "upset"); *People* v. *Doxie* (leading of 5-year-old child witness); *Hubbard* v. *State* (leading of adult rape victim); and *State* v. *Snow* (witness had difficulty with English language). For cases bearing on the trial judge's authority to question the witness, see *Furtando* v. *Mantebello Verified School District; State* v. *Simmons;* and *Commonwealth* v. *Butler.*

the speaker of an unusual style of English and the non-English speaker for whom interpretation is normally provided.[5] Ultimately, sensitivity to language variations might be incorporated into the law of evidence. The primary concern of the rules of evidence has been on questions of admissibility. Once ruled admissible, the form in which evidence is presented is subject only to very broad constraints. Evidentiary rules serve to ensure the reliability of the evidence being admitted. The law cannot serve this purpose if it ignores elements that, in the eyes of the jury, are as significant as the "facts" themselves. A question for the law to consider in dealing with all this is whether a witness should be held incompetent, for example, if he or she cannot present testimony in a style that will receive an unprejudiced hearing. It would seem that to the extent that speech style may distract jurors from a relatively objective assessment of the facts, the principles of equity, if not constitutional law, require that the courts develop a more active response to the problem.

Implications for Social Science

Research on language and law is in a rudimentary state. Only a handful of articles and books on legal language were available two decades ago. During the last decade, as a variety of researchers from several disciplines have studied diverse topics in language and law, the field has begun to take shape. Language in the courtroom has emerged as an area of specific interest. Yet, even today, our knowledge of the relation between language and law in all areas remains extremely limited. This book, through its specific focus on speech styles and their relation to legal processes, has attempted to identify and discuss some of these issues and, in doing so, to bring the matter of language in the courtroom to the attention of more social scientists, some of whom will, it is hoped, add to our understanding through their future work.

The study of courtroom language has provided an opportunity for a specific consideration of the utility of distinguishing between normative and pragmatic rules in competitive arenas. Although this distinction was originally applied to distinguish between the publicly agreed upon and morally sanctioned rules for political contests, as opposed to strategic

[5] In the long run, such recognition might even entail lesislative specification of uniform guidelines for the selection and use of such interpreters as has begun to be the case for the deaf and for non-English-speaking litigants.

rules about how one might actually maximize chances of winning, it has particular applicability to the trial courtroom. There are, as noted in Chapter 1 both publicly acknowledged rules of procedure and more private, often unarticulated or even unconscious rules for successful strategies. This distinction has led us directly to the study of frequently ignored, but critical parts of the legal process—at least those parts that occur within trial courtrooms.

It has been useful to combine this interest in pragmatic rules with a concern for language and the role it plays in the legal process. This linkage of concepts has led into an exciting, if unknown area for social science. And our findings here lead us to speculate about the generality of the processes involved. We suspect that the same, or at least similar strategic rules of language use, can be discovered in other professional domains such as education, medicine, and advertising as well as in the ordinary affairs of everyday life.

The study of pragmatic rules for courtroom strategy raises an interesting question about the vantage from which we have viewed this entire matter. The rules and strategies we have been considering, as well as those discussed in the trial practice manuals to which we have referred, consider the legal system from the viewpoint of lawyers. These are not the rules and strategies that are successful for witnesses in achieving THEIR goals in court. One of the most frequent complaints of witnesses, especially first-time witnesses, is that they had little opportunity during the trial to tell their version of the facts. Instead, they typically report, the lawyers asked only SOME of the relevant questions and consequently they only managed to tell part of their story (Linton 1965). Perhaps we have, like the lawyers who write strategy manuals, taken a one-sided perspective on the courtroom. What would it be like, for example, to ask another kind of question—to consider the rules of successful strategy for TESTIFYING in court?

This question can be examined profitably by considering the corollaries of the propositions regarding successful tactics recommended by lawyers. In Table 7.1, some of the techniques recommended in trial practice manuals are shown on the left. On the right side of the table are suggested the corresponding strategies that witnesses might use to wrest control of the courtroom interview from the examining lawyers. Just as there are two opposing sides in every courtroom contest, there are also two parties in the question–answer interview and they too have different vested interests, sometimes even different goals. The suggested strategies for witnesses in Table 7.1 are, of course, only hypotheses about what might work for witnesses. These notions are drawn from what lawyers believe works to help them achieve their own goals. Such a witness-

Table 7.1
A Comparison of Some Effective Strategies for Lawyers and Witnesses

Effective techniques for lawyers	Effective techniques for witnesses
1. Make effective use of variations in question format.[a]	1. Make effective use of variations in answer format.[b]
2. Allow more opportunity to one's own witnesses on direct examination to give longer, narrative versions of their testimony; restrict the opportunity of witnesses under cross-examination to short, direct answers to the specific questions asked.	2. Make every possible effort to give long answers whenever possible; require the opposition lawyer to stop you frequently during cross-examination so as to give the impression that he does not want your full story to be placed before the jury.
3. Convey a sense of organization in your interviews of witnesses and your remarks to the jury.	3. Attempt to confuse the organization which the opposition lawyer has planned for the cross-examination.
4. Adopt different styles of questioning with different kinds of witnesses, such as women, the elderly, children, expert witnesses.	4. Adopt different styles of answering questions asked by different questioners. Show great deference to the judge; avoid any hints of rehearsed answers while under direct-examination; do not get hostile with the opposition lawyer but maintain an attitude of politeness throughout.
5. Remain poker-faced throughout; do not reveal surprise even when an answer is totally unexpected; save dramatic reactions for special occasions.	5. Do not show surprise even when questions are unexpected. Save dramatic reactions for special moments (e.g., *Well, I'm finally glad you got around to asking me that*); then proceed with the answer.
6. Rhythm and pace are important; do not bore the jury with slowness; use silence strategically.	6. Use rhythm and pace to advantage. Upset the opposition lawyer's pace with variations in response timing (e.g., break the steady rhythm the lawyer may be attempting to achieve by asking, *Would you please repeat the question?* after an especially long or complex question).
7. Repetition can be useful for emphasis, but it should be used with care so as not to bore the jury. Some authors of trial manuals endorse repetition as a means of educating the jury; others think it unnecessary in most instances.	7. Turn a cross-examiner's repetition of material back on him or her (e.g., ask, *What's the matter, don't you understand my answer?* Or say, *You've asked me that before. As I said, the answer is . . .* Or ask, *Why do you keep asking the same question which I've already answered?*).

(Cont'd.)

Table 7.1 (continued)

Effective techniques for lawyers	Effective techniques for witnesses
8. Avoid interrupting a witness whenever possible. Interrupting a responsive answer may be as damaging as the content of the answer; it gives the impression you want to hide some of the facts.	8. Interrupt the opposition lawyer to volunteer answers when you begin to see whshe is getting at. It gives the impression that you are cooperative and will only serve to confuse his style.
9. Use objections sparingly; they not only call attention to the material being objected to but also convey an impression of attempting to conceal information.	9. Blurt out relevant facts and opinions on cross-examination even though the opposition lawyer may attempt to limit your answer. The lawyer's attempts to limit your answers will give the impression he is attempting to conceal some of the evidence you have to offer.

[a] Techniques for lawyers are based on materials contained in the trial practice manuals discussed in Chapter 3, pages 33–38.

[b] Techniques proposed for witnesses are assumed to be the reverse of those that would be successful strategies for lawyers on the opposing side. Lawyers are urged to vary questions for different types of witnesses. Consequently, it is suggested that variations in ANSWERS might be a useful witness technique.

centered view of courtroom strategy cannot be found in any books on courtroom technique, but it is a view the anthropologist must consider when attempting as complete a view of the courtroom contest as possible.[6]

Some questions about the processes involved in the way speech style works in the legal process remain unanswered to our full satisfaction. The experiments reported in Chapters 5 and 6 behaviorally demonstrate the effects of speech style on legal decision makers. Because of the consistency with which these results were found across a variety of speech styles and situations, there is little question that presentational form of testimony does indeed matter and is ultimately consequential in the legal process. Yet many specific questions about how these effects work remain unanswered by the research conducted up to now. For example, it is not known whether some of these effects are stronger than others—would the negative aspects of powerless speech override the

[6] This view is not likely to be received warmly at first by many practicing attorneys. However, further consideration might suggest that these techniques may be useful for THEIR witnesses when being examined by opposing counsel.

benefits of highly narrative testimony? Many questions like this can be answered only by additional research. In considering them, it should be remembered that we have not sought here to provide an exhaustive set of trial techniques validated through social science experimentation, but rather we have conducted these experiments to gather as much evidence as possible for the general significance of speech style in the courtroom.

Speech style does not exist in isolation from the content of the testimony delivered, from the larger context of the trial itself, and, especially, from the many efforts on the parts of persons to manage the meaning of style. Because juries do not make decisions as individuals, but as groups, many researchers have believed that theories of decision making must be modified to take account of the small-group context in which they occur before being applied to the courtroom. Similarly, we believe that a fuller understanding of speech style in legal decision making needs to include consideration of the context in which it occurs.

In a related vein, the experimental studies themselves need to be refined as much as possible to increase confidence in these findings. Although much of the theory of experimental social psychology is based on studies conducted with students, we must never be completely satisfied until we have replicated as closely as possible the real-world phenomena and persons being studied. Because the present study has demonstrated the general significance of speech style for legal contexts, future studies should begin testing hypotheses with subject populations who resemble more closely actual jurors in terms of demographic characteristics and in situations where the total context approximates more closely that of a typical trial. We do not believe that the subjects or the situation in which our studies were conducted limit or diminish in any way the significance of the general findings, but we welcome future refinements in related research.

For sociolinguistics in particular this research holds some specific implications. A frequent criticism of sociolinguistics is that the field has become obsessed with producing more and more elegant descriptions of language variation whereas little, if any, attention is paid to the consequences and significance of the variation. This research, we submit, provides a substantial answer to this question about variation: *So what?* It shows, for example, not only that language is patterned according to social dimensions in a court of law (an idea by no means unexpected or even new to the legal context) but also that these forms of variation are utterly consequential for the legal process. For those who might wish to argue that the particular variables selected for study have not been fully described or even understood completely (a criticism to which we are sensitive), we submit that we did find over and over again that form is critically important for the legal process. Whether or not we know all the finer details about "powerful" as opposed to "powerless" speech, narrative versus fragmented testimony styles, hypercorrection, or simultaneous speech, we do know that the particular variations in presentational form that were used in our experimental tapes and transcripts did elicit very different responses. We challenge others to assist in both the identification of further variables that might be even more important in courtroom presentational styles and the fuller understanding of those that have been studied thus far.

This research may be seen as part of a broad trend within sociolinguistics in the last few years that focuses on language in professional contexts.[7] Researchers in medicine, advertising, education, government, and other professional fields are studying the role of language and communication processes in the professional activities of these fields. Language and law is fast becoming one of the major areas of inquiry in these studies. As a specific field for inquiry, it stands to learn from as well as contribute to this broader development.

Finally, the perspective employed in this study of language and law deals with language as the means for explaining legal processes. It does not deal with the important question of what forensic uses of language may reveal about the nature of language itself. In the long run, a full study of language and law must deal with this as well as a broad range of more specific issues, such as: language and the conceptualization of law, reform of legal language, other "legal languages" besides English.

Further Questions

It is said that H. L. Mencken often complained about people who withhold criticism until they have a better alternative to offer. "One need not know," he is reported to say, "what to do in order to identify a problem." Whether these are Mencken's words or those attributed to him by someone else, they echo a sentiment that has informed all that we have said up to now. No fully adequate solution to the issue of speech style in the courtroom is in sight. Yet, we know it is a critical element in the overall chemistry of legal decision making. Perhaps no controls are necessary—for as the tradition of the case law interprets it, demeanor

[7] A book currently nearing completion will likely define this field and bring it squarely to the attention of both social scientists and professionals in such fields as law, medicine, and advertising. See Shirley Brice Heath, *Language and the Professions*, forthcoming.

evidence allows the decision makers to rely upon their humanity in evaluating evidence. But whether we see this process as a problem in need of control or merely as an element only dimly understood, speech style is unquestionably central to how the courtroom works. Hence, practical, theoretical, or possibly both concerns motivate interest in the role of form in courtroom communication.

Future research efforts can readily build upon what has already been accomplished here. Studies of the speech of lawyers are needed to complement our knowledge about witnesses' styles. It has practical relevance as well as theoretical interest—for as many lawyers are quick to point out, there often is not much they can do about a witness's style, but they might more readily, if they knew what to do, attempt to alter their own.

We have noted the possibility of diversifying subject populations in further studies now that the general effects of speech style are known. What this might lead to, however, is a serious questioning of the sacred cow of the concept of a jury of one's peers. We have noted, for example, that social science studies have shown persons tend to be more punitive toward people like themselves, especially when these people attempt to disguise ethnic accents or nonstandard speech styles. How would the law deal with the full implications of showing that juries composed of those persons most like us rely more heavily in making decisions about us on our manner of speaking? This will have to wait until we know more about such a situation, but its implications for the jury system are staggering.

We have discussed at some length the possibilities for controlling, limiting, or even extinguishing the effects of speech style. Experimental results to date have not been promising, but it should be noted that we have merely failed in our efforts thus far to find a means of control, and not that we have concluded that it is impossible within the framework of the American judicial system to do so. The effects are strong and they are persistent, but further research may well discover a reasonable means to exercise controls over speech style.

Although this research was undertaken for theoretical rather than practical reasons, its findings have interested a large number of trial lawyers. Presentations to groups of trial lawyers of the results of our studies about the effects of courtroom speech styles have been of interest to many of them—if we may draw such a conclusion from immediate reactions, letters, and word-of-mouth recommendations. The effort to discuss this research with attorneys has also been of great use to the project, providing a means for gathering new ideas for further research from attorneys who deal with matters of courtroom strategy daily. To illustrate the

Table 7.2
Some Practical Questions Asked by Lawyers about This Research

---

1. In cross-examination, does it help the cross-examiner to say to a witness, *I know you want to make a point, but I want some specific information from you; so would you please listen very closely and give your answer to the specific question to us?* Would making such a statement to a witness help point out that witness's bias to the jury?
2. Is it possible that "powerless" speech would be more credible to those who USE "powerless" speech themselves?
3. Do jurors react negatively to a lawyer they observe attempting to watch them?
4. How can a "powerless" witness be transformed into a "powerful" one?
5. Are people from some regions of the country more likely to use hedge words?
6. Is there any evidence to suggest that the interpretation of style is any more effective than an instruction to disregard it?
7. Do laypeople expect attorneys to be linguistically formal and precise, or do they view it as pedantic?
8. It is becoming common in federal courts for judges to require written stipulations of uncontested facts, background details, and foundation details rather than to allow oral testimony on these subjects. Is it fair to require a juror to weigh evidence by just hearing testimony concerning the contested facts?
9. When a witness gives very lengthy answers, should the lawyer interrupt to prevent the jury from losing attention?
10. When is it a good idea to avoid using a "powerless" witness?
11. What can a lawyer do to discredit a white male, "powerful," middle-class witness who narrates his testimony, who does not interrupt, does not "talk up," but who is LYING?

---

sophistication of their questions, several that were submitted in writing at a recent trial lawyers' association seminar are contained in Table 7.2. The questions not only are interesting in themselves but also suggest that joint theoretical and applied research on social science and the law will be of great benefit to both academicians and legal practitioners. A merger of practical legal issues with theoretical matters may produce in this case some findings of considerable significance for us all.

Finally, the following further questions are especially intended for those who still wonder at this point why an anthropologist who began his career by spending 2 years in an African village turned to research an American courtroom: How do legal systems that depend primarily on verbal settlement procedures differ from those using magic, oracles, feuds, warfare, and various forms of contest? Is the prowess of words all that different from brute force? How did verbal dispute settlement procedures evolve in the first instance? What can be learned from the socialization of children as they are taught to settle their arguments through language? Does demeanor and style matter to the same degree in all cultures? To what degree are the principles of language that are found strategically useful in an American courtroom universally effective?

1

TRANSCRIPTS OF "POWERFUL" AND "POWERLESS" STYLES

The study of "powerless" versus "powerful" speech styles involved four experimental tapes. One involved a female witness speaking in the "powerless" mode. This version was based on the actual testimony of a witness as recorded in court. Names, dates, and locations were changed in order to preserve anonymity. A few objections were eliminated as well.

The three other tapes involved various alterations of this replication of the original testimony. One involved a female witness speaking in a "powerful" mode (i.e., having the "powerless" speech characteristics removed). The remaining two tapes were replications of the two female-witness tapes with the role of the witness played by a male actor. All four versions are described in the text; see pages 71–73.

Because of the great similarity of the male and female versions, only the two female tapes are transcribed here. The male tapes differ as described in Table 5.2.

These transcripts were prepared by a free-lance court reporter who was asked to transcribe them as she would testimony actually presented in court. These are two of the four transcripts used in the study reported in Chapter 6. The spelling and punctuation conventions in these transcripts are those used by the court reporter. The transcripts were used in this form in the studies concerning possibilities for controlling the effects of speech style described in Chapter 6 on pages 94–96.

Powerless Style (Female Witness)

Whereupon,

MRS. JOAN S. GURNEY, Having been first duly sworn, was examined and testified as follows:

DIRECT EXAMINATION BY MR. CONNOR:

Q. Now, will you state your full name for the Court and the jury?
A. Joan S. Gurney.
Q. Mrs. Gurney, where do you live?
A. 210 Garrett Road in Durham.
Q. And where were you living on May the 3rd, 1973?
A. 210 Garrett Road in Durham.
Q. State whether or not, Mrs. Gurney, you were acquainted with or knew the late Mrs. Edith Davis?
A. Quite well.
Q. What was the nature of your acquaintance with her?
A. We were very close friends. Ah, she was even sort of like a mother to me.
Q. Did—in regard to where you live on Garrett Road, where did she live?
A. Right next door to me.
Q. State whether or not you had an occasion to be with her about 12:45 or 12:55 on the early morning hours of May the 3rd?
A. Yes, I did.
Q. Where was that?
A. We were in an ambulance. Now, I cannot give you the exact time. I can tell you that her nephew called me and said that she was quite ill.
Q. Now, as a result of a telephone call, state whether or not you went to her house?
A. Oh, yes, unh-hunh, I went to her house.
Q. And after you got to her house, did you thereafter go anywhere with her?
A. Yes, I surely did.
Q. Where did you go?
A. I went in an ambulance with her to the hospital.
Q. Where were you located in the ambulance?
A. Well, in the front seat.
Q. Do you know who was driving the ambulance?
A. Yes, I do. Mr. Norris.
Q. Do you see him in the courtroom?
A. Yes, he's here. There in the yellow shirt.
Q. Now, where was Mrs. Davis?
A. She was on a stretcher in the back of the ambulance. She was—well, strapped onto it, you know.

Q. Were you present when she was put in the ambulance?
A. I certainly was.
Q. Had you—were you conversing with her?
A. Oh, yes, unh-hunh.
Q. Was she able to talk?
A. Certainly she was.
Q. She was alive?
A. Very definitely.
Q. All right. Now, was anyone else in the back area of the ambulance with the cot?
A. Mr. Watson was in the back.
Q. Is that Mr. John D. Watson?
A. Right. He was the attendant in the back of the ambulance. So, let's see. Mr. Norris was driving, and I was riding in the front beside Mr. Norris.
Q. All right. Do you recall about the time that that was?
A. Oh, oh, well, that is somewhat of a problem. I think that Mr. Young who is Mrs. Davis' nephew called me, I think, around eleven. Maybe just a little bit after.
   Her son, you know, he has a little difficulty hearing, so that's why Mr. Young called me.
Q. You were at home when you got the call?
A. Yes.
Q. Then you went next door?
A. And then I went immediately next door, yes.
Q. Approximately how long did you stay there before the ambulance arrived?
A. Oh, it seems like it was about twenty minutes, just long enough to help my friend, Mrs. Davis get straightened out.
Q. Now, how long have you lived in Durham?
A. All my life, really.
Q. You are familiar with the streets?
A. Oh, yes.
Q. You know your way around?
A. Unh-hunh, I guess I do.
Q. When you got in the ambulance with Mrs. Davis, with Mr. Norris driving, where were you going, do you know?
A. Yeah, we were going to Duke Hospital, and we went—let's see—we went up—up Glenn, down Camden, if I'm not mistaken, down to Avondale Road and down Avondale to Roxboro Road. Then up Roxboro Road to Holloway Street, and that's when the horrible accident occurred.
Q. You were saying Holloway Street?
A. That's correct. Holloway.
Q. Is that West Holloway Street?
A. Let's see. You're asking—I think so.
Q. Well, do you recall which—were you headed—do you know which direction you were headed?

A. Yeah, which way do you go to Duke Hospital? Seems like you're headed west, is that right?

Q. You were headed west then?

A. All right, yes, I'm very sorry. I don't—I have such a terrible sense of direction.

Q. Now, was there any partition in the ambulance between the—where the patient was in the back and the front where you were riding?

A. No, you see, I was holding onto Mrs. Davis' hand, you know. I had my hand back like this (indicating) holding her hand, and when the collision occurred—

Q. (Interposing) Now, wait just a minute.

A. Excuse me.

Q. You were holding her hand?

A. Unh-hunh (yes), and I was talking to her.

Q. You—was she conversing with you?

A. Certainly.

Q. Now, do you recall the events immediately before the ambulance reached the intersection of Holloway Street while you were on Roxboro Road—

A. (Interposing) Yes, I do.

Q. —as best you can recall?

A. Excuse me.

Q. Now, would you tell the jury—do you know whether the ambulance light was on?

A. I don't believe it was.

Q. Well, it had a siren?

A. Not that I know of.

Q. You don't know?

A. No, it did not.

Q. Well, do you recall approaching that intersection?

A. I certainly do.

Q. State whether or not there is—how that traffic is controlled there; whether it's an electric light or a stop sign?

A. Stop lights.

Q. Electric lights?

A. Yes, and we—as we approached, as I said, I'm a very poor judge of distance, if you'll begging my pardon. The light was red as we approached it, but as I will explain to you, we were a little further away from it than—than the length of this courtroom.

So, it turned green, and Mr. Norris slowed up and then he approached— I mean—I mean it was red. It turned red, and as Mr. Norris approached it, it turned green and he kept going through, and that's when we got hit.

Q. Do you—do you have any idea of the speed that he was driving the ambulance?

A. No, sir, I'm not sure about that—you know—it couldn't have been too— too fast. Maybe thirty, thirty-five?

Q. And when you came to the intersection, right there at the intersection, what happened?
A. Just—just as we approached the intersection, like this, (indicating) Mr. Maxwell's car came across and—you know—caught the—some of the side or the back of the ambulance.
Q. Came across what?
A. Well, you know, Holloway Street.
Q. It was traveling on Holloway Street?
A. That's right, and it threw the ambulance around and around, I don't remember a thing after that.
But it threw the ambulance around, and Mr. Watson was thrown right out. And then poor Edith—Mrs.—Mrs. Davis was thrown out, too.
Q. Up to the moment of the collision, was Mrs. Davis alive?
A. Oh, very definitely.
Q. How do you know?
A. I know because she was talking to me.
Q. At the moment of impact, did anyone say anything?
A. Yes, she said, "Oh, my God, what's happening?" when she heard—you know—the crash.
Q. As a result of the accident, state whether or not you were rendered unconscious?
A. Afterwards, I was, yes, for a while.
Q. What is—what is the first thing you remember after the accident?
A. I guess I remember coming to in the Duke Emergency, and I thought I was at the police station because it seemed like there were so many policemen around, and I just couldn't figure out what I'd done to be taken to the police station, you know.
Q. You do not remember, in other words?
A. No, sir, I don't. And it shook me up, you know. And this very kind policeman came up, and he asked me if there was someone he could call for me, and I asked him if he would call my husband—you know—when I sort of had my wits back together again.
Q. Did you see Mrs. Davis after that?
A. No, sir.
Q. Did you ever see her alive after the moment of impact with Mr. Maxwell's car at Holloway and Roxboro Road?
A. No, I didn't.
Q. How long did you stay at the hospital?
A. Well, I stayed overnight because I wanted to come home so badly. I felt like I would—you know—be able to get along much better being at home rather than being in a hospital.
Q. Did you know what her condition was?
A. Well, my husband told me the next morning.
MR. CONNOR: Thank you. I have no further questions at this time.
THE COURT: You may cross-examine.

Powerful Style (Female Witness)

Whereupon,
   MRS. JOAN S. GURNEY, Having been first duly sworn, was examined and
   testified as follows:

Q. Now, will you state your full name for the Court and the jury?
A. Joan S. Gurney.
Q. Mrs. Gurney, where do you live?
A. 210 Garrett Road, in Durham.
Q. And where were you living on May the 3rd, 1973?
A. 210 Garrett Road.
Q. State whether or not, Mrs. Gurney, you were acquainted with or knew the
    late Mrs. Edith Davis?
A. Yes, I did.
Q. What was the nature of your acquaintance with her?
A. Well, we were close friends. She was like a mother to me.
Q. Did—in regard to where you live on Garrett Road, where did she live?
A. Next door.
Q. State whether or not you had an occasion to be with her about 12:45 or
    12:55 on the early morning hours of May the 3rd?
A. Yes, I did.
Q. Where was that?
A. Oh, we were in an ambulance. Sometime that night her nephew called me
    and said that she was ill.
Q. Now, as a result of a telephone call, state whether or not you went to her
    house?
A. Yes, I did.
Q. And after you got to her house, did you thereafter go anywhere with her?
A. Yes, I did.
Q. Where did you go?
A. In the ambulance with her to the hospital.
Q. Where were you located in the ambulance?
A. In the front seat.
Q. Do you know who was driving the ambulance?
A. Mr. Norris.
Q. Do you see him in the courtroom?
A. Yes, he's here in the yellow shirt.
Q. Now, where was Mrs. Davis?
A. She was on a stretcher in the back of the ambulance. She was strapped
    onto it.
Q. Were you present when she was put in the ambulance?
A. I was.
Q. Had you—were you conversing with her?
A. Yes.

Q. Was she able to talk?
A. Yes, she was.
Q. She was alive?
A. Yes.
Q. All right. Now, was anyone else in the back area of the ambulance with the cot?
A. Mr. Watson was in the back.
Q. Is that Mr. John D. Watson?
A. He was the attendant in the back of the ambulance.
   Mr. Norris was driving, and I was riding in the front beside Mr. Norris.
Q. All right. Do you recall about the time that was?
A. Well, Mr. Young, who was Mrs. Davis's nephew, called me around eleven. Her son has difficulty hearing, so that's why Mr. Young called me.
Q. You were at home when you got the call?
A. Yes.
Q. Then you went next door?
A. Yes.
Q. Approximately how long did you stay there before the ambulance arrived?
A. Twenty minutes. Long enough to help get Mrs. Davis straightened out.
Q. Now, how long have you lived in Durham?
A. All my life.
Q. You are familiar with the streets?
A. Yes.
Q. You know your way around?
A. Yes.
Q. When you got in the ambulance with Mrs. Davis, with Mr. Norris driving, where were you going, do you know?
A. Yeah, we were going to Duke Hospital. We went up Glenn, down Camden, down to Avondale Road, and down Avondale to Roxboro Road to Holloway Street, and that's when the accident occurred.
Q. You were saying Holloway Street?
A. Holloway.
Q. Is that West Holloway Street?
A. Yes.
Q. Well, do you recall which—were you headed—do you know which direction you were headed?
A. Yeah, well, if you're going to—ah—we were headed west.
Q. You were headed west then?
A. Yes, I have a poor sense of direction.
Q. Now, was there any partition in the ambulance between the—where the patient was in back and the front where you were riding?
A. No, I was holding Mrs. Davis's hand. I had my hand back like this (indicating) holding her hand, and when the collision occurred—
Q. (Interposing) Now, wait just a minute.
A. Yes.
Q. You were holding her hand?

A. Unh-hunh (yes), and I was talking to her.
Q. You—was she conversing with you?
A. Yes.
Q. Was she conscious?
A. Yes.
Q. Now, do you recall the events immediately before the ambulance reached the intersection of Holloway Street and—
A. (Interposing) Yes, I do.
Q. —while you were on Roxboro Road?
A. Yes.
Q. Would you tell the jury, do you know whether the ambulance light was on?
A. No, it wasn't.
Q. Well, it had a siren?
A. No.
Q. You don't know?
A. No, it did not have a siren.
Q. Well, do you recall approaching that intersection?
A. Yes, I do.
Q. State whether or not there is—how the traffic is controlled there; whether it's an electric light or a stop sign?
A. It's a stoplight.
Q. Electric lights?
A. Yes, and the light was red as we approached, and we were further away from it than the length of this courtroom, it was red, and Mr. Norris slowed up, and then as he approached it, it turned green, and he—he kept going, and that's when we got hit.
Q. Do you—do you have any idea of the speed that he was driving the ambulance?
A. It couldn't have been too fast. Thirty—thirty-five.
Q. And when you came to the intersection, right there at the intersection, what happened?
A. Just as we approached the intersection, Mr. Maxwell's car came across and caught some of the side or the back of the ambulance.
Q. Came across what?
A. Holloway Street.
Q. It was traveling on Holloway Street?
A. Right, it threw the ambulance around, I don't know how many times, because I don't remember anything after that.
    But it threw the ambulance around, and Mr. Watson was thrown out, and then Mrs. Davis was thrown out, too.
Q. Up to the moment of the collision, was Mrs. Davis alive?
A. Yes, she was.
Q. How do you know?
A. She was because she was talking to me.
Q. At the moment of impact, did anyone say anything?

A. Yes. She said, "Oh, my God, what's happening?", when she heard the car hit.
Q. As a result of the accident, state whether or not you were rendered unconscious?
A. Yes, I was.
Q. What is—what is the first thing you remember after the accident?
A. I remember coming to in the Duke Emergency, and I thought I was at the police station, because there were so many policemen around.
    And I couldn't figure out what I had done to be taken to the police station.
Q. You do not remember, in other words?
A. No, I don't. And it shook me up, and this policeman came up, and I asked him if he would call my husband when I had my wits back again.
Q. Did you see Mrs. Davis after that?
A. No.
Q. Did you ever see her alive after the moment of impact with Mr. Maxwell's car at Holloway and Roxboro Road?
A. No.
Q. How long did you stay at the hospital?
A. Well, I stayed only overnight, because I wanted to come home. I thought I would be able to get along better being at home rather than staying in the hospital.
Q. Did you know what her condition was?
A. My husband told me the next morning.
MR. CONNOR: Thank you. I have no further questions at this time.
THE COURT: You may cross-examine.

2

TRANSCRIPTS OF NARRATIVE AND FRAGMENTED STYLES

The study of narrative and fragmented testimony styles involved four experimental tapes. The experimental stimulus tapes were based on the testimony of a female witness who spoke in a highly FRAGMENTED style. Members of the research team worked together to alter the original testimony style so that it conformed more closely to the alternative NARRATIVE style used by many witnesses. Two experimental tapes thus presented the same female witness and the same male lawyer giving the "same" testimony in the two styles. Slight alterations were made so that two more tapes could be made in which a male witness gave this testimony in both narrative and fragmented styles. For these latter two tapes, the original "lawyer" continued in his role as the examining attorney. These styles and the experimental studies are described in the text on pages 76–82.

Since no transcript can render every aspect of speech behavior, judgments must be made regarding which features to represent and which to overlook in any particular transcript. The transcripts included in this appendix are provided for the primary purpose of demonstrating differences between the narrative and fragmented testimony styles. Ordinary English spelling and writing conventions are used whenever possible to make these transcripts readable and usable by as wide an audience as possible. Although no special effort has been made to represent elapsed time or pauses within speech, COMMAS are used to designate relatively short intervals (audible to members of the research team) and ELIPSES are used for intervals of longer duration. No attempt has been made to represent speakers' dialects or pronunciation idiosyncracies or to show any periods when the speech of two people overlaps—features that, along with many others, would be usefully represented for many other types of analysis. As in Appendix 1, Q and A refer to QUESTIONER (the attorney conducting the examination) and ANSWERER (the witness giving testimony). Other speakers are identified by their roles in the court.

Fragmented Style

CLERK: Do you swear that the testimony that you are about to give this court is the truth, the whole truth, and nothing but the truth, so help you God?

MRS. MARSHALL: I do.

JUDGE: Be seated.

Q. Will you please tell the court members of the jury your name?

A. My name is Carol Marshall.

Q. And where do you live?

A. I live at 311 Plum Street.

Q. And how long have you lived in Durham?

A. Oh, 2 years.

Q. Now, prior to the twenty-first day of November, 1974, uh, how long had you been employed at the Seven–Eleven store on Willowdale Avenue?

A. Um, I—I'd been employed, uh, we came to Durham in August of '73, the fifteenth or so.

Q. Alright, and uh, where did you first, what store were you employed at, at the beginning?

A. I started on Spruce.

Q. And then what?

A. And I uh, then I worked all the stores, you know, rotated all the stores in Durham, I—I mean the Seven–Eleven stores.

Q. When did you start working at the Willowdale store?

A. I made assistant manager on Spruce, and I stayed there for several months. Then I was transferred to Willowdale.

Q. So approximately how long before the twenty-first of November last year had you been working at the store on Willowdale?

A. Uh, about, uh—

Q. Approximately?

A. Several months.

Q. Now, calling your attention to the twenty-first day of November, a Saturday, what were your working hours that day?

A. Well, I was working from 7 to 3.

Q. Was that 7 A.M.?

A. Yes.
Q. And what time that day did you arrive at the store?
A. 6:30.
Q. 6:30. And did, uh, you open the store at 7 o'clock?
A. Yes, it has to be opened.
Q. Did you have, uh, any other employees with you that day?
A. No.
Q. Now sometime, during that morning, did you have occasion to see, uh, someone in the store?
A. Yes, about 9:20.
Q. Alright, who was that?
A. That man right there.
Q. You're pointing to the man sitting next to Mr. Williams?
A. Yes.
Q. Now prior to his being at the store, did you have any customers?
A. Oh, yes, customers came in the store, but after 9 there was no one in the store but me.
Q. What were you doing at that time?
A. I was talking on the telephone to my sister in Georgia.
Q. And how long did that conversation run?
A. It, about, uh, close to 20 minutes.
Q. And during that time did any customers come into the store?
A. That man, oh, John Barnes walked in, at about 20 after nine.
Q. Were you still on the telephone?
A. I was, yea I was still talking on the phone to my sister. I was still talking. He just walked in.
Q. Now would you please tell me where is this phone located in the building?
A. At the door, as you walk in the door.
Q. Where exactly?
A. The telephone is there on the wall, right at the door.
Q. And this gentleman who you described as the uh, pointed out as the defendant in this matter, when did you first notice him?
A. Well, when I was talking on the phone.
Q. What happened after you first saw him?
A. He walked into the store, and I was still talking.
Q. What was he doing?
A. He just walked in and he was walking around like he was going to buy something.
Q. You remained on the phone?
A. Well he never did come to the counter or anything, so I just kept talking to my sister.
Q. Were you still the only persons in the store?
A. No, a couple of minutes later, this, uh, two people came in the store.
Q. What did you do then?
A. I told my sister I had to go because I had some customers.
Q. So did you hang up the phone?

A. Yes.

Q. And then what happened?

A. Well, I waited on the couple and they went on out.

Q. Was there anyone in the store with you after that?

A. The defendant, and me.

Q. Uh, what if anything was he doing?

A. Well, he was, he was still looking around.

Q. Alright, then what.

A. Then he got some things and, uh, put them there on the counter.

Q. Was that while the couple was there?

A. No, they went out.

Q. Alright, then what did you do?

A. I went to ring up his things.

Q. Did he say anything to you?

A. Yes.

Q. What did he say?

A. Well, he said, well he kinda, kinda walked away and said, "I'd like to have a carton of Kool cigarettes."

Q. And what did you do?

A. Well, I said, "Three seventy-five, plus tax."

Q. Did he say anything else?

A. Yes, he said, he said "That's alright."

Q. And what happened then?

A. And then he walked over to the counter where the wine was.

Q. And did he bring anything back?

A. No, I thought he would, but he didn't.

Q. So what did you do?

A. Well I, I rung it all up and it, it came to 7 dollars and 5 cents.

Q. Had he come back to the counter where you rang it up?

A. I hadn't taxed the 7 dollars, and I was waiting for him to come back for more but he didn't bring any more.

Q. Alright, then he came back to the counter?

A. Yes.

Q. And then what if anything happened?

A. I, well, you know, had the cash register open.

Q. And, uh, what did the man do?

A. Well, he just leaned over with his gun and said, "I want all your money."

Q. Did he say anything else?

A. You know, like, yea, "Just hand it over."

Q. Did you give it to him?

A. Yes, he made me give it all to him.

Q. Alright now, did you, uh, what type of gun did he have?

A. Well, it was a small black gun.

Q. And uh, are you familiar with guns?

A. If I look at them very close, I uh . . .

Q. Was this, are you familiar with, with the difference between a revolver and a pistol?
A. Well, it was short, and it seems like, um, it's about about that size.
Q. And, when he, after he made that statement to you, what did you do?
A. I gave him the money!
Q. Did you say anything to him?
A. Yes I said, I said, "Don't shoot me."
Q. And was that all?
A. Then he said, "I'm not going to shoot you, just hand all the money over."
Q. Alright, how much, how much did you hand over to him? In dollars.
A. Oh, close to a hundred.
Q. Now, when you say he pointed a pistol at you, what part of your body, if any, did he point this?
A. Just, he just leaned over and just, you know, like that with the gun.
Q. And did you, do anything then?
A. Yes, I threw this hand up, and said, "Hey, don't shoot me."
Q. So you handed the money to him?
A. Yes.
Q. Then what happened?
A. Uh, well, I handed him all the money from there.
Q. Did he say anything?
A. Oh yea, he said, he said, "That one too."
Q. "That one too?"
A. Yes, I had to turn around and open the other cash register.
Q. Where is the other cash register?
A. Right behind.
Q. Alright, did you, uh, empty both cash registers?
A. Yes.
Q. All the bills?
A. Yes. All the bills, not the change.
Q. Was there any other money?
A. There was another box.
Q. Did you hand it to him?
A. Yes.
Q. And what did he do with it?
A. He took it and, um, put it down his—in his jacket.
Q. Alright, then what happened next?
A. Then he said, "Come on."
Q. Where did he go?
A. Well, then he made me go in the back room.
Q. Did he say anything?
A. He said, "Don't come out."
Q. And did—then what?
A. He, he closed the door, but I heard him.
Q. What did you hear?

A. Well it sounded like he got some more wine.
Q. Anything else?
A. Well, I know he got some more cigarettes and he got all the bag.
Q. What bag?
A. You know, all the stuff that I put in the bag for him.
Q. The bag of merchandise?
A. Yes, he'd, he'd taken all that and got away.
Q. Alright, where is this—you say he made you go to the back room.
A. Uh huh.
Q. Well, is this in the back of the store?
A. Yes, the stockroom.
Q. He didn't go in the room with you?
A. No, he just went and shoved the door.
Q. How?
A. Well, you know, he took his hand and pulled the door.
Q. Did you try to get back out inside the store?
A. No, I just stayed there by the door.
Q. Did he lock the door?
A. No, it doesn't lock, it just closes.
Q. Alright, when did you come out of that room?
A. Um, when I heard the bell on the door, I ran from back there.
Q. And did you see him then?
A. Yes.
Q. Where was he?
A. Um, he had just gotten in his car and went to Pike Street, and um . . .
Q. And did you get the license number?
A. I got some of the license number.
Q. What was it?
A. Five-o-nine.
Q. Now do you, would you describe how that was on the license plate? Was that the first three or the last three digits?
A. It was the last three.
Q. Alright. Now the car the man was driving, was it a brown, a brown 1972 Chevrolet Nova?
OPPOSITION LAWYER: Objection.
JUDGE: Sustained, leading the witness.
Q. Uh, did you remember what type of car, uh, could you describe the car?
A. Well, it was brownish tan, a Nova—a Chevy.
Q. Could you describe whether it looked like a new car or old car?
A. It was uh, it was '70—it was '72. It was '72 Chevy.
Q. Okay, then after the car went away, what happened?
A. I phoned the police.
Q. Alright, did any policemen come?
A. Yes.
Q. Approximately how soon after this happened did the policemen come?

A. Uh, just a few minutes.
Q. Well who came at that time?
A. Uh, I can't recall the name exactly, but they were kind of short. And then, uh, Detective Monroe came.
Q. Is this the gentleman sitting behind him?
A. Yes.
Q. And did he talk to you about what had gone on?
A. Yes.
Q. Alright, and what did you tell him had happened?
A. Um, I told him—what happened.
Q. After you talked to Detective Monroe, what did you do?
A. Um, I, I had to go home for the day.
Q. Why was that?
A. The manager told me to go on home.
Q. Now, uh, was there anything covering this person's face who was in the Seven–Eleven store at that time?
A. Um he had a beard under there. He still had the same—he's the same face.
Q. Did you have occasion after this day to see him?
A. I saw him after he, uh, robbed me at the store.
Q. How many days later was that?
A. I can't recall when exactly.
Q. About how many?
A. It was about a few days, a week maybe.
Q. And where was this that you had seen him?
A. I saw him at the K-Mart in Durham.
Q. Was this during the daytime or nighttime?
A. Oh, it was in the daytime about the middle of the day.
Q. And why were you there at K-Mart that day?
A. Well, I was just doing some shopping at that time.
Q. Did you see him in the store or where?
A. As I was coming out the door to come home, and that man, he, was coming in.
Q. Is that the defendant over there?
A. Yes.
Q. What if anything did you do when you saw him?
A. Well, I hurried to my car before he saw me.
Q. Did you see anything on the way to your car?
A. As I was going out the parking lot, I saw the same car, the one the robber used just sitting right there.
Q. You say the same car, what do you mean by that?
A. I had to pass this car, I had to pass the Chevy to get to my car.
Q. What Chevy?
A. The Chevy that John Barnes was driving.
Q. What happened after you saw the car?
A. I recognized the car and I, and I went to my car and I raced to the telephone.

Q. Where was the telephone?
A. About oh, half a mile down on Simmons, a little store down on Simmons Street.
Q. Whom did you call?
A. I called the police.
Q. Now, what did they say to you?
A. They told me to describe the car.
Q. And did you?
A. I gave them, the, you know, the make of the car and everything.
Q. Then you went home?
A. No, he told me to stay there until he got there.
Q. And then what?
A. And so I did and then uh, we both went to headquarters.
Q. Did you have occasion then to see Detective Monroe?
A. Uh, not that day.
Q. Did you then go home?
A. Uh, I went home.
Q. Now sometime later, did you have occasion to speak to some police officers in your home?
A. Yes.
Q. When was that?
A. Detective Monroe and two others came over to my house with that photograph book.
Q. Before you looked at that book, did he have any conversation with you relative to that book?
A. No, they just came to my apartment, and handed me the book.
Q. And then what happened?
A. We went and, you know, just looked at it.
Q. And you looked in the book and picked this picture?
A. Yes.
Q. This man does not have a beard in the picture.
A. Well, it was the face, it was the man that robbed me. I never forget a face.
Q. What did you say to uh, Detective Monroe or the other detectives?
A. I said, "That's the man."
Q. What else occured in the conversation?
A. They took the book and, and, you know, thanked me.
Q. Anything else?
A. No, they just, then they left.
Q. Alright, I have no further questions at this particular time.

Narrative Style

CLERK: Do you swear that the testimony that you are about to give this court is the truth, the whole truth, and nothing but the truth, so help you God?

MRS. MARSHALL: I do.
JUDGE: Be seated.
Q. Will you please tell the court members and the jury your name.
A. My name is Carol Marshall.
Q. And where do you live?
A. I live at 311 Plum Street.
Q. And how long have you lived in Durham?
A. Oh, 2 years.
Q. Alright, prior to the twenty-first day of November, 1974, uh, how long had you been employed at the Seven–Eleven store on Willowdale Avenue?
A. Um, I'd been employed uh, we came to Durham in August of '73, the fifteenth or so. I started on Spruce and I uh, then I worked all the stores, you know, rotated all the stores in Durham, the Seven–Eleven Stores. And then I made assistant manager on Spruce, and I stayed there for several months. Then I was transferred to Willowdale.
Q. So approximately how long before the twenty-first day of November last year had you been working at the store in Willowdale?
A. Uh, several months.
Q. Now, calling your attention to the twenty-first day of November, a Saturday, what were your working hours that day?
A. Well, I was working from 7 A.M. to 3 P.M. I arrived at the store at 6:30 and opened the store at 7.
Q. Did you have, uh, any other employees with you that day?
A. No.
Q. Now sometime, sometime during that morning, did you have occasion to see, uh, someone in the store?
A. Yes, about 9:20. I saw that man right there.
Q. You're pointing to the man sitting next to Mr. Williams?
A. Yes.
Q. Now prior to his being at the store, did you have any customers?
A. Oh, yes, customers came in the store, but after 9 there was no one in the store but me. And I was talking on the telephone to my sister in Georgia for about 20 minutes. I was still talking on the phone to my sister and then no one came in then until about 20 after 9 and this man came in, that man, John Barnes. I was still talking. He just walked in.
Q. Now would you please tell me where is this phone located in the building?
A. At the door, as you walk in the door. The telephone is there on the wall, right at the door.
Q. And this gentleman who you described as the uh, pointed out as the defendant in this matter, when did you first notice him?
A. Well, when I was talking on the phone.
Q. Alright, now please tell the court and members of the jury what happened after you first saw him.
A. Well, he walked into the store, and I was still talking. He just walked in and he was walking around like he was going to buy something. And, he never did come to the counter or anything, so I just kept talking to my

sister. And then a couple minutes later, this, uh, two people came in the store and I told my sister I had to go because I had some customers. So him and I were still in there, and I hung like I hung up the phone and went to the counter and waited on the couple and they went on out.

Q. Was there anyone in the store with you after that?

A. Well, the defendant and me were in there. And he was still looking around and then, as they went out, and then he, he got some things and set them on the counter, and I went to ring it up and then I was ringing it up and uh, he, he, he walked away and said, "I'd like to have a carton of Kool cigarettes." I said, "Three seventy-five plus tax." And he said, "That's alright." And then he walked back over to the counter where the wine was, and he brought uh, well didn't bring anything back. I thought he would, but he didn't. And so I rung it all up and it came to 7 dollars and 5 cents. I was waiting for more, you know. And I had it all in the bag, about the time he came back and uh I thought he was going to have something else, so I hadn't taxed the 7 dollars and 5 cents, but he didn't bring any more. And, you know, I had the cash register open, and he just leaned over with his gun and said, "I want all your money," you know, "just hand it over." And he made me give it all to him.

Q. Alright, now, did you, uh, what type of gun did he have?

A. Well, it was a small black gun.

Q. And uh, are you familiar with guns?

A. If I look at them very close, I uh . . .

Q. Was this, are you familiar with the difference between a revolver and a pistol?

A. Well, it was short, and it seems like, um, it's about that size.

Q. And, when he, after he made that statement to you, what did you do?

A. Well, I gave him the money. I just said, "Don't shoot me," you know. And he said, "I'm not going to shoot you, just hand me all the money over." I gave him close to a hundred dollars.

Q. Now, when you say he pointed the pistol at you, what part of your body if any did he point this?

A. Just, he just leaned over and just, you know, like that with the gun. And I threw this hand up and said, "Hey don't shoot me, don't shoot me." And uh, just hand him all the money from there and he said, "That one too." So I had to turn around and open the other cash register and give him that money too. Um the other cash register is right behind. And so I gave him all the bills, not the change, and then there is another box, he took it and put it down in his, like in his jacket. And then he said, "Come on." And he made me go in the back room and he closed the door and he said, "Don't come out." And, you know, and I went straight back and went to the side and I ran in there and I heard him, well, it sounded like he got some more wine and I know he got some more cigarettes and he got all the bag, you know, the stuff that I had put in the bag for him. He'd taken all that and got away.

Q. Alright, where is this—you say he made you go to the back of the room?

A. Uh huh. In the back of the store, the stockroom.
Q. Now did he go in the room with you?
A. No, he just he just went and shoved the door. And, you know, he took his hand and pulled the door, and then you know, well I—I didn't try to get back out—inside the store, I just stayed there by the door.
Q. Did he, did he lock the door?
A. No, it doesn't lock, it just closes. When I heard the bell on the door, I—I ran from back there and he had just gotten in his car, and went to Pike Street. And I got some of the license number: It was five-o-nine from his car. It was the last three numbers.
Q. Alright. Now the car the man was driving, was it a brown, a brown 1972 Chevrolet Nova?
OPPOSITION LAWYER: Objection.
JUDGE: Sustained, leading the witness.
Q. Uh, did you remember what type of car, uh, could you describe the car?
A. Well, it was a brownish tan Nova, a Chevy. It was, it was '70—it was '72. It was '72 Chevy.
Q. Okay, then after the car went away, what happened?
A. Well, I phoned the police, and they came right, I guess, a few minutes later. Uh, I can't, I can't recall who came, but they were kind of short. And then, Detective Monroe came. That's him sitting behind that man. I told him, Detective Monroe, I told him what happened and then, uh, well I went home for the day. Well, the manager told me to go on home.
Q. Alright, now was there anything covering this person's face who was in the Seven–Eleven store at that time?
A. Um, he had a beard under here. He still had the same—he's the same face.
Q. And did you have occasion sometime after this day to see him?
A. I saw him after he, uh, robbed me at the store. I can't recall when exactly, but it was about a few days, a week maybe. I saw him at K-Mart in Durham. It was in the daytime about the middle of the day. I was just doing some shopping at that time and uh, I was coming out the door to come home, and that man, he was coming in. I hurried to my car before he saw me. And uh, as I was going out the parking lot, I saw the same car, the one the robber used, just sitting right there. I had to pass this car, I had to pass the Chevy to get to my car. The Chevy that John Barnes was driving. I recognized the car and I, and I went to my car and I raced to the telephone about oh, half a mile down on Simmons, a little store down on Simmons Street and I called the police and they told me to describe the car, and I, I gave them, the, you know, the make of the car and everything. And he told me to stay there until he got there, and so I did and then uh, we both went to headquarters.
Q. Did you have occasion then to see Detective Monroe?
A. Uh, not that day. I went home and sometime later Detective Monroe and two others came over to my house with that photograph book.
Q. Alright, now before you looked at that book, did he have any conversation with you relative to that book?

A. No, they just came to my apartment and handed me the book, and we went and, you know, just looked in it.

Q. And you looked in the book and picked this picture?

A. Yes. This, this man does not have a beard in the picture but it was the face. Like it was the man that robbed me. I never forget a face.

Q. And what did you say to Detective Monroe and the other detectives?

A. I said, "That's the man," and then they took the book and, you know, thanked me and then they left.

Q. Alright, I have no further questions as this particular time.

3

TRANSCRIPTS OF HYPERCORRECT AND FORMAL STYLES

The study of hypercorrect and formal speech styles involved two experimental tapes. The experimental stimulus tapes were based on the testimony of a male witness who spoke in a HYPERCORRECT style similar to that of several other witnesses we observed during the Summer of 1974. The experimental tape in the hypercorrect style closely replicates the original testimony on which it is based, whereas the experimental tape using the formal style represents a ''doctored'' version of the original testimony in which hypercorrect vocabulary and grammar are eliminated as much as possible. Both hypercorrect and formal styles and the experimental study of their effects are discussed in the text on pages 83–87.

The transcripts of the hypercorrect and formal styles of testifying are intended primarily to demonstrate differences of vocabulary and grammar between the two styles. As in Appendix 2, ordinary English spelling, punctuation, and writing conventions are used whenever possible.

Hypercorrect Style

CLERK: Do you solemnly swear that the evidence you shall now give the court and the jury in the case being heard to be the truth, the whole truth, and nothing but the truth, so help you God?

A. I do.
Q. What is your full name please sir?
A. John D. Watson, Junior.
Q. Mr. Watson, how old are you?
A. Twenty-five years old, sir.
Q. Mr. Watson, where do you live?
A. Forty-one-thirty Missouri Street, Durham, North Carolina.
Q. On June tenth, 1974, by whom were you employed, and in what capacity?
A. Smithfield Ambulance Service, ambulance attendant.
Q. Did you have occasion to be working at or about 12 o'clock midnight?
A. Yes sir, I did.
Q. Uh, on the night of June the ninth and the early morning hours of June the tenth?
A. Yes sir.
Q. How many hours had you been on duty that day?
A. Eight hours. We were just ready to go off duty when a call came in.
Q. At that time, did you have occasion to go to a residence on Sheridan Avenue?
A. Yes sir, we did.
Q. Where was that sir?
A. Four-twelve West Sheridan.
Q. And whom did you see there?
A. Well, the patient, uh, Mrs. Edith Davis was in a reclining position. She was lying on a bed.
Q. Were you working alone?
A. No, I was assisting Mr. Delbert Norris.
Q. And did you often work with Mr. Norris?
A. Yes sir.
Q. Would you say that you and Mr. Norris have become friends as a result of your working together?
A. Yes sir, I would say that.
Q. What did you and Mr. Norris do after you arrived?
A. Well, I had a very very rudiment knowledge of medicine, or . . .
Q. Of . . . very what? Excuse me.
A. Ah, I was a novice more or less . . . in this, uh working at this position. And Mr. Norris was very proficient at this, uh, because he had quite a bit of previous training with it, and uh . . . he examined her initially of course. And I just watched.
Q. After Mr. Norris's initial examination of Mrs. Edith Davis, what was done with her, if anything?
A. After Mr. Norris determined that she was in somewhat less than a dire condition, I returned to the emergency vehicle.
Q. What was the purpose of returning to the ambulance?
A. I brought a stretcher.
Q. And what was the purpose of bringing the stretcher?

A. We had to transport her on a stretcher because the patient was not ambulatory.
Q. Was she put onto the stretcher in the house?
A. Yes sir, she sure was.
Q. And where was she taken thereafter?
A. She was taken out the uh front door to the vehicle, which was on the left . . . a matter of yards, just a few steps.
Q. And was she placed in the ambulance?
A. Yes sir, she was.
Q. Through which doors was she placed in it?
A. The rear doors sir. Double doors in the rear.
Q. In what side of it was she placed?
A. The left side of the vehicle, facing . . . the rear.
Q. Now, will you describe how, if in anyway, the stretcher is held in place on the left side of the uh . . .
A. Yes sir, it certainly is. It's moored. In other words, ah, there are clamps . . . on the uh panel of the van. The strecher slid into the vehicle, and these clamps are encircled around the uh, stretcher. In other words, it holds it in place with two clamps.
Q. Of what material are the clamps?
A. They are made of some type of metal.
Q. And was the stretcher moored to the steel or metal clamps?
A. Yes sir, the stretcher was moored to the clamps, because you push it into place and it snaps. It locks tight.
Q. Are the clamps affixed to the body of the vehicle itself?
A. Yes sir. Yes sir. They are.
Q. Are you absolutely sure that when you and Mr. Norris put Mrs. Davis into the ambulance that you secured the stretcher?
A. Yes sir, I am sure I did.
Q. After the patient was put into the ambulance, did you get in?
A. Yes sir, I did.
Q. And in what area of the ambulance were you riding?
A. I was sitting, opposite of Mrs. Davis. Uh, she was on the left. Her stretcher was moored to the panel, to the vehicle. I was on the right-hand side, setting on another stretcher, over there on the right-hand side, facing Mrs. Davis, attending to Mrs. Davis.
Q. Then you would be on the right-hand side, looking to the left-hand side of the ambulance?
A. Yes sir. Right.
Q. Where did Mr. Norris, uh, what was his position in the vehicle?
A. (cough) Excuse me, he was sitting in the front left, driving the vehicle.
Q. Was anyone else in the ambulance?
A. Yes sir, there was a lady on the right. Mrs. Gurney.
Q. Now, after Mrs. Davis was placed in there in the ambulance, where were you going?

A. We were going towards Duke Hospital.

Q. Did Mr. Norris turn on the siren?

A. Mr. Norris always turns on the siren when we have a serious case.

Q. Are you sure that Mr. Norris turned on the siren on this particular occasion?

A. Yes sir, I believe he did.

Q. And was it on during the entire trip?

A. Yes sir, I believe it was.

Q. Did you complete your travel to Duke Hospital?

A. No, no sir, we never got to Duke Hospital.

Q. In the course of traveling to the hospital, did you have an occasion to be on Academy Street at or near its intersection with Roxboro Road in the city of Durham?

A. Yes sir, we did.

Q. Prior to the entering of the intersection of Roxboro Road, on what street was the ambulance traveling?

A. We were headed west, on Academy.

Q. Immediately prior to entering the intersection, was Mrs. Davis alive?

A. Yes sir, she was.

Q. Do you remember entering the intersection?

A. Well, I was not absolutely cognizant of my surroundings, because, I was attending to the patient. I was facing the patient. I was facing south . . . and the patient was facing east.

Q. That was in a direction toward uh . . .

A. In a direction toward . . .

Q. East on Academy Street.

A. Yes sir, east on Academy Street. And I was attending to the patient. I had my head in a somewhat tilted position because I was comforting and soothing the patient. And . . . and I didn't have occasion to look up prior to impact. Although I did see some reflections of lights.

Q. Did you hear anything?

A. Yes sir, I, I did hear brakes.

Q. And uh, you saw . . . you observed what?

A. Well, after I heard, I can't, I can't really, I can't definitely state whether the lights or the brakes came first, but, I rotated my head slightly to the right, and looked directly behind Mr. Norris, and I saw reflections of lights, and uh, very very very instantaneously after that, I heard a very very loud explosion, from my standpoint of view it would've been an implosion because everything was forced out like this, like a grenade thrown into a room. And uh, it was, it was, it was terrifically loud.

Q. When you first heard the brakes, could you tell which direction you heard them coming from?

A. Well, since I was not cognizant of my location, I could not ascertain from which direction the vehicle was coming from.

Q. Well, were you able to tell the direction from the lights?

A. No sir, it would be impossible to tell that.

Q. Did you happen to observe the condition of the traffic light as the emergency
    vehicle entered the intersection?
A. Yes sir, I did.
Q. And what was its condition?
A. It was green as we entered, sir.
Q. Now, how is it that you remember so well about the condition of the light
    if you were busy attending to the patient?
A. Well, I just happened to look up as I saw the reflection of the automobile
    headlights.
Q. Immediately after the collision, what happened to you?
A. Well, directly after the implosion . . . I vaguely remember being hurled in
    some direction. I know not where, but . . . I went . . . I hurdled through
    the air some distance. I must have been unconscious at the time. I did
    awake briefly, and during that interim, Mr. Norris was standing over me
    . . . uh, perhaps more than likely, getting ready to administer first aid. But
    I, I relapsed into a comatose state, and, I, I can't remember anything after
    that for the next 72 hours or so.
Q. Immediately prior to the entry of the ambulance in the intersection of Rox-
    boro and Academy, was Mrs. Edith Davis alive?
A. Yes sir, she was.
Q. And do you have any independent knowledge of your own as to what
    happened to Mrs. Davis after the accident?
A. No, not of my own knowledge.
Q. I have no further questions to ask of this witness.

Formal Style

CLERK: Do you solemnly swear that the evidence you shall now give the
    court and the jury in the case being heard to be the truth, the whole truth,
    and nothing but the truth, so help you God?
A. I do.
Q. What is your full name please sir?
A. John D. Watson, Junior.
Q. Mr. Watson, how old are you?
A. Twenty-five, sir.
Q. Mr. Watson, where do you live?
A. Forty-one-thirty Missouri Street, Durham, North Carolina.
Q. On June tenth, 1974, by whom were you employed, and in what capacity?
A. Smithfield Ambulance Service, ambulance attendant.
Q. Did you have occasion to be working at or about 12 o'clock midnight?
A. Yes sir, I did.
Q. On the night of June the ninth and the early morning hours of June the
    tenth?

A. Yes sir.

Q. How many hours had you been on duty that day?

A. Eight hours. We were just ready to go off duty when a call came in.

Q. At that time, did you have occasion to go to a residence on Sheridan Avenue?

A. Yes sir, we did.

Q. Where was that sir?

A. Four-twelve West Sheridan.

Q. Whom did you see there?

A. Well, the patient, uh, Mrs. Edith Davis, was lying down. She was lying on a bed.

Q. Were you working alone?

A. No, I was assisting Mr. Delbert Norris.

Q. Did you often work with Mr. Norris?

A. Yes sir.

Q. Would you say that you and Mr. Norris have become friends as a result of your working together?

A. Yes sir.

Q. What did you and Mr. Norris do after you arrived?

A. Well, I had only a limited knowledge of how to examine patients, but Mr. Norris had had quite a bit of previous training with it, so he examined her initially, of course. And I just watched.

Q. After Mr. Norris's initial examination of Mrs. Edith Davis, what was done with her, if anything?

A. After Mr. Norris determined that she was in a condition to be moved, I returned to the emergency vehicle.

Q. What was the purpose of returning to the ambulance?

A. I brought a stretcher.

Q. What was the purpose of bringing the stretcher?

A. We had to move Mrs. Davis on a stretcher, because she was in no condition to walk.

Q. Was she put onto the stretcher in the house?

A. Yes sir, she was.

Q. And where was she taken thereafter?

A. She was taken out the front door to the ambulance which was a few yards away to the left.

Q. And was she placed in the ambulance?

A. Yes sir, she was.

Q. Through which doors was she placed in it?

A. The double doors in the rear, sir.

Q. In what side of the vehicle was she placed?

A. The left side, facing . . . the rear.

Q. Now, will you describe how, if in any way, the stretcher is held in place on the left side of the . . .

A. Yes sir. There are clamps . . . on the panel of the van. The stretcher slides into the van and these clamps encircle the stretcher and hold it in place.

Q. Of what material are the clamps?
A. They are made of some type of metal.
Q. Was the stretcher moored to the steel or metal clamps?
A. Yes sir, the stretcher was moored to the clamps. You push it into place and it snaps. It locks tight.
Q. Are the clamps affixed to the body of the vehicle itself?
A. Yes sir. They are.
Q. Are you absolutely sure that when you and Mr. Norris put Mrs. Davis into the ambulance that you secured the stretcher properly?
A. Yes sir, I am.
Q. After the patient was put into the ambulance, did you get in?
A. Yes sir, I did.
Q. In what area of the ambulance were you riding?
A. I was sitting opposite Mrs. Davis. She was on the left. Her stretcher was moored to the floor. I was on the right-hand side, sitting on another stretcher, facing Mrs. Davis, and attending to her.
Q. Then you would be on the right-hand side, looking to the left-hand side of the ambulance?
A. Yes.
Q. Where did Mr. Norris, what was his position in the ambulance?
A. (cough) Excuse me, he was sitting in the front left, driving.
Q. Was anyone else in the ambulance?
A. Yes sir, there was a lady on the right. Mrs. Gurney.
Q. Now, after Mrs. Davis was placed in there in the ambulance, where were you going?
A. We were going to Duke Hospital.
Q. Did Mr. Norris turn on the siren?
A. Mr. Norris always turns on the siren when we have a serious case.
Q. Are you sure, though, that he did turn on the siren on this particular occasion?
A. Yes sir, I believe he did.
Q. Was it on during the entire trip?
A. Yes sir, I believe it was.
Q. Did you complete your travel to Duke Hospital?
A. No sir, we did not.
Q. In the course of traveling to the hospital, did you have an occasion to be on Academy Street at or near its intersection with Roxboro Road in the city of Durham?
A. Yes sir, we did.
Q. Prior to entering the intersection of Roxboro Road, on what street was the ambulance traveling?
A. We were headed west on Academy.
Q. Immediately prior to entering the intersection, was Mrs. Davis alive?
A. Yes sir, she was.
Q. Do you remember entering the intersection?
A. Well, I was not aware of the surroundings because I was attending to the

patient. I was facing the patient. I was facing the side of the ambulance, and the patient was facing the back.

Q. That was in a direction toward . . .

A. In a direction toward . . .

Q. East on Academy Street?

A. Yes sir, east on Academy Street. My head was tilted somewhat because I was comforting and soothing the patient. And um . . . and I didn't have occasion to look up prior to impact, although I did see some lights.

Q. Did you hear anything?

A. Yes sir, I did hear ah brakes.

Q. And uh, you saw . . . you observed what?

A. Well, after I heard, I can't definitely state whether the lights or the brakes came first, but I turned slightly to the right, and looked directly behind Mr. Norris, and I saw some lights, and uh, immediately after that, I heard a very loud explosion, like a grenade thrown into a room. And uh, it was, it was terrifically loud.

Q. When you first heard the brakes, could you tell which direction you heard them coming from?

A. Well, since I was not aware of our location, I could not tell which direction the vehicle was coming from.

Q. Were you able to tell the direction from the lights?

A. No sir, it was impossible to tell.

Q. Did you happen to observe the condition of the traffic light as the emergency vehicle entered the intersection?

A. Yes sir, I did.

Q. What was its condition?

A. It was green as we entered, sir.

Q. Now, how is it that you remember so well about the condition of the light if you were busy attending to the patient?

A. Well, I just happened to look up as I saw the reflection of the automobile headlights.

Q. Immediately after the collision, what happened to you?

A. Well, directly after the collision . . . I vaguely remember being hurled in some direction. I don't know where, but . . . I went . . . I hurled through the air some distance. I must have been unconscious at the time. I did awake briefly, and during that time, Mr. Norris was standing over me, uh, probably getting ready to administer first aid. But uh, I lost consciousness, and I can't remember anything after that for the next 3 days or so.

Q. Immediately prior to entry of the ambulance in the intersection of Roxboro and Academy, was Mrs. Edith Davis alive?

A. Yes sir, she was.

Q. Do you have any independent knowledge of your own as to what happened to Mrs. Davis after the accident?

A. No, not of my own knowledge.

Q. I have no further questions to ask of this witness.

TRANSCRIPTS OF OVERLAPPING AND NONOVERLAPPING SPEECH

The study of INTERRUPTIONS and SIMULTANEOUS SPEECH involved four experimental tapes. By their nature, cross-examinations of witnesses are more hostile than direct examinations. They contain more verbal clashes: interruptions of the witness by the lawyer (or vice versa), both parties speaking at once, and aggressive questioning. The experimental stimulus tapes were based on the testimony of a male witness who was involved in several types of verbal clashes with the examining attorney during cross-examination.

As explained in the text on pages 87–91, one tape included about equal domination of lawyer and witness in these clashes.[1] Two additional tapes contain a similar number of clashes, but differ with regard to which party dominates. In one, called *Overlapping Speech—Lawyer Dominates,* the attorney perseveres roughly three-quarters of the time. In another, called *Overlapping Speech—Witness Dominates,* the attorney perseveres only one-quarter of the time.

The form chosen to show overlaps is the simplest one I could devise. Intervals of overlapping speech are italicized, underlined, and numbered

---

[1] Persons with interest in CONVERSATIONAL ANALYSIS (see Sacks *et al.* 1974) may wish to note that overlaps are distributed randomly with regard to which party is speaking at the time the overlap begins. In addition, approximately half of the overlaps occur at TURN RELEVANCE PLACES and half do not. This replicates rather closely the actual situation we observed in the original testimony on which all experimental stimulus tapes are based.

in sequence within each transcript. Readers wishing to study patterns of dominance and acquiescence can easily locate the beginning and end of each overlap and thereby note which party, if any, was already speaking and which party persists.

The three transcripts included here are the NONOVERLAPPING STYLE (used for control purposes in the experiments) and the OVERLAPPING STYLE—LAWYER DOMINATES and the OVERLAPPING STYLE—WITNESS DOMINATES. It seemed needless duplication to include the transcript of the experimental tape in which neither dominates since its characteristics can easily be imagined after studying the ones included here.

Nonoverlapping Style

CROSS-EXAMINATION

Q. Now, Mr. Nesbitt, how far, uh, do you say you live from your father's house?

A. The third house.

Q. The third house?

A. Yes.

Q. Are you married?

A. Yes.

Q. Do you live with your wife?

A. Yes, I do.

Q. Now, Mr. Nesbitt, uh, you and your father have had considerable trouble, haven't you?

A. The fact is that if my father would leave us alone and quit messing with guns and if he'd stop his drinking, we wouldn't have any trouble. I have a wife and two children that we, I mean, when you're called at 1, 2, 3, 4 o'clock in the morning, and he come, have someone coming up, beating on your door, yeah, there's trouble when he's drunk.

Q. All right, I asked you if there hadn't just a few days or weeks, just a short time before this incident . . . you beat your father up?

A. No. No, I didn't.

Q. You did not?

A. No, I didn't.

Q. Well, did you have any controversy at all?

A. No!

Q. Did not?

A. No.

Q. All right, I ask you if you haven't beaten him up in the last week?

A. Yes, and do you know why? Another gun episode.

Q. Another gun episode?

A. That's right.

Q. And, if you didn't cut, put a cut on his face here and break his ribs?
A. Well, when you start, gonna shoot somebody, you doggone right better, threatening me, gonna shoot me, sue me . . .
Q. All right. You got it in for your father haven't you?
A. After all these things which comes from guns and his drinking, yes I do. When I'm threatened, when I haven't done anything, when I'm tending to my own business, got my own family, and yet I can't be left alone . . .
Q. Oh, but you do have it in for your father, don't you? You've had a controversy going with him for a long time, haven't you?
A. Not until I'm threatened that I'm going to be shot, or sued by his 24-year-old girlfriend. It's not just that I'm his son.
Q. Now, on this particular incident that we've talked about, it was early in the morning, wasn't it?
A. Yeah, it was.
Q. It was about 6 o'clock in the morning, wasn't it?
A. No, it started before then.
Q. Well, what time did it start?
A. It started between 4:30 and 5. He waited until after 5 to usually start his trouble.
Q. Now what trouble did you say he started on this particular morning?
A. On this particular morning?
Q. That's correct.
A. Well, he had my mother call me, and in the background he was threatening her, he has a foul mouth when he gets drunk.
Q. Well, did you talk to your father at all that morning?
A. He couldn't have talked; all he could do was slur, but I could understand what he was saying. But my mother had already told me if she called, if she needed help, and I knew she did—I could hear it, because he'd start hitting her, that I was to call the police.
Q. I'm talking about on this particular morning, sir, could you stick to this particular morning?
A. I'm talking about this particular morning. I knew I had to call the police.
Q. On this particular morning, did you have any conversation at all with your father?
A. No. Because he wouldn't talk, he made my mother talk. He told her what to say.
Q. Oh, he made your mother talk?
A. Yeah, and he told her what to say.
Q. All right, now, you were at home all this time, were you not?
A. Yes, I was.
Q. Three doors down?
A. On the telephone you can hear someone standing beside another person telling 'em what to say, yeah, you can hear it.
Q. All right, but all this was on the telephone was it not, because you said, because he never, at one time, went on your premises, did he, on that particular morning, on April the first?

A. I wouldn't swear to it.

Q. Well, would you swear that he did not?

A. . . . No.

Q. Did you ever see him at any time, on April the first during the morning on your premises?

A. No.

Q. Did you ever go to his house, other than the occasion that you mentioned you went down with the police officer?

A. Yes, I went down with the officer, and that was it.

Q. I mean other than that.

A. No.

Q. Now, and if he never talked to you on the telephone?

A. No.

Q. And he never, he never went to your house, and you never went to his house?

A. Only with the officer.

Q. All right, now, how can you, how do you, uh, what is the basis upon your position that he was bothering you or threatening you at any time?

A. Well, they're my father and mother. I heard the conversation on the phone, and I know what's going on. That's why . . .

Q. Your mother called you on the telephone, did she?

A. That's right.

Q. And what did she call you about?

A. She called me because of him. He told her . . . oh, he wanted his gun.

Q. He wanted you, uh, to return his rifle that you took from him, did he not?

A. Mm-hmm. Yeah, he did.

Q. All right, did he make any threats to you through your mother?

A. All I knew she needed help and that was it. I heard enough of it.

Q. What did she tell you that would indicate to you that she needed help?

A. She told me a long time ago that if she called, and I knew there was trouble, to definitely call the police right away so she could leave.

Q. All right. But this call, did I understand you to tell the jury, that because your mother called up, and told you that your father wanted you to return the rifle, that was sufficient evidence for you to call the police department?

A. Yes, because he was drunk.

Q. Well, how do you know he was drunk? When was the last time you'd seen him?

A. Because my father goes to bed when he's not. He doesn't—he's a different person. There's two different people.

Q. When is the last time before this incident that you had seen your father?

A. Oh, probably the day before.

Q. And you, uh, you did not see him from the day before until the police officer came down and opened the door, and you give this court the opinion that he was drunk, is that correct?

A. Well, he is my father, and I know him quite well.

Q. You, you just assume that he was drunk, is that correct?

A. No, I'm not assuming, no.

Q. Well, what now, what do you base your testimony on that he was drunk?

A. Well, I know him, that's the difference. When you've lived with a person, when you've grown up with him all your life, you know him.

Q. And you know he's always drunk, is that correct?

A. I know when he is, and when he isn't.

Q. Wha—, even though you don't see him or don't talk to him?

A. That's right, that's right.

Q. All right. Now . . . what did you tell the police officer when you called on the telephone?

A. I asked him to come to 1720 Sarris Avenue.

Q. That's the home of your father, or your home?

A. That's my father's home.

Q. And what did you tell 'em the reason that you wanted him to come there?

A. Because I wanted my mother to be able to leave safely.

Q. Well, did your mother ever state to you that she could not leave the house?

A. He has, he has kept her in it before, yes.

Q. Did your mother, on this particular instance over the telephone to you, state that she could not leave the house?

A. I asked her, I told my mother to come on up here. She said she couldn't.

Q. Well, did she tell you the reason she couldn't come, was it something with her husband?

A. She couldn't say that in front of him.

Q. How do you know she couldn't?

A. Because when I had lived at home she couldn't say anything, neither could I . . . on those occasions when he's like that you can't, not unless you want to get hit.

Q. All right, but your mother made no indication to you on this particular occasion?

A. Yes, I asked her if she wanted to leave, and she said, "Uh-huh," and that was it.

Q. Well . . . she said she wanted to leave?

A. That's right.

Q. And, did she tell you there was any trouble between her and her husband?

A. Now listen, when you're going through things like this you don't have time to go into details. If you'd never been through that such you would know.

Q. Well, do you mind to take a little time and go into details now?

A. No, but I'm just trying to tell you how it is.

Q. Well now I ask you sir, if you can tell this court, this jury of this court, as to what exactly what your mother said to you that would indicate there was need of a police officer?

A. I said to her, "Do you want to leave, do you need help?" She said, "Uh-huh."

Q. I see, it's now that, "You need help."

A. That's right.

Q. . . . Now uh, what time did you make the call?

A. I don't know.
Q. Well, how long was it before the police officer came down?
A. I don't know that either.
Q. Well, was it light when you came down?
A. No, it was dark.
Q. It was early in the morning; it was dark.
A. Yes, it was.
Q. All right, and then, uh, did uh, how many police officers arrived on the scene?
A. At first it was just the one.
Q. Just Edward Browning?
A. Yes.
Q. This fellow right here?
A. Uh-huh.
Q. Now, whenever you arrived at the house, uh, you were already there, I mean with the police officer?
A. No, I was not there. Oh, when what?
Q. When the police officer arrived at the house, you were already down there.
A. No, I wasn't. I said I was in front of my home, flagging him down.
Q. Oh, your home.
A. I don't go down there anymore when he's drunk.
Q. Oh, I see. Mr., uh, Mr. Nesbitt, uh, did the officer go to your house or to his house?
A. He went on down to Sarris, um, where my father was, I told him I was walking on down there, and um, he drove his car on down.
Q. Did you, did you go up to the porch before he got there, or after?
A. Um, we more or less went together.
Q. He waited to talk to you first?
A. Yes.
Q. All right, and then he went up to the porch. Is that right, the officer did? Where were you?
A. I was right there with him.
Q. All right now, your father's house has a step on the porch, does it not?
A. Yes.
Q. And it's a front door—has a front door, does it not?
A. Storm door, and then the front door.
Q. Storm door, and the door has a venetian blind type thing on it, does it not?
A. Mm-hmm.
Q. And at the time you went up there the venetian blinds were closed, were they not?
A. Yeah.
Q. All right, now at the time that you went up to the door, I ask you if the officer did not bang on the door vigorously?
A. I knocked.
Q. Did the officer knock?
A. I knocked to begin with. I wanted to make sure my mother was all right.

Q. Well, where was the officer when you knocked?
A. He was standing right beside me or behind me.
Q. All right. And then, uh, whenever the, uh, I ask you if the blinds had just cracked open, is that correct?
A. To me they stretched open, they lifted open.
Q. Stretched open, and when they stretched open you saw this pistol, didn't you?
A. Yes, I did.
Q. And it was pointed directly at you, wasn't it?
A. Yes, it came out. He, see, he thought it was me rather than the police officer.
Q. He thought it was you. He didn't have any idea it was a police officer out there.
A. No, because he knew that my mother had just called me.
Q. All right. And uh, what did, uh, what did you do after you saw that?
A. What did I do when I saw that? I backed up.
Q. Backed up. Now what did your father do?
A. He . . . um, he ran, then started running all over the house.
Q. He didn't open the door, did he?
A. No.
Q. He closed the blinds and went back in the house, didn't he. As far as you can tell.
A. He ran to the kitchen where there's no blinds.
Q. All right then, uh, what happened after that? Now I ask you if the door didn't open immediately after that?
A. No, uh, that's when the other officers came and I went behind the car because I didn't want to be in line with any gun fire.
Q. Well, did uh Officer Browning go out and make a call for other officers?
A. They had come up while we were on the porch.
Q. They all came up about the same time.
A. That's right.
Q. And Officer Browning remained on the porch, did he not?
A. I believe so. Well, no, he started, he got down off the porch too, after he saw the gun.
Q. . . . Did the officer before he knocked on the door or at the time that he knocked on the door, did you hear him state or tell or notify the person then that he was a police officer?
A. Yes.
Q. What did he say?
A. He told him to put the gun away, that he wanted to talk to him.
Q. All right. Well, that was after the gun came through the venetian blinds.
A. That's right.
Q. Now, before you knocked, or at the time you knocked did the police officer say anything that would attempt to identify himself as a police officer?
A. I . . . right then I can't really state what was said by the police officer. I don't know.

Q.   . . . Now, uh, Mr. Nesbitt, I meant to ask you at the time, I should have asked you, at the time you made this telephone call to the police officers, did you identify yourself?

A.   Yes, I think they usually ask who's calling.

Q.   I ask you if you didn't tell 'em. You, you refused to tell 'em.

A.   No. I don't refuse to tell the police who I am when I make a call. They usually want to know who's calling and your address, and I give it to 'em.

Q.   Do you recall exactly what you told the officer, the person who answered the telephone over at the police station what was going on at the house?

A.   Ah yes, I would think I told that, uh, I wanted my mother to be able to leave the house because my father was drinking.

Q.   You told 'em that your father was drunk. Drinking, you said. You said, you wanted your mother to get out.

A.   That's right.

Q.   Did you tell the police officer that your mother had asked you to help her get out?

A.   No, I don't remember exactly what I said at the time.

Q.   All right . . . Would uh, your mother when she called, the reason she called was to ask you to bring the gun, wasn't it?

A.   Yes, probably.

Q.   And then you begin to ask her these other questions about, well, as you say you asked her.

A.   Mm-hmm.

Q.   All right . . . That's all I have to ask.

Overlapping Style—Lawyer Dominates

CROSS-EXAMINATION

Q.   Now, Mr. Nesbitt, how far, uh, do you say you live from your father's house?

A.   The third house.

Q.   The third house?

A.   Yes.

Q.   Are you married?

A.   Yes.

Q.   Do you live with your wife?

A.   Yes, I do.

Q.   Now, Mr. Nesbitt, uh, you and your father have had considerable trouble, haven't you?

A.   The fact is that if my father would leave us alone and quit messing with guns and if he'd stop his drinking, we wouldn't have any trouble. I have a wife and two children that we, I mean, when you're called at 1, 2, 3, 4

o'clock in the morning, and he come, have someone coming up, beating on
your door, yeah, there's trouble *when*—

                    1
Q. *All right,* I asked you if there hadn't just a few days or weeks, just a short

    1
time before this incident . . . you beat your father up?
A. No. No, I didn't.
Q. You did not?
A. No, I didn't.
Q. Well, did you have any controversy at all?
A. No!
Q. Did not?
A. No.
Q. All right, I ask you if you hadn't beaten him up in the last week?
A. Yes, and do you know why?
Q. Well, I—*I didn't ask you that.*

                    2
A. *Another gun episode.*

                    2
Q. Another gun episode?
A. That's right. But *I*—

                    3
Q. *And* if you didn't cut, put a cut on his face here *and break* his ribs?

    3   4
A. *Well,* when you start, gonna shoot somebody, you doggone right better,

    4
threatening me, gonna shoot me, *sue*—

                              5
Q. *All right.* You got it in for your father, haven't you?

    5
A. After all these things which comes from guns and his drinking, yes I do.
Q. And *you been beating him up?*

                    6
A. *When I'm threatened,* when I haven't done anything, when I'm tending to

                    6
my own business, got my own family, and yet I can't be left alone . . .
Q. Oh, but you do have it in for your father, don't you? You've had a con-
    troversy going with him for a long time, haven't you?
A. Not until I'm threatened that I'm going to be shot, or sued by his 24-year-
    old girlfriend. It's not just that I'm his son.
Q. Now, on this particular incident that we've talked about, it was early in the
    morning wasn't it?
A. Yeah, it was.
Q. It was about 6 o'clock in the morning, wasn't it?

A. No, it started before then.

Q. Well, what time did it start?

A. It started between 4:30 and 5. He waited until after 5 to usually start his trouble.

Q. Now what trouble did you say he started on this particular morning?

A. On this particular morning?

Q. That's correct.

A. Well, he had my mother call me, and in the background he was threatening her, he has a foul mouth when he gets drunk.

Q. Well, did you talk to your father at all that morning?

A. He couldn't have talked; all he could do was slur, but I could understand what he was say *in—*
$$\overline{7}$$

Q. *Well* if you did not talk *to him on the telephone—*
$$\overline{7}\overline{8}$$

A. *But my mother had already* told me if she called, if she needed help, and
$$\overline{8}$$
I knew she did—I could hear it, because he'd start hitting her, that I was to call the police.

Q. I'm talking about on this particular morning, sir, *could you stick to this particular morning?*
$$\overline{9}$$

A. *I'm talking about this particular morning. I knew* I had to call the police.
$$\overline{9}$$

Q. On this particular morning, did you have any conversation at all with your father?

A. No. Because he wouldn't talk, he made my mother talk. *He—*
$$\overline{10}$$

Q. *Oh,* he made your mother talk?
$$\overline{10}$$

A. Yeah, and he told her what to say.

Q. All right, now, you were at home all this time, were you not?

A. Yes, I was.

Q. Three doors down?

A. On the telephone you can hear someone standing beside another person telling 'em what to say, yeah, you can hear it.

Q. All right, but all this was on the telephone was it not, because you said, because he never, at one time, went on your premises, did he, on that particular morning, *on April the first?*
$$\overline{11}$$

A. *I wouldn't swear* to it.
$$\overline{11}$$

Q. Well, would you swear that he did not?

A. . . . No.

Q. Did you ever see him at any time, on April the first during the morning on your premises?
A. No.
Q. Did you ever go to his house, other than the occasion that you mentioned you went down with the police officer?
A. Yes, I went down with the police officer, _and—_
                                                    12
Q. _I mean_ other than that.
        12
A. No.
Q. Now, and if he never talked to you on the telephone?
A. No.
Q. And he never, he never went to your house, and you never went to his house?
A. Only with the officer.
Q. All right, now, how can you, how do you, uh, what is the basis upon your position that he was bothering you or threatening you at any time?
A. Well, they're my father and mother. I heard the conversation on the phone, and I know what's going on. That's why . . .
Q. Your mother called you on the telephone, did she?
A. That's right.
Q. And what did she call you about?
A. She called me because of him. He told her . . . oh, he wanted his gun.
Q. He wanted you, uh, to return his rifle that you took from him, did he not?
A. Mm-hmm. Yeah, he did.
Q. All right, did he make any threats to you through your mother?
A. All I knew she needed help and that was _it. I—_
                                                    13
Q. _Now what did_ she tell you that would indicate to you that _she needed_
        13
    help?
     14
A. _She told me a long_ time ago that if she called, and I knew there was trouble,
        14
    to definitely call the police right away so she could leave.
Q. All right. _But this call—_ Did I understand you to tell this jury, that because
                15
    your mother called up, and told you that your father wanted you to return the rifle, that was sufficient evidence for you to call the police department?
A. _So she could leave._
        15
A. Yes because he was drunk _and—_
                16

Q. <u>*Well, how*</u> do you know he was drunk? When was the last
16
time you'd seen him?
17

A. <u>*Because my, my father*</u> goes to bed when he's not. He doesn't—he's a dif-
17
ferent person. There's two <u>*differ—*</u>
18

Q. <u>*When is the*</u> last time before this incident that you had seen your father?
18

A. Oh, probably the day before.

Q. And you, uh, you did not see him from the day before until the police officer down and opened the door, and you give this court the opinion that he was drunk, is that correct?

A. Well, he is my father, and I know him quite well.

Q. You, you just assume that he was drunk, is that correct?

A. No, I'm not assuming, no.

Q. Well, what now, what do you base your testimony on that he was drunk?

A. Well, I know him, that's the difference. When you've lived with a person, when you've grown up with him all your life, you know him.

Q. And you know he's always drunk, is that correct?

A. I know when he is, and when he isn't.

Q. Wha—, even though you don't see him or <u>*don't talk to him?*</u>
19

A. <u>*That's right,*</u> that's right.
19

Q. All right. Now . . . what did you tell the police officer when you called on the telephone?

A. I asked him to come to 1720 Sarris Avenue.

Q. That's the home of your father, or your home?

A. That's my father's home.

Q. And what did you tell 'em the reason that you wanted him to come there?

A. Because I wanted my mother to be able to leave safely. Now <u>*whe—*</u>
20

Q. <u>*Well, did*</u> your mother ever state to you that she could not leave the house?
20

A. He has, he has kept her in it before, yes.

Q. Did your mother, on this particular instance over the telephone <u>*to you, state that she could not leave the house?*</u>
21

A. <u>*I asked her, I told my mother to come on*</u> up here. She said she couldn't.
21

Q. Well, did she tell you the reason she couldn't come, was it <u>*something with her husband?*</u>
22

A. *She couldn't, she couldn't* say that in front *of—*
         22   23

Q. *How do* you know she couldn't?
       23

A. Because when I had lived at home she couldn't say anything, neither could
    I . . . on those occasions when he's like that you can't, not unless you want
    to get hit.

Q. All right, but your mother made no indication to you on this particular
    occasion that she couldn't?
                     24

A. *Yes, I asked her if she* wanted to leave, and she said, "Uh-huh," and that
           24
    was it.

Q. Well . . . she said she wanted to leave?

A. That's right.

Q. And, did she tell you there was any trouble between her and her husband?

A. Now listen, when you going through things like this you don't have time
    to go into details. If you'*d nev—*
                     25

Q. *Well, do* you mind to take a little time and go into details now?
       25

A. No, but I'm just trying to tell *you—*
                             26

Q. *Well, now* I ask you sir, if you can tell this court, this jury of this court,
       26
    as to what exactly what your mother said to you that would indicate
    there was need of a police officer?
                   27

A. *I said to her, "Do you want* to leave, do you need help?" She said, "Uh-
                   27
    huh."

Q. I see, it's now that, "You need help."

A. That's right.

Q. . . . Now uh, what time did you make the call?

A. I don't know.

Q. Well, how long was it before the police officer came down?

A. I don't know that either.

Q. Well, was it light when you came down?

A. No, it was dark.

Q. It was early in the morning; it was dark.

A. Yes, it was.

Q. All right, and then, uh, did uh, how many police officers arrived on the
    scene?

A. And first it was just the one, and um, *h—*
                                             28

Q. *Just* Edward Browning?
        28
A. Yes.
Q. This fellow right here?
A. Uh-huh.
Q. Now, whenever you arrived at the house, uh, you were already there, I
        mean with the police officer?
A. No, I was not there. Oh, when what?
Q. When the police officer arrived at the house, you were already down there.
A. No I wasn't. I said I was in front of my home, *flaggi—*
                                                            29
Q. *Oh, your home.* All right did you *go with him?*
                29   30
A. *I don't go down there* anymore when he's drunk.
                30
Q. Oh, I see. Mr., uh, Mr. Nesbitt, uh, did the officer go to your house or to
        his house?
A. He went on down to Sarris, um, where my father was, I told him I was
        walking on down there, and um, he drove his car on down.
Q. Did you, did you go up to the porch before he got there, or after?
A. Um, we more or less went together.
Q. He waited to talk to you first?
A. Yes.
Q. All right, and then he went up to the porch. Is that right, the officer did?
        Where were you?
A. I was right there with him.
Q. All right now, your father's house has a step on the porch, does it not?
A. Yes.
Q. And it's a front door—has a front door, does it not?
A. Storm door, and then the front door.
Q. Storm door, and the door has a venetian blind type thing on it, does it not?
A. Mm-hmm.
Q. And at the time you went up there the venetian blinds were closed, were
        they not?
A. Yeah.
Q. All right, now at the time that you went up to the door, I ask you if the
        officer did not bang on the door vigorously?
A. I knocked.
Q. Did the officer knock?
A. I knocked to begin with. I wanted to make sure my mother was all right.
Q. Well, where was the officer *when you* knocked?
                                            31
A. *He was* standing right beside or behind me.
        31

Q. All right. And then, uh, whenever the, uh, I ask you if the blinds had just cracked open, is that correct?

A. To me they stretched open, *they*—
  32

Q. *Stretched* open, and when they stretched open you saw this pistol, didn't
  32
you?

A. Yes, I did.

Q. And it was pointed directly at you, wasn't it?

A. Yes, it came out. He, see, he thought it was me rather than the police officer.

Q. He thought it was you. He didn't have any idea it was a police officer out there.

A. No, because he knew that my mother had just called me.

Q. All right. And uh, what did, uh, what did you do after you saw that?

A. What did I do when I saw that? I backed up.

Q. Backed up. Now what did your father do?

A. He . . . um, he ran, then started running all over the house.

Q. He didn't open the door, did he?

A. No.

Q. He closed the blinds and went back in the house, didn't he? As far as you can tell.

A. He ran to the kitchen where there's no blinds and started *t*—
  33

Q. *All right,* then, uh, what happened after that? Now I ask you if the door
  33
didn't open immediately after that?

A. No, uh, that's when the other officers came and I went behind the car because I didn't want to be in line with any gun fire.

Q. Well, did uh Officer Browning go out and make a call for other officers?

A. They had come up while we were on the porch.

Q. They all came up about the same time.

A. That's right.

Q. And Officer Browning remained on the porch, *did he not?*
  34

A. *I believe so.* Well, no he started, he got down off the porch too, after he
  34
saw the gun.

Q. . . . Did the officer before he knocked on the door or at the time that he knocked on the door, did you hear him state that *he was an officer?*
  35

A. *He, he want*—, he tried to talk to him.
  35

Q. Did you hear the officer state or tell or notify the person then that he was a police officer?

A. Yes.

Q. What did he say?

A. He told him to put the gun away, that he wanted to talk to him.

Q. All right. Well, that was after the gun came through the venetian blinds.

A. That's right.

Q. Now before you knocked, or at the time you knocked did the police officer say anything that would attempt to identify himself as a police officer?

A. I . . . right then I can't really state what was said by the police officer. I don't know.

Q. . . . Now, uh, Mr. Nesbitt, I meant to ask you at the time, I should have asked you, at the time you made this telephone call to the police officers, did you identify yourself?

A. Yes, I think they usually ask who's calling.

Q. I ask you if you didn't tell 'em. You, you refused to tell 'em.

A. No. I don't refuse to tell the police who I am when I make a call. They usually want to know who's calling and your address, and I give it to 'em.

Q. Do you recall exactly what you told the officer, the person who answered the telephone over at the police station what was going on ·at the house?

A. Ah yes, I would think I told that, uh, I wanted my mother to be able to leave the house because my father was drinking.

Q. You told 'em that your father was drunk. Drinking, you said. You said, you wanted your mother to get out.

A. That's right.

Q. Did you tell the police officer that your mother had asked you to help her get out?

A. No, I don't remember exactly what I said at the time.

Q. All right . . . Would uh, your mother when she called, the reason she called was to ask you to bring the gun, wasn't it?

A. Yes, *prob—*
　　　36

Q. *And* then you begin to ask her these other questions about, well, as you
　　36
say you asked her.

A. Mm-hmm.

Q. All right . . . That's all I have to ask.

Overlapping Style—Witness Dominates

CROSS-EXAMINATION

Q. Now, Mr. Nesbitt, how far, uh, do you say you live from your father's house?

A. The third house.

Q. The third house?
A. Yes.
Q. Are you married?
A. Yes.
Q. Do you live with your wife?
A. Yes, I do.
Q. Now, Mr. Nesbitt, uh, you and your father have had considerable trouble, haven't you?
A. The fact is that if my father would leave us alone and quit messing with guns and if he'd stop his drinking, we wouldn't have any trouble. I have a wife and two children that we, I mean, when you're called at 1, 2, 3, 4 o'clock in the morning, and he come, have someone coming up, beating on your door, yeah, there's trouble *when he's drunk.*
                                                                         1
Q. *All right. I asked* you if there hadn't just a few days or weeks, just a short
        1
    time before this incident . . . you beat your father up?
A. No. No, I didn't.
Q. You did not?
A. No, I didn't.
Q. Well, did you have any controversy at all?
A. No!
Q. Did not?
A. No.
Q. All right, I ask you if you haven't beaten him up in the last week?
A. Yes, and do you know why?
Q. Well, *I—*
          2
A. *Ano*ther gun episode.
     2
Q. Another gun episode?
A. That's right. But *that was just last week.*
                                          3
Q. *And if you didn't cut, put* a cut on his face here and *brea—*
             3   4
A. *Well,* when you start, gonna shoot somebody, you doggone right better,
     4
    threatening me, gonna shoot me, *sue me*
                                        5
Q. *All right.* You got it in for your father, haven't you?
     5
A. After all these things which comes from guns and his drinking, yes I do.
Q. And *you been*
         6

A. _When I'm thr_eatened, when I haven't done anything, when I'm tending to
6
my own business, got my own family, and yet I can't be left alone . . .

Q. Oh, but you do have it in for your father, don't you? You've had a controversy going with him for a long time, haven't you?

A. Not until I'm threatened that I'm going to be shot, or sued by his 24-year-old girlfriend. It's not just that I'm his son.

Q. Now, on this particular incident that we've talked about, it was early in the morning, wasn't it?

A. Yeah, it was.

Q. It was about 6 o'clock in the morning, wasn't it?

A. No, it started before then.

Q. Well, what time did it start?

A. It started between 4:30 and 5. He waited until after 5 to usually start his trouble.

Q. Now what trouble did you say he started on this particular morning?

A. On this particular morning?

Q. That's correct.

A. Well, he had my mother call me, and in the background he was threatening her, he has a foul mouth when he gets drunk.

Q. Well, did you talk to your father at all that morning?

A. He couldn't have talked; all he could do was slur, but I could understand what he was say_in—_
7

Q. _Well,_ if you did not talk _to_
7   8

A. _But_ my mother had already told me if she called, if she needed help, and
8
I knew she did—I could hear it, because he'd start hitting her, that I was to call the police.

Q. I'm talking about on this particular morning sir, _could you_
9

A. _I'm talking_ about this particular morning. I knew I had to call the police.
9

Q. On this particular morning, did you have any conversation at all with your father?

A. No. Because he wouldn't talk, he made my mother talk. _He told her what to say._
10

Q. _Oh, he made_ your mother talk?
10

A. Yeah, and he told her what to say.

Q. All right, now, you were at home all this time, were you not?

A. Yes, I was.

Q. Three doors down?

A. On the telephone you can hear someone standing beside another person telling 'em what to say, yeah, you can hear it.

Q. All right, but all this was on the telephone was it not, because, you said, because he never, at one time, went on your premises, did he, on that particular morning, *on Ap—*

11

A. <u>*I wouldn't swear*</u> to it.

11

Q. Well, would you swear that he did not?

A. . . . No.

Q. Did you ever see him at any time, on April the first during the morning on your premises?

A. No.

Q. Did you ever go to his house, other than the occasion that you mentioned you went down with the police officer?

A. Yes, I went down with the officer, <u>*and that was it.*</u>

12

Q. <u>*I mean other than*</u> that.

12

A. No.

Q. Now, and if he never talked to you on the telephone?

A. No.

Q. And he never, he never went to your house, and you never went to his house?

A. Only with the officer.

Q. All right, now, how can you, how do you, uh, what is the basis upon your position that he was bothering you or threatening you at any time?

A. Well, they're my father and mother. I heard the conversation on the phone, and I know what's going on. That's why . . .

Q. Your mother called you on the telephone, did she?

A. That's right.

Q. And what did she call you about?

A. She called me because of him. He told her . . . oh, he wanted his gun.

Q. He wanted you, uh, to return his rifle that you took from him, did he not?

A. Mmm-hmm. Yeah, he did.

Q. Alright, did he make any threats to you through your mother?

A. All I knew she needed help and that was <u>*it. I heard enough of it.*</u>

13

Q. <u>*Now what did she tell you*</u> that would indicate to you that <u>*she*</u>

          13   14

A. <u>*She to*</u>ld me a long time ago that if she called, and I knew there was trouble,

  14

to definitely call the police right away.

Q. All right. *But*
                 —
                 15
A. *So she could leave.*
     ———————
         15
Q. Did I understand you to tell this jury, that because your mother called up, and told you that your father wanted you to return the rifle, that was sufficient evidence for you to call the police department?
A. Yes, because he was drunk, *and I know how he gets.*
                                 —————————————
                                         16
Q. *Well, how do you know* he was drunk? When was the last *time you'd*
     ——————————————   ——————————
             16   17
A. *Because my,* my father goes to bed when he's not. He doesn't—he's a
     —————————
         17
different person. There's two *different people.*
                                ————————————
                                       18
Q. *When is the last* time before this incident that you had seen your father?
     ———————————
           18
A. Oh, probably the day before.
Q. And you, uh, you did not see him from the day before until the police officer came down and opened the door, and you give this court the opinion that he was drunk, is that correct?
A. Well, he is my father, and I know him quite well.
Q. You, you just assume that he was drunk, is that correct?
A. No, I'm not assuming, no.
Q. Well, what now, what do you base your testimony on that he was drunk?
A. Well, I know him, that's the difference. When you've lived with a person, when you've grown up with him all your life, you know him.
Q. And you know he's always drunk, is that correct?
A. I know when he is, and when he isn't.
Q. Wha—, even though you don't see him or *don't—*
                                             ——————
                                               19
A. *That's right,* that's right.
     —————————
         19
Q. All right. Now . . . what did you tell the police officer when you called on the telephone?
A. I asked him to come to 1720 Sarris Avenue?
Q. That's the home of your father, or your home?
A. That's my father's home.
Q. And what did you tell 'em the reason that you wanted him to come there?
A. Because I wanted my mother to be able to leave safely. Now *when he's drunk, he keeps her in.*
     ——————————————————————————
                  20
Q. *Well, did your mother ever state* to you that she could not leave the house?
     ——————————————————————
                  20

A. He has, he has kept her in it before, yes.

Q. Did your mother, on this particular instance over the telephone *to you—*
   <u>   21</u>

A. *I ask*ed her, I told my mother to come on up here. She said she couldn't.
   21

Q. Well, did she tell you the reason she couldn't come, was it
   something with—
   <u>   22</u>

A. *She couldn't,* she couldn't say that in front *of him when he's like that.*
   <u>   22</u>   <u>   23</u>

Q. *How do you know she couldn't?*
   <u>   23</u>

A. Because when I had lived at home she couldn't say anything, neither could
   I . . . on those occasions when he's like that you can't, not unless you want
   to get hit.

Q. All right, but your mother made no indication to you on this particular
   occa*sion?*
   <u>   24</u>

A. *Yes,* I asked her if she wanted to leave and she said, "Uh-huh," and that
   24
   was it.

Q. Well . . . she said she wanted to leave?

A. That's right.

Q. And, did she tell you there was any trouble between her and her husband?

A. Now listen, when you going through things like this you don't have time
   to go into details. If you'*d never been through that such that*
   you would know.
   <u>   25</u>

Q. *Well, do you mind to take a little time* and go into details now?
   <u>   25</u>

A. No, but I'm just trying to tell *you how it is.*
   <u>   26</u>

Q. *Well, now I* ask you sir, if you can tell this court, this jury of this court,
   <u>   26</u>
   as to what exactly what your mother said to you that would indicate
   there was need—
   <u>   27</u>

A. *I said to her,* "Do you want to leave, do you need help?" She said, "Uh-
   <u>   27</u>
   huh."

Q. I see, it's now that, "You need help."

A. That's right.

Q. . . . Now uh, what time did you make the call?

A. I don't know.

Q. Well, how long was it before the police officer came down?
A. I don't know that either.
Q. Well, was it light when you came down?
A. No, it was dark.
Q. It was early in the morning; it was dark.
A. Yes, it was.
Q. All right, and then, uh, did uh, how many police officers arrived on the scene?
A. At first it was just the one, and um, *he didn't expect any troub*le.
　　　　　　　　　　　　　　　　　　　　　　　　28

Q. *Just Edward Browning?*
　　　28
A. Yes.
Q. This fellow right here?
A. Uh-huh.
Q. Now, whenever, you arrived at the house, uh, you were already there, I mean with the police officer?
A. No, I was not there. Oh, when what?
Q. When the police officer arrived at the house, you were already down there.
A. No, I wasn't, I said I was in front of my home, *flagging him* down.
　　　　　　　　　　　　　　　　　　　　　　　　29

Q. *Oh, your home.* All right, did you *go—*
　　29　　　　　　　　　　　　　30
A. *I* don't go down there anymore when he's drunk.
　 30
Q. Oh, I see. Mr., uh, Mr. Nesbitt, uh, did the officer go to your house or to his house?
A. He went down to Sarris, um, where my father was, I told him that I was walking on down there, and um, he drove his car on down.
Q. Did you, did you go up to the porch before he got there, or after?
A. Um, we more or less went together.
Q. He waited to talk to you first?
A. Yes.
Q. All right, and then he went up to the porch. Is that right, the officer did. Where were you?
A. I was right there with him.
Q. All right now, your father's house has a step on the porch, does it not?
A. Yes.
Q. And it's a front door—has a front door, does it not?
A. Storm door, and then the front door.
Q. Storm door, and the door has a venetian blind type thing on it, does it not?
A. Mm-hmm.
Q. And at the time you went up there the venetian blinds were closed, were they not?
A. Yeah.

Q. All right, now at the time that you went up to the door I ask you if the officer did not bang on the door vigorously?

A. I knocked.

Q. Did the officer knock?

A. I knocked to begin with. I wanted to make sure my mother was all right.

Q. Well, where was the officer *when you—*
<u>31</u>

A. *He was* standing right beside me or behind me.
<u>31</u>

Q. All right. And then, uh, whenever the, uh, I ask you if the blinds had just cracked open, is that correct?

A. To me they stretched open, *they lifted open.*
<u>32</u>

Q. *Stretched open,* and when they stretched open you saw this pistol, didn't
<u>32</u>
you?

A. Yes, I did.

Q. And it was pointed directly at you, wasn't it?

A. Yes, it came out. He, see, he thought it was me rather than the police officer.

Q. He thought it was you. He didn't have any idea it was a police officer out there.

A. No, because he knew that my mother had just called me.

Q. All right. And uh, what did, uh, what did you do after you saw that?

A. What did I do when I saw that? I backed up.

Q. Backed up. Now what did your father do?

A. He . . . um, he ran, then started running all over the house.

Q. He didn't open the door, did he?

A. No.

Q. He closed the blinds and went back in the house, didn't he? As far as you can tell.

A. He ran to the kitchen where there's no blinds and started *yelling and screaming.*
<u>33</u>

Q. *All right, then, uh,* what happened after that? Now I ask you if the door
<u>33</u>
didn't open immediately after that?

A. No, uh, that's when the other officers came and I went behind the car because I didn't want to be in the line with any gun fire.

Q. Well, did uh Officer Browning go out and make a call for other officers?

A. They had come up while we were on the porch.

Q. They all came up about the same time.

A. That's right.

Q. And Officer Browning remained on the porch, *did h—*
<u>34</u>

A. *I belie*ve so. Well, no, he started, he got off the porch too, after he saw
    34
    the gun.
Q. . . . Did the officer before he knocked on the door or at the time that he
    knocked on the door, did you hear him state that he *wa*—
                                                          35
A. *He,* he wanted, he tried to talk to him.
    35
Q. Did you hear the officer state or tell or notify the person then that he was
    a police officer?
A. Yes.
Q. What did he say?
A. He told him to put the gun away, that he wanted to talk to him.
Q. All right. Well, that was after the gun came through the venetian blinds.
A. That's right.
Q. Now, before you knocked, or at the time you knocked did the police officer
    say anything that would attempt to identify himself as a police officer?
A. I . . . right then I can't really state what was said by the police officer. I
    don't know.
Q. . . . Now, uh, Mr. Nesbitt, I meant to ask you at the time, I should have
    asked you, at the time you made this telephone call to the police officers,
    did you identify yourself?
A. Yes, I think they usually ask who's calling.
Q. I ask you if you didn't tell 'em. You, you refused to tell 'em.
A. No. I don't refuse to tell the police who I am when I make a call. They
    usually want to know who's calling and your address, and I give it to 'em.
Q. Do you recall exactly what you told the officer, the person who answered
    the telephone over at the police station what was going on at the house?
A. Ah yes, I would think I told that, uh, I wanted my mother to be able to
    leave the house because my father was drinking.
Q. You told 'em that your father was drunk. Drinking, you said. You said,
    you wanted your mother to get out.
A. That's right.
Q. Did you tell the police officer that your mother had asked you to help her
    get out?
A. No, I don't remember exactly what I said at the time.
Q. All right . . . Would uh, your mother when she called, the reason she called
    was to ask you to bring the gun, wasn't it?
A. Yes, *prob*ably.
            36
Q. *And* then you begin to ask her these other questions about, well, as you
    36
    say you asked her.
A. Mm-hmm.
Q. All right . . . That's all I have to ask.

REFERENCES

Cases

Abbott v. *Church*
   288 Ill. 91, 123 N.E. 306 (1919).
Apodaca v. *Oregon*
   406 U.S. 404 (1972).
Ballew v. *Georgia*
   435 U.S. 223 (1978).
Bartholomew v. *Universe Tankships, Inc.*
   168 F. Supp. 153 (S.D.N.Y. 1953).
Commonwealth v. *Butler*
   448 Pa. 128, 291 A. 2d 89 (1972).
Creamer v. *Bivert*
   214 Mo. 473, 113 S.W. 1118 (1908).
First Federal Savings & Loan Ass'n. v. *Commercial Union Ins. Co.*
   156 S.E. 2d 101 (Ga. App. 1967).
Furtando v. *Mantebello Verified School Dist.*
   206 Cal. App. 2d 72, 23 Cal. Rptr. 476 (1962).
Hubbard v. *State*
   2 Md. App. 364, 234 A. 2d 775 (1967).
Johnson v. *Louisiana*
   406 U.S. 356 (1972).
Kovacs v. *Szentes*
   130 Conn. 229, 33 A. 2d 124 (1943).
Murphy v. *Roux*
   352 Mich. 97, 89 N.W. 2d 532 (1958).

National Labor Relations Board v. *Dinion Coal Co.*
    201 F. 2d 484 (2d Cir. 1951).
People v. *Doxie*
    34 Cal. App. 2d 511, 93 P. 2d 1068 (1939).
People v. *Nitti*
    312 Ill. 73, 143 N.E. 448 (1924).
Rotolo v. *United States*
    404 F. 2d 316 (5th Cir. 1968).
State v. *Simmons*
    98 N.J. Super. 430, 237 A. 2d 639, *cert. denied,* 395 U.S. 924 (1968).
State v. *Snow*
    98 N.H. 1, 93 A. 2d 831 (1953).
Swain v. *Alabama*
    389 U.S. 202 (1965).
Turner v. *Fouche*
    396 U.S. 346 (1969).
United States v. *Littlewind*
    551 F. 2d 244 (8th Cir. 1977).
Williams v. *Florida*
    399 U.S. 78 (1970).

Books and Articles

Aiken, Ray J. 1960. Let's not oversimplify legal language. *Rocky Mountain Law Review* 32:358–364.

American Law Reports. 1920. Annotation on Effect of witness qualifying his testimony with "I think," "I believe," or the like, when expressing thereby indistinct observation or recollection. *American Law Reports* 4:979–990.

Ardener, Edwin (ed.). 1971. *Social Anthropology and Language.* ASA Monograph No. 10. London: Tavistock Publications.

Atkinson, J. Maxwell, and Paul Drew. 1979. *Order in Court.* Atlantic Highlands, N.J.: Humanities Press.

Austin, J. L. 1962. *How to Do Things with Words.* London: Oxford University Press.

Bailey, F. G. 1969. *Strategems and Spoils.* New York: Schocken.

Bailey, F. Lee, and Henry B. Rothblatt. 1971. *Successful Techniques for Criminal Trials.* Rochester, N.Y.: The Lawyers Co-operative Publishing Co.

Barth, Frederik. 1966. Models of social organization. *Royal Anthropological Institute Occasional Paper* No. 23. London.

Bauman, Richard, and Joel Sherzer (eds.). 1974. *Explorations in the Ethnography of Speaking.* New York: Cambridge University Press.

Beardsley, Charles A. 1941. Beware of, eschew, and avoid pompous prolixity and platitudinous epistles. *Journal of the State Bar of California* 16:65–69.

Bishin, William R., and Christopher D. Stone. 1972. *Language, Law, and Ethics: An Introduction to Law and Legal Method.* Mineola, N.Y.: The Foundation Press.

Black, Mary, and Duane Metzger. 1965. Ethnographic description and the study of the law. *American Anthropologist* 67:141–165.

Bloch, Maurice (ed.). 1975. *Political Language and Oratory in Traditional Society.* New York: Academic Press.

Bohannan, Paul. 1969. Ethnography and comparison in legal anthropology. In *Law in Culture and Society*. Laura Nader (ed.). Chicago: Aldine.

Bowman, B. A. 1970. Are lawyers lousy writers? *Georgia State Bar Journal* 6:285–289.

Bricker, Victoria A. 1974. The ethnographic context of some traditional Mayan speech genres. In *Explorations in the Ethnography of Speaking*. R. Bauman and J. Sherzer (eds.). New York: Cambridge University Press.

Brown, Roger W., and Marguerite Ford. 1961. Address in American English. *Journal of Abnormal and Social Psychology* 62:375–385.

Brown, Roger W., and Antonio Gilman. 1960. The pronouns of power and solidarity. In *Style in Language*. T. Sebeok (ed.). Cambridge, Mass.: M.I.T. Press.

Charrow, Robert P., and Veda R. Charrow. 1979a. Making legal language understandable: a psycholinguistic study of jury instructions. *Columbia Law Review* 79:1306–1374.

Charrow, Veda R., and Robert P. Charrow. 1979b. Characteristics of the language of jury instructions. In *Language in Public Life*. James E. Alatis and G. Richard Tucker (eds.). Georgetown University Roundtable on Language and Linguistics 1979. Washington, D.C.:Georgetown University Press.

Chomsky, Noam. 1957. *Syntactic Structures*. The Hague: Mouton.

Chomsky, Noam. 1965. *Aspects of the Theory of Syntax*. Cambridge, Mass.: The M.I.T. Press.

Conley, J. M., W. M. O'Barr, and E. A. Lind. 1978. The power of language: presentational style in the courtroom. *Duke Law Journal* 78:1375–1399.

Crystal, David, and Derek Davy. 1969. *Investigating English Style*. Bloomington: Indiana University Press.

Danet, Brenda. 1976. Speaking of Watergate: language and moral accountability. *Centrum* (Working Papers of the Minnesota Center for Advanced Study in Language, Style, and Literary Theory) 4:105–138.

Danet, Brenda. 1980a. "Baby" or "fetus"? Language and the construction of reality in a manslaughter trial. *Semiotica* 32:187–219.

Danet, Brenda. 1980b. Language in the legal process. *Law and Society Review* 14:445–564.

Dellinger, David T. 1970. *Contempt: Transcript of the Contempt Citations, Sentences, and Responses of the Chicago Conspiracy 10*. Chicago: Swallow Press.

de Saussure, Ferdinand. 1916. *Cours de linguistique generale*. Paris: Payot. [*Course in general linguistics* (translated by Wade Baskin). New York: Philosophical Library, 1958.]

Doob, A. N. 1976. Evidence, procedure, and psychological research. In *Psychology and the Law*. G. Bermant, C. Nemeth, and N. Vidmar (eds.). Lexington, Mass.: D. C. Heath.

Edelman, Murray. 1964. *The Symbolic Uses of Politics*. Urbana: University of Illinois Press.

Ellis, J., and J. N. Ure. 1969. Language Varieties: register. In *Encyclopedia of Linguistics, Information, and Control*. London: Pergamon.

Elwork, A., B. D. Sales, and J. J. Alfini. 1977. Juridic decisions: In ignorance of the law or in light of it? *Law and Human Behavior* 1:163–189.

Erickson, Bonnie, E. Allan Lind, Bruce C. Johnson, and William M. O'Barr. 1978. Speech style and impression formation in a court setting: the effects of "powerful" and "powerless" speech. *Journal of Experimental Social Psychology* 14:266–279.

Ervin–Tripp, Susan M. 1964. An analysis of the interaction of language, topic and listener. *American Anthropologist* 66:86–102.

Fallers, Lloyd A. 1969. *Law without Precedent*. Chicago: University of Chicago Press.

Ferguson, Charles A. 1976. The collect as a form of discourse. In *Language in Religious Practice*. William J. Samarin (ed.). Rowley, Mass.: Newbury House.

Fischer, J. L. 1958. Social influence in the choice of a linguistic variant. *Word* 14:47–56.

Fox, James J. 1974. "Our ancestors spoke in pairs": Rotinese views of language dialect and code. In *Explorations in the Ethnography of Speaking*. R. Bauman and J. Sherzer (eds.). New York: Cambridge University Press.

Frake, Charles O. 1969. "Struck by speech": the Yakan concept of litigation. In *Law in Culture and Society*. Laura Nader (ed.). Chicago: Aldine.

Gerhart, Eugene C. 1954. Improving our legal writing. *American Bar Association Journal* 40:1057–1060.

Giles, H. and P. F. Powesland. 1975. *Speech Style and Social Evaluation*. New York: Academic Press.

Gluckman, Max. 1969. Concepts in the comparative study of tribal law. In *Law in Culture and Society*. Laura Nader (ed.). Chicago: Aldine.

Grice, H. P. 1975. Logic and conversation. In *Syntax and Semantics*, Vol. 3. New York: Academic Press.

Haas, M. R. 1944. Men's and women's speech in Koasati. *Language* 20:142–149.

Hager, John. 1959. Let's simplify legal language. *Rocky Mountain Law Review* 32:74–86.

Heath, Shirley Brice. Forthcoming. *Language and the Professions*.

Hoebel, E. Adamson. 1964. *The Law of Primitive Man*. Cambridge, Mass.: Harvard University Press.

Hurwitz, J. I., A. F. Zander, and B. Hymovitch. 1953. Some effects of power on relations among group members. In *Group Dynamics*. D. Cartwright and A. Zander (eds.). Evanston, Ill.: Harper & Row.

Hymes, Dell. 1962. The ethnography of speaking. In *Anthropology and Human Behavior*. T. Gladwin and W. C. Sturtevant (eds.). Washington, D.C.: Anthropological Society of Washington.

Jeans, James W. 1975. *Trial Advocacy*. St. Paul, Minn.: West Publishing Company.

Jones, E. E. 1964. *Ingratiation*. New York: Appleton–Century–Crofts.

Jones, E. E., and E. E. Davis. 1965. From acts to dispositions: The attribution of process in person perception. In *Advances in Experimental Social Psychology*. L. Berkowitz (ed.). New York: Academic Press.

Jones, E. E., K. E. Davis, and K. J. Gergen. 1961. Role playing variations and their informational value for person perception. *Journal of Abnormal and Social Psychology* 63:302–310.

Judicial Council of California. 1976. *A Report to the Judicial Council on the Needs of Non-English Speaking Persons in Relation to the State's Justice System*. Sacramento, Cal.: Arthur Young and Company.

Kalven, Harry. 1970. "Introduction." In *Transcript of the Contempt Citations, Sentences, and Responses of the Chicago Conspiracy 10*. David T. Dellinger. Chicago: Swallow Press.

Kalven, Harry, and Hans Zeisel. 1966. *The American Jury*. Boston: Little, Brown.

Kapferer, Bruce (ed.). 1976. *Transaction and Meaning*. Philadelphia: Institute for the Study of Human Issues.

Keesing, Roger M. 1981. *Cultural Anthropology: A Contemporary Perspective*. 2d ed. New York: Holt, Rinehart & Winston.

Keeton, Robert E. 1973. *Trial Tactics and Methods*, 2d. ed. Boston: Little, Brown.

Kelley, H. H. 1967. Attribution theory in social psychology. *Nebraska Symposium on Motivation* 14:192–241.

Kessler, J. B. 1975. *The Jury System in America*. Beverly Hills, Cal.: Sage Publications.

Key, M. R. 1975. *Male/Female Language*. Metuchen, N.J.: Scarecrow Press.

Labov, W. 1966. *The Social Stratification of English in New York City*. Washington, D.C.: Center for Applied Linguistics.

Labov, W. 1972a. Hypercorrection as a factor in linguistic change. In *Sociolinguistic Patterns*. W. Labov (ed.). Philadelphia: University of Pennsylvania Press.

Labov, W. (ed.). 1972b. *Sociolinguistic Patterns*. Philadelphia: University of Pennsylvania Press.

Lakoff, Robin. 1973. Language and woman's place. *Language in Society* 2:45–79.

Lakoff, Robin. 1975. *Language and Woman's Place*. New York: Harper & Row.

Lambert, W. E., R. C. Hodgson, R. C. Gardner, and S. Fillenbaum. 1960. Evaluational reactions to spoken languages. *Journal of Abnormal and Social Psychology* 60:44–51.

Levine, Murray, Michael P. Farrell, and Peter Perrota. 1980. The impact of rules of jury deliberation on group developmental processes. In *The Trial Process*. B. D. Sales (ed.). New York: Plenum.

Levi–Strauss, Claude. 1968. *Structural Anthropology*. New York: Basic Books.

Lind, E. A., B. Erickson, J. M. Conley, and W. M. O'Barr. 1978. Social attributions and conversational style in trial testimony. *Journal of Personality and Social Psychology* 36:1558–1567.

Lind, E. A., and W. M. O'Barr. 1979. The social significance of speech in the courtroom. In *Language and Social Psychology*. Howard Giles and Robert St. Clair (eds.). College Park, Md.: University Press.

Lind, E. A., J. Thibaut, and L. Walker. 1976. A cross-cultural comparison of the effect of adversary and inquisitorial processes on bias in legal decision making. *Virginia Law Review* 62:271–283.

Linton, N. K. 1965. The witness and cross-examination. *Berkeley Journal of Sociology* 10:1–12.

Loftus, Elizabeth. 1974. Reconstructing memory: the incredible eye-witness. *Psychology Today* 8:117–119.

Loftus, Elizabeth. 1979. *Eyewitness Testimony*. Cambridge, Mass.: Harvard University Press.

Loftus, Elizabeth, and John Palmer. 1974. Reconstruction of automobile destruction: An example of the interaction between language and memory. *Journal of Verbal Learning and Verbal Behavior* 13:585–589.

McConnell–Ginet, Sally. 1980. Linguistics and the feminist challenge. In *Women and Language in Literature and Society*. Sally McConnell–Ginet, Ruth Borker, and Nelly Furman (eds.). New York: Praeger.

McConnell–Ginet, Sally, Ruth Borker, and Nelly Furman (eds.). 1980. *Women and Language in Literature and Society*. New York: Praeger.

McElhaney, J. W. 1974. *Effective Litigation—Trials, Problems, and Materials*. St. Paul, Minn.: West Publishing.

Malinowski, Bronislaw. 1935. *Coral Gardens and Their Magic*, Vol. 2. New York: American Book Company.

Mellinkoff, David. 1963. *The Language of the Law*. Boston: Little, Brown.

Mills, J. 1966. Opinion change as a function of the communicator's desire to influence and liking for the audience. *Journal of Experimental Social Psychology* 2:152–159.

Mills, J., and J. M. Jellison. 1967. Effect on opinion change of how desirable the communication is to the audience the communicator addressed. *Journal of Personality and Social Psychology* 5:459–463.

Morrill, A. E. 1971. *Trial Diplomacy*. Chicago: Court Practice Institute.

Morton, Robert A. 1941. Challenge made to Beardsley's plan for plain and simple legal syntax. *Journal of the State Bar of California* 16:103–106.

Nader, Laura. 1965. The anthropological study of law. *American Anthropologist* 67:3–32.

Nader, Laura. (ed.). 1980. *No Access to Law: Alternatives to the American Judicial System*. New York: Academic Press.

Naroll, Raoul, and Ronald Cohen (eds.). 1973. *A Handbook of Method in Cultural Anthropology*. New York: Columbia University Press.

Nemeth, C. 1976. Rules governing jury deliberations: A consideration of recent changes. In *Psychology and the law*. G. Bermant, C. Nemeth, and N. Vidmar (eds.). Lexington, Mass.: D. C. Heath.

Newcombe, Nora, and Diane B. Arnkoff. 1979. The effects of speech style and sex of speaker on person perception. *Journal of Personality and Social Psychology* 37:1293–1303.

O'Barr, William M. 1981. The language of the law. In *Language in the U.S.A.* Charles A. Ferguson and Shirley Brice Heath (eds.). New York: Cambridge University Press.

O'Barr, William M., and Bowman K. Atkins. 1980. "Women's language" or "powerless language"? In *Women and Language in Literature and Society*. S. McConnell-Ginet, R. Borker, and N. Furman (eds.). New York: Praeger.

O'Barr, William M., and John M. Conley. 1976. When a juror watches a lawyer. *Barrister* 3:8–11, 33.

O'Barr, William M., and E. A. Lind. 1981. Ethnography and experimentation—partners in legal research. In *The Trial Process*. B. D. Sales (ed.). New York: Plenum.

O'Barr, William M., and Jean F. O'Barr (eds.). 1976. *Language and Politics*. The Hague: Mouton.

O'Barr, William M., Laurens Walker, John M. Conley, Bonnie Erickson, and Bruce R. Johnson. 1976. Political aspects of speech styles in American trial courtrooms. In *Working Papers in Culture and Communication* (Philadelphia: Temple University Department of Anthropology) 1:27–40.

Padawer–Singer, A. M., A. Singer, and R. Singer. 1977. An experimental study of twelve v. six member juries under unanimous v. nonunanimous decisions. In *Psychology in the Legal Process*. B. D. Sales (ed.). Jamaica, N.Y.: Spectrum Publications.

Pelto, Pertti J., and Gretl H. Pelto. 1978. *Anthropological Research: The Structure of Inquiry*, 2d. ed. New York: Cambridge University Press.

Philbrick, Frederick A. 1949. *Language and the Law: The Semantics of Forensic English*. New York: Macmillan.

Philips, Susan U. 1980. Sex differences and language. *Annual Review of Anthropology* 9:523–544.

Poythress, Norman G. 1979. A proposal for training in forensic psychology. *American Psychologist* 34:612–621.

Pousada, Alicia. 1979. Interpreting for language minorities in the courts. In *Language in Public Life*. James E. Alatis and G. Richard Tucker (eds.). Georgetown University Round Table on Language and Linguistics 1979. Washington, D.C.: Georgetown University Press.

Rosen, Lawrence. 1977. The anthropologist as expert witness. *American Anthropologist* 79:555–578.

Sacks, Harvey, Emanuel Schegloff, and Gail Jefferson. 1974. A simplest systematics for the organization of turn-taking in conversation. *Language* 50:696–735.

Sales, B. D., A. Elwork, and J. Alfini. 1977. Improving jury instruction. In *Perspectives in Law and Psychology, Vol. 1: The Criminal Justice System*. B. D. Sales (ed.). New York: Plenum.

Searle, John R. 1969. *Speech Acts*. London: Cambridge University Press.

Tambiah, S. J. 1968. The magical power of words. *Man* (N.S.) 3:175–208.

Thibaut, John, and Laurens Walker. 1975. *Procedural Justice: A Psychological Analysis*. Hillsdale, N.J.: Lawrence Erlbaum Associates.

Thorne, B., and N. Henley (eds.). 1975. *Language and Sex*. Rowley, Mass.: Newbury House.

Trudgill, Peter. 1974. *Sociolinguistics: An Introduction*. Baltimore, Md.: Penguin Books.

Turton, David. 1975. The relationship between oratory and the exercise of influence among the Mursi. In *Political Language and Oratory in Traditional Society*. Maurice Bloch (ed.). New York: Academic Press.

Varenne, Herve. 1978. Culture as rhetoric: patterning in the verbal interaction between teachers and administrators in an American high school. *American Ethnologist* 5:635–650.

Whorf, Benjamin Lee. 1956. *Language, Thought and Reality*. John Carroll (ed.). Cambridge, Mass.: M.I.T. Press.

Younger, Irving. 1976. In praise of simplicity. *American Bar Association Journal* 62:632–634.

INDEX

A

Accent, 4, 55n, 82, 94
Age
  blindness of law to, 11
  as factor in courtroom strategy, 35
  reflected in speech, 4
Anthropology
  and studies of language, 7–10, 7n, 15,
    26–28, 125
  and studies of legal processes, 12, 54
Attribution theory, 77–78, 81

C

Class
  blindness of law to, 11
  and speech style, 87
Children, as witnesses in court, 6, 120
Comprehension
  of jury instructions, 22
  of legal language, 19, 26–27
Contests, 118
  Eskimo headbutting, 10
Control
  of courtroom interviews, 77
  and simultaneous speech, 87–88

of speech style effects, 93–96, 110–111,
    117, 125
Conversational analysis, 29, 88n
Court talk, 25, 40, 40n
Credibility, 41
  as determined by demeanor, 42–43, 49
  and testimony style, 74, 79–82, 86,
    95–96, 125
Cross-examination, 6, 34n, 35, 35n, 65n,
    88

D

Decision making, by persons with legal
    training, 79–82
Demeanor
  appropriate, for courtroom, 101–102
  evidence, 42, 123–124
  treatment of, by law, 2, 41–49
Depositions, as alternative to oral
    testimony, 94
Dialect, 41
Direct examination, 34n, 35, 35n

E

Ethnography, 51–53, 111
  definition, 51

189

and study of courtroom speech, 61, 63, 76–77, 88
Examination, *see* Cross-examination; Direct examination
Experimentation, 12, 51–55, 111
  definition, 52
  and study of effects of speech styles, 59, 61, 63, 71–75, 78–82, 84–91, 93–95

F

Form, in language, 1–5, 2n
Formality, 5
Formal style, *see* Hypercorrection
Fragmented style, *see* Narrative versus fragmented style

G

Gender, and language, *see* Sex differences

H

Hearsay, 6
Hedges, 47–49, 65–67, 125
Hypercorrection, 58, 61, 83–87, 114
  definition, 83
  effects of, 84–86
  related studies, 86–87
  transcripts used in experiments, 149–156

I

Interpretation, 3, 19, 125
  by lawyers in closing arguments, 33, 114, 114n
  of legal language, 23
  and management of style, 97–110
  for non-English speakers, 39–40, 39n, 116
  of silence, 108–110
Interruptions, 36, 82, 121, *see also* Simultaneous speech

J

Jury instructions, 17–18, 22, 26–27, 27n, 41

as means of controlling effects of speech style, 94–96
Jury of one's peers, 87, 124

L

Language
  anthropological studies of, 7–10, 7n, 15, 26–28
  and behavior, 28–29
  and comprehension, 19, 22, 26–27
  and conceptualization, 27–28
  in courtroom, 25, 118
  and culture, 7n
  foreign, 10
  and justice, 10–11
  legal, 4, 15–29, 123
    American, 16
    assumptions about, 31–49
    history of, 16, 18, 20–21, 23, 26
    simplification of, 20–23
    spoken, 16, 21n, 23–29
    written, 16–26, 25n
  and legal process, 2, 10, 15, 23–24, 24n, 28
  and politics, 9–10
  and psychology, 27, 27n
  and speech, 24n
  and strategy, 5–10, 8n, 31–38, 114, 118–119, 124–125
Leading
  questions, 6, 34
  of witness, in style, 83
Legal facts, 1
Legalese, 21–22, 21n, *see also* Language, legal

M

Manipulation
  of silence, 107–108
  of words, 11
Meaning, 2n, 100, 110, *see also* Interpretation
  management of, 104
Method of data collection, 56–59

N

Narrative versus fragmented style, 58, 61, 76–83, 114

definition, 76
effects of, 78–82
related studies, 82
transcripts used in experiments,
137–148
Nonverbal communication, 1, 42, 67
Normative rules, *see* Rules, normative

O

Objections, 36, 102–104
Oratory, 7, 9–10
Overlapping speech, *see* Simultaneous
speech

P

Paralinguistic features, 1
Participant observation, 12, 56–58, 103
Pauses, 82, 106
Powerful versus powerless style, 58,
61–75, 116, 125
attempts to limit effects of, 94–96, 114
definition, 70
effects of, 71–75
patterns of use, 70–71
previous studies of, 62–64
related studies, 6
transcripts used in experiments,
127–135
"women's language," 63–64
Pragmatic rules, *see* Rules, pragmatic
Procedural rules, *see* Rules, procedural
Pronouns, information communicated by,
7, 36–37

Q

Questions, 35–36, 40n, 120
leading, 6, 34
relation to their answers, 29, 34, 76

R

Race
blindness of law to, 11
and speech style, 87
Rate of speech, 4, 7, 82, 120
Register, 4, 4n, 25
Response
lag, 105–106

lengthy, by witness, in testifying, 76
matching, 82
Rhetoric, 7
Rules
of evidence, 6, 43, 118
normative, 5, 118–119
pragmatic, 5, 118–119
of procedure, 5, 39–40, 53
about silence, 103–104

S

Semantic principles, of legal documents,
19
Semantics, *see* Meaning
Sex differences
blindness of law to, 11
reflected in speech, 4, 63–75
Silence, 33, 36
interpretation of, 98–110
manipulation of, 107–108
of record, 102–104
refusal to maintain, 101–102
right to, 98–110
during trial, 104–107
Simultaneous speech, 58, 61, 87–91, *see
also* Interruptions
definition, 88
effects of, 88–91
patterns of, 88
transcripts used in experiments,
157–180
Social information, communicated by
form, 4–5
Social psychology, 12, 78
and studies of legal process, 54–55,
54n, 55n, 59, 77–78, 85, 122
Sociolinguistics
development of, 8–9
and study of gender differences in
language, 62–64, 62n
and study of legal process, 53–54,
122–123
Strategy, language, *see* Language, and
strategy
Style, 2, 2n, 4, 4n, 52, 54n, 55, 75, *see
also* specific speech styles: Hypercorrection; Narrative versus
fragmented style; Powerful versus
powerless style; Simultaneous
speech

of courtroom language, 25–26, 55n
of legal documents, 19
management of, 97
of questioning, 35
of testifying, 41–49, 55, 55n, 118

T

Tactics, 6, 31, *see also* Language, and
strategy
Testimony, *see also* specific testimony
styles
eyewitness, 29
style of, 44
Trial
model of, 11

practice, 113
Trial practice manuals, 6, 6n, 31–38, 32n,
34n, 35n, 56, 119

V

Variety, of language, *see* Register; Style

W

Women
perceptions of, when using narrative
versus fragmented styles, 80–82
questioning style, appropriate for,
34–35, 120
speech style of, 61–71

Date Due